PQ
6144
.S65
1996

D1502757

Post-Totalitarian Spanish Fiction

Post-Totalitarian Spanish Fiction

Robert C. Spires

University of Missouri Press
Columbia and London

Copyright © 1996 by

The Curators of the University of Missouri

University of Missouri Press, Columbia, Missouri 65201

Printed and bound in the United States of America

5   4   3   2   1   00   99   98   97   96

Library of Congress Cataloging-in-Publication Data

Spires, Robert C.
    Post-totalitarian Spanish fiction / Robert C. Spires.
        p.   cm.
    Includes bibliographical references and index.
    ISBN 0-8262-1071-6 (alk. paper)
    1. Spanish fiction—20th century—History and criticism.
    I. Title.
    PQ6144.S65   1996
    863'.91409—dc20   96-18447
                                                        CIP

∞™ This paper meets the requirements of the
American National Standard for Permanence of Paper
for Printed Library Materials, Z39.48, 1984.

Text design: Stephanie Foley
Cover design: Mindy Shouse
Typesetter: BOOKCOMP
Printer and Binder: Thomson-Shore, Inc.
Typeface: Minion

This work is brought to publication with the assistance of the Program for Cultural
Cooperation between Spain's Ministry of Culture and United States' Universities.

To Carolyn and John Brushwood, friends

Contents

Acknowledgments

Although I may be accused of stating the obvious, I feel compelled to assert that all books are the product of a community effort. Even the most extensive bibliography imaginable could not begin to recognize adequately those who have contributed to a given project. Notwithstanding the impossibility of the task, I must make an effort to name a few whose contributions to this study are especially obvious. First, thanks to Roberta A. Spires for her continued support. A very special expression of appreciation goes to Nina Molinaro, a former student who over the years has taught me so much and whose critique of this manuscript was invaluable. Also among the contributors are the students who in my graduate courses and seminars helped me think through the specific readings and general focus of this book. Because of space limitations they must remain anonymous here, but in my mind their individual identities could not be more sharply drawn. I appreciate as well the intellectual stimulation of my departmental colleagues. For their friendship and hospitality while I was in Spain during February and March 1993, my deep gratitude goes to Julián Companys, Luis Goytisolo, Eva and John Kronik, Cathy Larson, and Anita and Carmen Martín Gaite. Finally, I would like to recognize the Program for Cultural Cooperation between Spain's Ministry of Culture and United States' Universities for a grant that enabled me to spend the time in Spain and to the Hall Center for the Humanities of the University of Kansas for a fellowship during fall semester 1992.

Post-Totalitarian Spanish Fiction

Introduction

It seems to be virtually impossible to define current modes of existence without resorting to prefixed terms such as *postmodernism, poststructuralism, postculturalism, postcolonialism, postmarxism,* and *postcapitalism.* I am now guilty of extending the list by proposing the label *post-totalitarianism* for the body of fiction discussed here. There is a limitation imposed by attaching a prefix, of course, for it means that whatever follows is defined in terms of a previous definition. That being the case, some may consider the current flair for prefixing symptomatic of a preference to imitate and circumvent rather than create and invent. Yet I would like to propose that it may merely point to a growing awareness that all creation and invention departs from a previous model. Even if we eschew all "post" labels, including *post-totalitarianism,* and instead, for example, limit our explanations of current international political events by referring to fragmentation, decentralization, and subversion of authority, we cannot understand what these terms mean except in relationship to what preceded them: *political unity, centralization,* and *authoritarianism.* As I have delineated my task here it is not primarily to create or debate labels (though certainly I attempt to define the terms I employ) but rather to offer my own version of *épistémocritique*—an approach that analyzes the literary text as an expression of its epistemic context. I will identify some of the bonds connecting disparate academic disciplines and sociopolitical events with an eye to demonstrating how the world of fiction serves as a register of the nonfictional world and to demonstrate how this body of fiction offers its own representations of these connections.

The fiction I analyze in this study was published in Spain between 1975 and 1989, with the exception of *Tiempo de silencio* (A time of silence), a novel appearing in 1962 and whose inclusion here will be discussed shortly. The year 1975 has a familiar ring for Hispanists since it marks the death of Francisco Franco and the end of thirty-six years of dictatorship. For a more general audience, the second date should connote the culmination of the breakdown of the Eastern European totalitarian state (and in a less spectacular manner, of its Latin American, Asian, and African counterparts). The attempt in my initial sentence to link the year 1975 with 1989, fiction with politics, and the end of the Spanish ultra-Right regime with the collapse of the Soviet ultra-Left bloc, points to my goal with this project of identifying some of the connections between a culturally bound poetics and a culturally dispersed politics. I will argue in the following pages, however, that the relationship is not causal. In visiting Spain for a firsthand view of how that country managed the transition from totalitarianism to democracy, at first glance it may seem that Mikhail Gorbachev's trip to the Iberian Peninsula signaled a direct link between Soviet and Spanish political change. Yet it would be absurd to assert that the end of the Franco dictatorship led directly to the breakup of the former Soviet bloc, or to the fall of the Stroessner regime, or to the bloody demonstrations in Tiananmen Square. But all of these events, separated in time and space, form part of a common connecting grid, or episteme.

Foucault, to whom we owe the current use of the term *episteme*, refers to it as that "totality of relations that can be discovered, for a given period, between the sciences when one analyzes them at the level of discourse," and on another occasion he states it is an "open and doubtless indefinitely describable field of relationships." As if to open the term even further, Karlis Racevskis claims that its existence seems to be "founded on its non-existence, it dissolves as soon as it is identified."[1] But whereas the "indefinitely describable" approaches the status of nondefinable, it certainly is *not* nonexperiential. We often experience what we cannot define, which serves as well as anything to explain what a literary text has to offer us. Literature, then, allows us to experience the nondefinable, and criticism provides us with the tools to attempt to put into words that experience. Whereas I believe that there are universal or consensus human experiences, clearly we have not developed universal or consensus means for expressing

1. Quoted respectively from Michel Foucault, *The Archaeology of Knowledge and the Discourse on Language,* 191, and Michel Foucault, *The Foucault Effect: Studies in Governmentality* (55). Subsequent citations will indicate the page number in parentheses. The final reference is to Jeanne P. Brownlow, "Epochal Allegory in Galdós's *Torquemada: The Ur-Text and the Episteme,*" 295.

them. We must recognize, therefore, that our analyses, rather than leading to univocal interpretations, can at best only partially or inaccurately reexpress the literary text, which in turn can only partially or inaccurately reexpress some specific human experiences that the artist has transformed into blocks of sensations. But no matter how far from the original intent our readings may be, the experience re-created by the critic may turn out to be as satisfying (or even more satisfying) than its literary referent. It follows from what I have said that no work of literature or criticism can convey a totalized vision. Yet the combination of these two modes (literary and critical) may be the best source we have for expressing in language the episteme of any given epoch.

We cannot speak adequately of episteme without discussing the related concept, "field." Whereas intellectual communities since the Greeks have explained reality as a linear or causal process, the current community increasingly conceives of it as an interconnected network or field. In *The Archaeology of Knowledge and the Discourse on Language*, Foucault himself makes frequent reference to discursive fields as a system of dispersion involving statements, objects, concepts, thematic choices, and events (21– 39). According to N. Katherine Hayles, scientists use field model theory to refer to a reality that has no detachable parts, that is composed of "events" as opposed to particles. Gilles Deleuze and Félix Guattari argue that philosophical concepts "are fragmentary wholes that are not aligned with one another, because their edges do not match up. They are not pieces of a jigsaw puzzle but rather the outcome of throws of the dice."[2] Everything is interconnected but not in a linear order. Whether speaking of discourse or matter, the links and movements are multidirectional; each cause is also an effect and vice versa. The new science argues that humans define fields but also are defined by them—the person who discovers an area of knowledge is influenced by previously discovered fields that to one degree or another predetermined his or her discovery and that in turn will, to one degree or another, predetermine future discoveries. We should reject the illusion of true objectivity, for the observing subject cannot separate himself or herself from the observed object. Indeed, the language itself employed to

---

2. See respectively, N. Katherine Hayles, *The Cosmic Web: Scientific Field Models and Literary Strategies in the Twentieth Century*, 15–27, and Gilles Deleuze and Félix Guattari, *What Is Philosophy?* 35.

describe an object, concept, or event helps determine the reality of that object, concept, or event. In short, matter and discourse form and are formed by a web of ecological nexuses transcending molecular, academic, temporal, social, and geopolitical boundaries.

The term *geopolitical boundaries* connotes nationalism, which in turn relates directly to my growing concern with the political, social, and literary isolation of the Hispanic world. In the sociopolitical arena, observers and commentators from the rest of Europe and North America tend to treat the Hispanic world as if it were disconnected from world events. In this century we need only think in terms of the Mexican Revolution, whose relationship to its Russian counterpart would come as a complete surprise to many people. Although a few historians have recognized that the Spanish civil war of 1936–1939 served as a dress rehearsal for World War II, in general the Spanish conflict merits little more than a footnote in most histories of the war. In 1968 the Tlaltelolco massacre in Mexico City was absurdly overshadowed in world awareness by the demonstrations the same year in Paris and at the Democratic National Convention in Chicago. Conceding that the historical reasons for such dissociations are complex, I think we have now reached a point when there is a predisposition to accept the thesis that the Mexican Revolution, the Spanish civil war, the Tlaltelolco massacre, and a plethora of other Hispanic sociopolitical events formed an integral part of events occurring elsewhere in the world.

As critics we naturally have the greatest opportunity in our own area of literary studies to change the way others tend to look at or, perhaps more accurately, ignore the Hispanic world. But I would argue first that we critics have contributed to the Hispanic cultural isolation with our penchant for parochialism. As a profession we tend to create exclusive literary categories, with the result that we sometimes discourage the interest of general readers and of scholars in other disciplines. The Generation of '98 and *Modernismo* are two glaring examples of Hispanic parochialism. For the rest of the literary world, the first has virtually no meaning, while the second, Hispanists repeatedly have to point out to colleagues in other literatures, is not to be confused with the English term *modernism.* Such Hispanic exclusivity tends to inhibit non-Hispanists from exploring avenues of comparison and may explain a sometimes disdainful attitude on the part of critics in other literatures toward all post-*Quixote* Hispanic works. Even conceding that the Spanish American "boom" may well represent the most obvious exception to such an anti-Hispanic bias, there are those who argue that people in other Western countries were attracted more by the stereotypes than by the artistic value of "boom" fiction—"magic realism," they claim, corroborates North American and European images of Latin America as an exotic continent. If this attraction of alien Hispanic modes does explain to some degree the phenomenon of the "boom," even Fuentes, Vargas Llosa, and García Márquez have failed to free Hispanists from the corner of the world into which they have helped paint themselves.

Beginning in this country in the 1950s, and thanks largely to the efforts of René Wellek, comparative literature became the primary tool in our profession for transcending literary isolation. With this study I propose to accomplish a similar integrative goal by focusing on discourse. In his effort to offer a definition of that concept, Paul Bové conveys its interconnecting essence when he says that discourse aims "to describe the surface linkage between power, knowledge, institutions, intellectuals, the control of populations, and the modern state as these intersect in the functions of systems of thought."[3] While concentrating on Spanish fiction, I explain how the works analyzed serve as registers of events, trends, ideas, attitudes, and artistic styles that have come to define current Western rather than merely Spanish reality. Whereas I do not wish to deny what is uniquely Spanish in this body of fiction, I intend to emphasize how it forms part of an ecological discursive system encompassing the rest of the globe.

With an eye to keeping the communicative code as clear as possible, it may be appropriate to take a moment to expand on a couple of the ideas just stated. When I say that I emphasize how these works define current reality, I do not mean to imply that our historical, cultural, and intellectual past has no bearing on what I discuss. To the contrary. But the past always comes to us filtered through the present, and so my attention is on the current expression of our discursive heritage. I want to emphasize also that I refer to fiction as a register rather than as a reflection of certain concerns. By employing the word *register*, I hope to avoid the implication of causal relationships. Of course I am fully aware of novels such as *Jurassic Park*, in which the author self-consciously tries to develop a story based on chaos

3. Paul A. Bové, *Mastering Discourse: The Politics of Intellectual Culture*, 6–7.

and fractal theories, and of the numerous works in which philosophical and historical theories are discussed, debated, and sometimes demonstrated. But I do not propose to emphasize here such intertextual references with their cause-and-effect intents. When I equate a novelistic pattern with fractal geometry, for example, I do not mean to imply that the author has or has not heard of the geometrical hypothesis concerning fractals. What interests me in this project is how we can apply a theory from one discipline to help explain an effect created by another. When we can do that convincingly, again with fractals serving as an example, I think we can argue that similar epistemic forces inspire the mathematician and the novelist in their efforts to define reality at a given point in time.

As noted, I am not interested in determining to what degree the writers whose works I discuss in this study may consciously attempt to reflect, appropriate, or imitate certain scientific, social, or philosophical theories or activities—indeed, one's level of consciousness at best is difficult to measure and document. My goal is merely to demonstrate some of the ways in which fiction corresponds to events and methodologies in nonliterary areas. As I define my own position on this point, I should recognize that others have applied concepts such as "chaos" and "entropy theory" to literary works written outside our present episteme, and in doing so they have contributed new critical insights into those texts. Yet my goal is to avoid prescriptively applying any of the theories discussed to a given novel or story. I merely try to draw connections or analogies, to demonstrate some of the ways in which a specific work or body of fiction serves as yet another register—no more or less significant than the other disciplines mentioned—of how reality is conceived at a given moment in time.

Since textual analysis itself has become controversial, it seems only fair to underscore here that this study involves analysis and interpretation (I hope that it will be clear in all cases that it is *my* interpretation, with no implication that it is *the* interpretation of the work). James Mandrell, for example, argues that Hispanists in general and peninsularists in particular do little more than hammer out, year after year, yet another reading of the same canonical works, with each new reading contributing minimally, if at all, to our intellectual needs. His thesis echoes, consciously or not, that of William Paulson, who in a study of Anglo-French literary studies claims that the production of ever more complex formal analyses is no more intellectually dynamic than the production of biographical studies of thirty years ago.[4]

Most of the novels and stories I analyze in this study are new, and, for the most part, they have not been subjected to detailed critical analysis. As a result, I could claim innocence and ignore the charges by Mandrell and Paulson. Yet both scholars primarily address methodology rather than canonicity, and their thoughtful remarks deserve more than a flippant response.

First there is the issue of whether as literary scholars we should label ourselves *critics* or *theorists*. Although that neat division has been sanctioned by tradition, I question whether it continues to be viable. Most if not all of the literary texts I have read posit theoretical concepts, while much theory relies on literary texts for demonstrating its concepts. Increasingly in my own work I find it almost impossible to divorce literature from theory, and in this study I have made a conscious effort to combine the two. Yet many no doubt will label the product of that combination *criticism* and not *theory*. If so, I am comfortable with that label, about which I will have more to say in the Epilogue.

Whereas Mandrell laments our practice of producing multiple readings of a single text, I celebrate such readings as irrefutable evidence of the dynamic essence of literature. In this book, however, I am trying to offer more than "just another reading," a phrase that applies equally to the until now virtually nonanalyzed *Todas las almas* (All souls) as it does to *Tiempo de silencio*, a novel with an extensive critical bibliography. Even though I closely examine internal systems of signification in each work of fiction, I do not limit my scope to a structural analysis. My goal is to project a view of how this collection of texts forms an integral part of an international discursive field; to demonstrate how the aesthetic experiences this fiction creates can help us better understand, and perhaps give more meaning to, the world in which we exist. In effect, I aspire to demonstrate the aggregative participation of these works in a global interdisciplinary dialogue that voices new or different ideas about, and constructs new or different approaches

---

4. The references are to James Mandrell, "Peninsular Literary Studies: Business as Usual," 291; and William R. Paulson, *The Noise of Culture: Literary Texts in a World of Information*, 165.

to, reality. In addition to demonstrating how these works collectively create an ontological effect, I propose by means of individual analyses to examine how the reader becomes an active participant in these processes and how reading a work of literature helps bring into focus and contextualize the forces linking literature and mathematics, the natural sciences, the social sciences, the other humanities, and of course the nonacademic world of political revolutions and civic evolutions.

Of course implicit in what I have said to this point is the question of critical position and interpretative authority. I employ the first-person singular and the word *reader(s)* essentially as synonyms. In referring to reader experience, I do not mean to claim any kind of ultimate authority for my interpretations. Other than resorting to an abuse of qualifiers such as "perhaps," "maybe," "apparently," and "it seems," it is difficult to avoid statements that convey a didactic tone or a totalizing implication. If I am guilty of making such statements, I only hope that my reader understands that I merely wish to allude to what is variously called "consensus reality" or "communally acquired knowledge." That is to say, I have applied my acquired knowledge and faculties of logic and ask my readers to validate or challenge my readings according to their own acquired knowledge and faculties of logic. Although we work from a common base dictated by our culture, as individuals we acquire different kinds and levels of information and powers of reasoning, differences that ensure each of us reads and interprets to one degree or another differently. By defining my own reading and demonstrating how I arrive at it, my goal is to encourage a play of differences rather than to impose a law of uniformity.

Only three of the novels included in this study are securely in the canon: *Tiempo de silencio, Juan sin Tierra* (Juan the Landless), and *El cuarto de atrás* (The back room). The selections by Luis Goytisolo, Eduardo Mendoza, José María Guelbenzu, and Juan José Millás are waiting their turn, which may or may not come. The rest of the fiction is either too little analyzed to date or too new to have received the scrutiny necessary for canonization. Temporal and spatial constraints explain why I do not include several other works of fiction that I mention. I can easily imagine someone else writing a book with a similar approach and concerned with the same period yet drawing on a significantly different body of fiction (consisting of both other texts by the same author and texts by other authors). In addition, many readers no doubt will discover that one or two of their own favorites have been overlooked. Since it is beyond my capacity to write a study that is both analytic and comprehensive, I can only hope that the discussions of the works included serve to justify their selection. Of course that justification will depend on the success of the analyses in projecting a reasonably convincing picture of the discursive currents in post-totalitarian Spanish fiction. But even if the view I project is not as convincing as I would like, at the very least I hope that this book will serve as a useful point of departure for future studies of this novelistic period.

The organizational and selective process in a study such as this is always problematic and subject to second-guessing. First of all, I begin with an analysis of Martín-Santos's *Tiempo de silencio*, which was published in 1962. I include a novel published in the midst of rather than after the Spanish dictatorship because it introduced many of the discursive practices I analyze in the more recent works. If not the first, certainly Martín-Santos's was the most successful Spanish fiction of its time to introduce global discursive practices in a self-conscious manner. As I turn my attention to the post-totalitarian period, I divide it chronologically into three five-year segments: 1975–1979, 1980–1984, and 1985–1989. The order of analyses within these periods, however, responds to the discursive practices the works project rather than to the chronological sequence in which they were published. Although I believe that epistemes shift—just as a prevailing order tends toward disorder or entropy—over a period of time, I do not wish to suggest that the changes occur necessarily in five-year cycles. I created such a chronological division here merely as a means of tracing the process of the shift. If there is a significant temporal pattern, I believe that it more typically concerns decades (and even here I suspect there may be as much randomness as pattern over an extended period of time).

The combination of chronological divisions and a nonchronological order of analyses within the divisions, then, allows me to demonstrate the various means by which the novels published from 1975 through 1979 concentrate on subverting the authority of totalitarian discourse. There is a slight shift in the works drawn from the first five years of the decade of the 1980s. They evince different textual strategies for transcending a fascist mind-set that was at or near the point of exhaustion. Finally, the selections from the period 1985 through 1989 no longer project a need to nod to Franco's ghost presumably lurking in the background. Instead of totalitarianism and fascism, this fiction addresses in various ways the issues of power, ideology, gender, and identity.

The motive for the gradual disappearance of the Franco legacy in these works is an open question. An idealist may claim that it signals a sociopolitical coming-of-age for the nation. A cynic may opine that it represents a generational suppression of a guilty past. Perhaps a more realistic commentator would see it as a sign that the obsession with Francoism has recessed into the collective unconscious or has become dispersed in more immediate and topical issues. But whatever the motives, the fiction examined here does project a shift of emphasis in the discourse. In the pages that follow I will attempt to demonstrate how we as readers experience that process of change.

1

The Post–World War II Episteme

THE CURRENT TREND toward ethnic and regional as opposed to national identity serves as perhaps the most dramatic
register of our present episteme. We are witness to a worldwide political
process of fragmentation, decentralization, and pluralism that is challenging
and dismantling many of the established centers and hierarchies of power.
In effect, the trend now in intellectual circles and perhaps society in general
is not merely to tolerate but to celebrate difference, perhaps as a reaction
against the old order, for as one critic states it, the "reduction of difference
is the major totalitarian enterprise of both societies and individuals."[1] It
would not be excessively adventurous to predict that historians will label
the last quarter of the twentieth century as the *post-totalitarian era*—or
some nonprefixed synonym such as *the era of political decentralization*.
A brief review of the political events occurring since 1975 in Spain, the
former Soviet bloc, Latin America, and China indicates why I feel justified
in predicting such a label.

Certainly the year 1989 will live in memory since it marked the end of
the Soviet bloc. What happened in Eastern Europe, however, was part of
a much wider movement whose most immediate political antecedent was
Spain. When Franco declared himself supreme commander of the country

---

1. Leo Bersani, "The Subject of Power," 20. It may be important to underscore that I am
trying to report political changes and at the same time avoid value judgments concerning
the move toward decentralization. If on balance most observers see the changes in Spain
and the Soviet bloc as positive, few would praise the effect of decentralization and the
emphasis on ethnic identity in the former Yugoslavia. Even within Spain and the former
Soviet Union these changes have come with a high price tag, which could very well increase
tragically in the near future.

at the end of the civil war in 1939, he also promised that Spain would eventually return to a monarchy with Juan Carlos, the son of exiled King Don Juan, on the throne. Since Franco had Juan Carlos under his tutelage, it seemed certain that a Spanish totalitarian regime would continue well into the twenty-first century.

Franco himself unwittingly undermined his master plan for the next century with the decision in the 1950s to incorporate members of Opus Dei into strategic positions in the government. Opus Dei, a Catholic lay organization, echoed the regime's religious conservatism while also advocating economic and technological progress. By the late 1950s Opus Dei technocrats were firmly positioned in the government, and they deserve major credit for the dramatic increases in tourism, foreign investments, and international political influence as the decade of the 1960s began.[2] In addition to the flow of money and tourists into the peninsula from northern Europe, in November 1959 President Eisenhower arrived in Madrid to sign a pact with Franco to allow American military bases in the country. For its cooperation, Spain reaped the benefits of increased American foreign aid, and the U.S. State Department ceased its unofficial opposition to American citizens' visiting the country. But foreign influences and the drive to modernize slowly began to diminish the power of the centralized government to control and discipline its citizens.

By the 1970s Franco's health was visibly failing, and ETA, the militant Basque organization dedicated to political autonomy, manifested its power to the world by assassinating Franco's right-hand man, Carrero Blanco, in 1973. Even the pessimists sensed that the Spanish totalitarian regime, which had more than thirty years to build and fortify its infrastructure, might not be able to resist the forces of pluralism and decentralization.

After the dictator's death on November 20, 1975, King Juan Carlos, contrary to Franco's master plan and to what most Spaniards expected, set in motion the reforms that would end fascist rule in Spain. First, he responded to the growing sentiment toward decentralization by granting partial and then much broader amnesty to political prisoners, in July 1976

2. Charles F. Gallagher, "Culture and Education in Spain Part 6: Franco Spain (1936–1975)," states unequivocally that 1960 represented a whole new phase in Spanish social and educational development. Even though the Stabilization Plan recommended by the World Bank and administered by Opus Dei technocrats was issued in the summer of 1959, it was not until the following year that it began to take full effect (8–9).

and March 1977 respectively. Even more significant is that on December 15, 1976, he allowed a national referendum on political reform. The June 15, 1977, general parliamentary elections followed that vote. Not surprisingly, the first party to emerge with a majority was the Center Democratic Union, and its leader, Adolfo Suárez, was named prime minister. Suárez was a carryover from the Franco regime. This symbolic tie to the old center was short-lived, however, because in 1982 the formerly marginalized Socialists Workers' Party headed by Felipe González won the election. The forces for decentralization have continued since 1977, most dramatically with the Basque Separatist Party's demand for independence underscored by terrorist attacks, but also with the increasing autonomy granted to Cataluña, Galicia, and the other provinces.[3]

If ethnic plurality is but one of the forces that helps explain the drive for a decentralized government in Spain, it is perhaps the overriding factor in what occurred in the Soviet Union and its satellites. The dramatic changes in the Russian Republic began with Gorbachev's presidency in 1985 and glasnost, his program of reconciliation with the West. By October 1987 observers detected a significant increase in television-news autonomy just as the regime announced perestroika, a program of economic restructuring.[4] Following the election of a new parliament in March 1989, the 110-member Central Committee resigned in May (a resignation that Gorbachev "requested"). Yet the coal strikes and increasing ethnic rebellions in July and August 1989 threatened Gorbachev's own power. In September the Kiev Popular Movement called for independence for the Ukraine, and the inexorable tide of ethnic pluralism signaled the end of Gorbachev's presidency and of the Soviet Union.

Simultaneous with the drive for independence on the part of the ethnic regions within the old Soviet Union, the Warsaw Pact members also broke from the centralized control of Moscow. Contrary to the 1956 Polish and 1968 Czechoslovakian revolutions when Russian invasion and occupation reasserted Soviet domination, in 1989 the central government not only lacked the power to intervene but indeed glasnost and perestroika tended to

3. For an example of how political regionalism has spread in recent times, see Angeles Espinosa, "Barrer para casa," *El País* (Madrid), January 31, 1993, p. 10.

4. See David Wedgwood Benn's "Glasnost, Dialogue and East-West Relations," and the interview by Anthony Gardner, "The Media under Gorbachev (Interview with Vitalii Alekseevich Korotich, Editor of *Ogonek*)."

encourage independence movements. When the Communist leaders of the satellite countries saw that they could no longer count on Moscow, they were forced to seek compromises within their own borders. Poland serves as a prime example. In the summer of 1988 Solidarity held strikes, and as a result the government banned the party. In April 1989 the government yielded to pressures and restored full legal rights to the labor party and agreed to general elections for June of the same year. The overwhelming victory of Solidarity marked the end of Communist rule and the independence of Poland from Russia.

Similar changes occurred in the other satellite countries. On November 24, 1989, the Communist Party leadership in Czechoslovakia resigned under pressure. Kádár was ousted from the Communist Party of Hungary in May 1988; in October 1989 the party dissolved itself, and elections were scheduled for spring 1990. Zhivkov was removed from power in Bulgaria, which had previously been considered a model satellite, in November 1989. Outside Russia, the most dramatic changes occurred in East Germany, where the exodus of citizens to West Germany forced Honecker to retire in October, and then the following month the Berlin Wall was dismantled. If at first glance the reunification of East and West Germany seems to challenge the general pattern of decentralization, it is well to remember that the imposed division had nothing to do with ethnic composition. Indeed, one political observer noted in a 1990 article that "the composition of the larger Germany will remain federated and decentralized."[5] Also in 1989 Slovenia declared its independence from Yugoslavia (a prelude to the bloodiest ethnic division in Europe during and after that period). Only Ceauşescu in Romania survived the decentralization of 1989, and he paid with his life for resisting for so long the tides of change.

One could argue that the shifts within the Soviet bloc were not merely interrelated but indeed causal. Yet similar challenges to centralized total-itarian regimes occurred that same year in Latin America and Asia that logically had no direct causal relationship to Russia and the Warsaw Pact. Stroessner of Paraguay was ousted in February 1989, the first dictator to fall in that key year. In April and May the whole world focused on the student demonstrations in Tiananmen Square in Beijing. Although squelched by

5. Thomas Kielinger, "Waking Up in the New Europe—with a Headache," 250.

a bloody show of force, the protest indicated the force of the opposition to China's centralized power. Other key events in the movement toward decentralization in 1989 include the election of Menem in Argentina in May, the Mexican state election of non-PRI candidates in Baja California in July, the union strikes and protests in Peru in October, and the Chilean elections marking the definitive end to the Pinochet rule in December. Finally, though nothing as dramatic as the events previously mentioned occurred in the United States, there is no question that Americans have experienced their own expression of decentralization. In the 1992 presidential elections (as was the case in 1980, 1984, and 1988), first the Republicans and then the Democrats offered party platforms stressing less government control and more autonomy for individual states. As the 1994 congressional elections clearly demonstrated, the 1996 presidential candidates from both parties in this country will feel obliged to embrace even more publicly the worldwide climate of decentralization.

The political changes that I have plotted leading from the former Soviet Union to China, to Latin America, and to the United States do not form a straight line of cause and effect but, rather, a jagged series of lines connecting scattered points on an international field. I now propose to expand that field by switching the focus of inquiry from spatial to temporal interconnections, from plotting the geographical points where totalitarian regimes fell to tracing the historical roots of the disciplining state.

For many people the term *disciplining society* conjures educational, penal, and mental institutions, but these facilities are merely physical manifestations of social attitudes. Indeed, attitudes and institutions are interconnected, and together they form part of a discursive practice; the corrective institutions emerge and evolve in response to the need to control citizens within the social unit. For example, Foucault relates how in the Middle Ages punishment was a public spectacle involving torture and grotesque executions, while prisoners were hidden away in underground dungeons. Increasingly in our century executions are being carried out in seclusion and by supposedly painless injection, while prisoners are housed for full display in high-rise cell blocks known as "panopticons."[6]

---

6. Of course witnesses normally are present at executions in this country, but the punishments are not open to the general public. It is not unreasonable to generalize that the only spectacle now occurs outside the facility and usually concerns demonstrations for

These contrasting systems project two distinct discursive practices. The shift from public spectacle to secret punition, from morbid beheadings to behavioral modifications, may have signaled the end of absolutism but not of discipline. Foucault argues that the modern nation-state has discovered that it can rule more effectively by means of psychological rather than physical punishment. The architectural design of the panopticon—prison cells built around a central observation tower in which a single guard can observe, without being observed, any prisoner at any given moment—is the physical expression of a social attitude. That attitude, extended to society at large, creates a sensation in each citizen that someone is always secretly watching—in addition to spies and agents of the police, the government, collection agencies, and cameras in stores, banks, schools, and hospitals, the computer has become an even more insidious all-seeing "eye." The principle behind such a surveillance system is to encourage civic self-discipline and conformity. Also, it becomes the duty of everyone to scrutinize the activities of neighbors. The panoptic system evolved, according to his theory, because it is more efficient than the gallows for controlling large masses.

Foucault's theory is as controversial as it is provocative. Recent statistics revealing a worldwide increase in crime would seem to refute the thesis that a panoptic system encourages civic self-discipline, and there is an ongoing debate as to whether psychology is a more effective deterrent of crime than the gallows. In fact, many argue that one of the earmarks of current society, along with an increasing crime rate, is a growing lack of self-discipline. I would not want to dismiss the notion that Foucault can be faulted for overstating the effect of a panoptic system. Yet I am prepared to argue that his analyses of the apparatuses created to implement the system, and of the intent behind their implementation by the state, are valid. Furthermore, the rise in crime rates may not signal that Foucault's theory on self-discipline is erroneous but rather that we are now witness to a growing resistance to the prevailing panoptic discourse.

Although the panoptic system has survived the decline of totalitarianism, clearly a dictatorship provides the most propitious context for it to operate at maximum efficiency. The current international antitotalitarian movement

---

and against capital punishment. The concept of self-discipline and the panopticon—to be discussed shortly—comes from Michel Foucault's *Discipline and Punish: The Birth of the Prison*.

can be interpreted, therefore, as an expression of a new (in the sense of "different") discursive practice. In effect it functions as a counterdiscourse to the disciplining authority of the nation-state—whether a dictatorship or a democracy—that has prevailed essentially since the medieval period and that has undergirded the ideals of national unity and centralized power.

Franco's speeches serve as a revealing register of how Spain expressed in its unique way the panoptic system that Foucault describes for Western Europe. In fact, the same basic discursive practice that led to the auto-da-fé during the Inquisition helps to explain the clandestine police state that evolved during the Franco dictatorship.[7] Even before he became dictator, the general himself assumed major responsibility for implanting the concept of a self-disciplining society. Indeed, the discursive link between Foucault and Franco clearly emerges in one of the general's addresses delivered in April 1937 in which he promised to give "to the people what truly interests it: *see and feel itself governed.*"[8] By stressing visual and sensorial phenomena, the soldier Franco actually seemed to be anticipating the philosopher Foucault and his panoptic thesis. But Franco was definitely not a philosopher and functioned as a voice of his time perhaps even more than as a military leader. A similar role obtains in another 1937 speech in which he declared that "A stable and firm government, capable of imposing its will on the people, and capable of directing the country, is all that Spaniards need and want" (177). Rather than merely defining the regime he had in mind for Spain when the war ended, obviously he initiated in this speech a discourse designed to convince the people that they were, or would be, responsible

7. In corroboration of the secrecy with which punishment was administered by the Franco forces both during and after the war, a continuing debate concerns the number of people executed by the regime. Not only were the executions carried out in secret, but to date no records have been found indicating how many victims were involved. On the Republican side, by way of contrast, executions were well documented in the press, which many feel helped justify the Allies' refusal to aid the Republican cause. For more on this debate and other issues see the series "1936–1939: La guerra de España," ed. Juan Luis Cebrián and Edward Malefakis, in *El País Semanal* (Madrid), issues 1–18 in 1986, pp. 1–288.

8. Falange Publications, *Palabras del Caudillo,* 14 (emphasis added). Subsequent citations will indicate the page number in parentheses. I will be limiting myself here to Franco's own statements. This and all other translations from Spanish in his study are my own. For examples of how other representatives of the regime express the same philosophy, see Amando de Miguel's *Sociología del franquismo: Análisis ideológico de los ministros del régimen.* For a discussion of Spanish fascism as defined primarily by Franco's followers, see Julio Rodríguez Puértolas, *Literatura fascista española: I/Historia,* 15–72.

for the type of government that emerged. That strategy formed a link with his emphasis on national and individual discipline.

Along with the words *faith* and *unity, discipline* was one of Franco's favorite prescriptions for ensuring the glory of Spain. In one of his later annual speeches, he devoted a whole section to "Disciplina y Orden."[9] Of course within the context of a fascist regime, discipline is synonymous with obedience to the central authority, which he insisted was "the responsibility of each and every Spaniard" (112). By tying obedience to individual and collective responsibility, once again he seemed to be pointing at a panoptic system in which each citizen has the duty to monitor neighbors, with the obvious result that every monitor is also monitored. All this leads to a self-perpetuating system, since the best defense against possible accusations made by others is to be in a position to return the accusations.

To ensure that the collective surveillance focused on the most insidious threats, the regime launched a discursive campaign against the advocates of political decentralization and religious and ethnic plurality, in short against anything that might undermine the hegemony championed in the constantly repeated "one Spain, one race, one language." That discursive campaign, moreover, included visual signs as well as verbal pronouncements. For example, the symbol of the Catholic Kings, five arrows bound by a yoke to signify unity, was appropriated by the Falange and became a ubiquitous highway poster—similar to the presence of Burma Shave advertisements in this country some forty years ago.

For resistance to be a vital force, it must have a formidable opponent; the more real and present the danger, the more effective the appeal to patriotic duty. During the war years it presented no problem to define the danger in terms of the enemy's ideologies, but Franco tended to eschew any mention of their Spanish nationality, an eschewal facilitated by the label *rojo* that he attached to them. His other strategy for avoiding the delicate "the enemy is us" paradox was to focus on the foreign elements in the Republican ranks. Taking advantage of Independence Day, May 2, 1937, he primarily targeted international communists as he praised the people for their courage to take up arms "to fight what was not Spanish but foreign."[10] The same collection of Franco's speeches reveals that the following year, at a celebration of the

9. Antonio Cillán Apalategui, ed., *Discursos y mensajes del jefe del estado (1968–1970)*, 63. Subsequent citations will indicate the page number in parentheses.
10. Falange Publications, *Palabras del Caudillo*, 85.

second anniversary of the *Alzamiento,* or Rebellion, he attacked the foreign brigades: "The foreign invasion is what opens the Catalan border and opens the door to undesirable international forces that plunder and destroy" (137). Obviously Franco hoped to exploit the emotional appeal of xenophobia to rally the people in the name of national unity. In doing so, he conveniently ignored the key role that non-Spanish troops and supplies played in his own major military campaigns: Moorish and Italian soldiers along with German air power and armaments. But the future dictator knew that in bellicose Spain the conditions were ideal for him to mold the discourse into his own version of reality, and xenophobia served him well to that end, as it continues to serve some politicians in this country.

The American Republicans particularly since 1992, as the Spanish Nationals of 1937, have equated liberalism with pernicious foreign influence. Both parties appealed to xenophobia as they spoke of national unity as a defense against the deunifying force of foreign influences. George Bush, for example, alluded to the time his Democratic opponent Bill Clinton spent studying at Oxford as reason to suspect some sinister foreign plot lurking behind Clinton's economic plan. The right wing of the Republican Party voiced even more militantly antiforeign sentiments. In addition to advocating trade embargoes for Japanese products, the ultraconservatives advocated constructing a wall on the border between the United States and Mexico. Although the Pat Buchanan wing cited economics as the official motive for its proposals, no one can deny that these policies appealed to racial xenophobia. Again we see an example of discourse fusing time and space.

Shifting the focus back to 1937 and Spain, Franco decided that because of the makeup of the Spanish Republican forces, communism offered the best target for his attacks. But even during the war, and definitely after it, he tried to create an even more pejorative connotation for the term *liberal.* He could apply liberalism, after all, to both sides of the postwar communist/capitalist conflict, since one ideology was as much a threat as the other to his dream of realizing the Falangist motto of "One country. One nation-state. One Leader."[11] Almost from the beginning he ranted that the liberals were out

11. The Spanish expression is "Una patria. Un estado. Un Caudillo," as cited by Javier Tusell, *La dictadura de Franco,* 103. Tusell gives an account of Franco's somewhat uneasy relationship with the Falange until he eliminated Hedilla. Tusell notes that in the early years, when Hedilla referred to the "Caudillo" of the party motto, he clearly had in mind José Antonio Primo de Rivera, the founder of the party, and not Franco (95).

to destroy traditional Spanish values: "And after the liberal exploitation of Spaniards there will be a rational participation by all as the State draws from families, municipalities and trade unions to progress."[12]

Franco made many references to what could be labeled *family values.* His dictatorship and the Republican Party of this country represent very different, basically opposite institutions, far removed in time and space. Yet the evils of liberalism seem to represent a cornerstone for a discursive field encompassing Spain of the 1930s to the mid-1970s and the United States of the 1990s. Indeed, during the 1992 elections the Republicans tried to exploit the issue of family values, a unifying force threatened by liberalism, according to them. In championing the "traditional family," implicitly if not explicitly they, like Franco, defined its values as patriarchy and patriotism, devoutness and deference. Obviously the Francoist as well as the Republican goals were to fuse the hearth with the heartland under the rubric of national unity and political conservatism. The recent congressional and approaching presidential elections in this country indicate their success as the Democrats demonstrate that they also intend to lay claim to family-values issues.

Whereas the association of family and religion applies to a plethora of religious denominations in the United States, in Spain the fusion is only with Catholicism. Franco contended that the liberals threatened religious orthodoxy, and he insisted that Catholic fanaticism directed against liberalism was a virtue that distinguished Spain from the rest of the world:

> Sépanlo también, en su egoísta frialdad, esas democracias cristianas (menos cristianas que democracias), que, infectadas de un liberalismo destructor no aciertan a comprender esta página sublime de la persecución religiosa española que, con sus millares de mártires, es la más gloriosa de las que haya padecido la Iglesia.

> (Let those Christian democracies [although they are less Christian than democratic] be aware, in their egotistic stoicism that, because they are infected by a destructive liberalism, they do not understand this sublime story of Spanish religious persecution that, with its thousands of martyrs, is the most glorious of all that the Church has suffered.) (48)

Since liberalism, to Franco's way of thinking, subverted Spanish religious as well as political unity, he responded by fusing state and church, a strategy

12. Falange Publications, *Palabras del Caudillo,* 14.

by which he proposed to create a uniquely Spanish trinity consisting of "unity, discipline, and faith."[13] As the rest of the world dedicated itself to ending the war, redefining national boundaries, and rebuilding razed cities and industries, Franco launched a new counterreformation designed to seal off the peninsula from all outside liberal influences.

He referred to foreigners in general, with their liberal and atheistic ideas and customs, as evil forces threatening the hegemony of Spain. His basic message never varied from the defiant declaration, "Those who believe that Spain needs to import anything from abroad are mistaken."[14] In a 1943 message to the Cortes, the dictator referred to the French occupation at the turn of the nineteenth century as a liberal plot typical of countries lacking the moral fortitude of Spain. His 1946 message to the Cortes consisted in large part of an attack against those countries that labeled his government a dictatorship, and he was still saying in 1955 that a liberal democracy, which goes hand-in-hand with marxism, would be the worst possible system for Spain.[15] His appeals to xenophobia did not exempt economics, as demonstrated by his 1949 attack on liberal capitalists (105). But as the decade of the 1950s progressed, national economic and international political issues began to usher in an inevitable change in the regime's policy of isolation.

In the mid-1950s the United Nations finally accepted Spain as a member, and Opus Dei asserted its influence as the country bore witness to the influx of northern European, American, Japanese, and eventually Arab investments and tourists. Eisenhower's visit in November 1959 marked a significant change in public and official attitudes toward non-Spanish presences in the country. As a result, Franco was forced to attenuate somewhat his antiforeign rhetoric. His address to the Cortes in 1967 serves as a good example. While defending the "Organic Law of the State," which named the Fascist Party (Movimiento Nacional) as the only legitimate political alliance in Spain, Franco felt obliged to concede that multiple political parties may have their place in other countries. At the same time, he insisted that such

---

13. Falange Publications, *Franco y España: 25 años de Caudillaje*. The Spanish reads, "la unidad, la disciplina y la fe" (21).

14. Falange Publications, *El Movimiento Nacional: Textos de Franco*, 18.

15. Antonio Cillán Apalategui, *El léxico político de Franco en las cortes españolas*, 108–9. Subsequent citations will indicate the page number in parentheses.

fragmentation would threaten the "social unity" of Spain and dismissed the calls for plurality as examples of rigid and dogmatic imported ideologies (122). It is highly significant, however, that in his 1969 annual address to the nation, Franco spoke with pride of an increase in tourism from 4 million to 21 million visitors over a ten-year span.[16] Suddenly, foreign invasions took on a very positive economic connotation.

As the leader of his country Franco was increasingly caught in a dilemma as Spain began the decade of the 1970s. Nothing demonstrates his plight more dramatically than his decision in 1970 to commute the death sentences of several ETA terrorists. In doing so, he tacitly admitted that the separatist movement of that organization was a significant force. In a public address after the commutation, however, he tried to negate the implications of his capitulation. While thanking the people for the display of homage "in all of Spain that you have rendered recently not only to me but to the Spanish Army and to our institutions," he pathetically claimed that such a display had reinforced his authority (178).[17]

The combination of Spain's increasingly active membership in the international marketplace and the decentralizing ethnic and democratic pressures from within the country created ideological and practical problems that Franco had never faced before. His personal dilemma serves as a register of the epistemic change that insidiously undermined the state system he had helped create, a system he tried desperately to maintain intact.[18]

With the assassination of Carrero Blanco in 1973, the infirm dictator must have realized that the fate of the country was in the hands of the robust Juan Carlos. Almost certainly he did not realize that in some five short years the protégé would help transform the mentor's dream of national unity into a nightmare of regional heterogeneity.

The preceding summary has traced the ecological connections between Spanish political history, the international breakup of the totalitarian state,

16. Cillán Apalategui, *Discursos*, 113.
17. As Tusell, *La dictadura*, notes: "El Franco de la guerra civil tiene poco que ver con ese anciano de voz atiplada sobre el que se hacían chistes innumerables a comienzos de la década de los setenta" (The Franco of the civil war has very little resemblance to that squeaky-voiced old man about whom innumerable jokes were made at the beginning of the decade of the '70s, 388).
18. In spite of the changes, the regime continued its discursive campaign in the press by means of what were sometimes very subtle manipulations. See Jean Alsina, "Une couverture: *Ya* (17-2-70)," for an interesting analysis of pictorial juxtapositions of a 1970 issue of this regime-sponsored newspaper.

Foucault's thesis on panoptic systems, and Franco's official addresses to the people. Now I propose to extend those interconnections by turning the focus to other disciplines. In doing so, I am not suggesting causal relationships but, rather, common approaches to and concepts of reality as evident in chaos, entropy, and information theories as well as in that elusive term *postmodernism*.

By virtue of its centralized authority and imposed conformity, totalitarianism creates the illusion of order and predictability. Yet Spain serves as a useful lesson of how illusions are indeed deceptions. Whether a question of politics or matter, order tends to disintegrate into disorder over a period of time, rendering predictable only that every linear pattern will, at some point, function in a nonlinear fashion. Indeed, recognition of randomness and its role in the universe constitutes one of the salient characteristics of our current episteme.[19]

In the world of science, the new order appears most dramatically in quantum mechanics and its law of probability.[20] For centuries any theory linking science and probability would have been considered an oxymoron; science dedicated itself to universal and linear truths, and any variance or perturbation was considered a flaw in the formula or in its application. Without question the advent of computers all but forced the scientific community to accept the reality of such perturbations, and along with the change created by microchips, discursive practices in general shifted, thereby facilitating the acceptance of hypotheses based on statistics rather than absolutes.[21]

19. See, for example, N. Katherine Hayles's article "Virtual Bodies and Flickering Signifiers."

20. I am bypassing the "Theory of Relativity" since, as Hayles notes, Einstein at one point considered calling his hypothesis the "Theory of Invariance" (*Cosmic Web*, 45), and his theory does not accommodate the concept of probability as a law. Carlos P. Otero, "The Cognitive Revolution and the Study of Language: Looking Back to See Ahead," offers a useful overview linking relativity to other contemporary scientific theories.

21. What I am suggesting also corresponds to *archive*, which, like *episteme*, is a term that resists reification. Foucault, *Archaeology of Knowledge*, seems to indicate, however, that by "archive" he means those forces or practices that allow certain things to happen at given moments in time (130). For example, when Newtonian linearity dominated science, perturbations or loops may have appeared, but scientists most likely dismissed them as flaws in the scientific model being applied. A new archive had to be created before such anomalies could be considered part of the pattern. Roberto González Echevarría, *Myth and Archive: A Theory of Latin American Narrative*, provides a more detailed discussion of archive, and his study offers a model for application of the concept to literary texts.

The path leading from probability to unpredictability, from quantum mechanics to chaos theory, does not form a line but a loop. Researchers in the mathematical, physical, chemical, biological, and ecological sciences have discovered that many linear patterns, some of which had been accepted for centuries as absolute laws, are subject at unpredictable intervals to "strange attractors" that twist the lines into loops. In addition, without actually rejecting causal relationships, chaos theory emphasizes that effects can be disproportionate to their causes. Related to that concept is fractal geometry, which allows us "to trace big effects back to minuscule causes"[22] or, conversely, to relate the local to the global by means of scale models.

Chaos theory encountered some resistance from the scientific community in its early stage, but that resistance has decreased significantly in recent years. Sometimes referred to as "orderly disorder," its advocates consider it a "precursor and partner" to order rather than its opposite.[23] As far as the resisting academy is concerned, Hayles claims that "the crucial turn comes when chaos is envisioned not as an absence or void but as a positive force in its own right" (3). The words "positive force in its own right" again suggest that the new science has come to be seen as a "sign of the times," which is another way of saying that it is interconnected with other discursive practices of recent years.

Entropy, or the "tendency for all things to become less orderly when left to themselves," forms one of the subcategories of this scientific theory. Entropy refers to the inclination "for energy to undergo certain transformations in the natural course of events, making it more disorganized and not so useful, degrading its qualities without diminishing its quantity."[24] As the quoted remarks suggest, a paradox arises since equilibrium signals disorder, and disequilibrium, order. Maximum entropy is a state of equilibrium, and it is difficult to channel matter to produce work when it is in a state of equilibrium. Even though there is an enormous amount of change under the surface, on the small scale of its particles, from the human point of view, it is useless change, banal, producing nothing of interest. In this

22. Elizabeth Sánchez, "*La Regenta* as Fractal," 257.

23. N. Katherine Hayles, *Chaos Bound: Orderly Disorder in Contemporary Literature and Science*, 9. Subsequent citations will indicate the page number in parentheses.

24. Jeremy Campbell, *Grammatical Man: Information, Entropy, Language, and Life*, 18. Subsequent citations will indicate the page number in parentheses.

sense equilibrium, because it resists being harnessed or conducted to an end or providing information, represents nonproductive "disorder." Minimum entropy, on the other hand, signals disequilibrium, and matter in a state of flux can more easily be channeled to produce work. Disequilibrium, then, since it has the potential to be organized to perform some task, is equated with "order." Counteracting the negative effect of entropy (equilibrium and disorder) is cybernetics, or "the science of maintaining order in a system, whether that system is natural or artificial" (22–23).

The insight that order has value serves as the focal point for the second law of thermodynamics. Jeremy Campbell notes that order enables new forms to be created out of old forms; it is one of the forces in biology that makes life possible. Furthermore, order provides the foundation on which civilized societies exist (41).

Because it is more difficult to produce than disorder, society places more value on order. Chaos represents the easiest, most predictable, and most probable state, and it lasts indefinitely. Order is improbable and hard to create. Time functions as its enemy, because entropy tends to increase with time. As noted, orderly energy can do work, but in the very process of working, it decays into disorderly energy (41–42). The formula, then, can be summarized as follows: low entropy = high order; high entropy = low order. Low entropy/high order allows for a maximum not only of work but also of information, the implications of which have led to information theory, a whole new discipline.

Shifting the focus from the science of physics to the science of language, entropy serves as a measure of a receiver's uncertainty concerning the contents of a message. In this sense, entropy equates with disorder.[25] Yet language and living systems are complex and resist disorder by relying on their internalized rules in the form of deep structures or a set of base rules and codes.[26] Paradoxical forces—on the one hand, excessive order, repetition, and redundancy; on the other, excessive complexity, variety, and information—oppose these deep structures. Since every information system "involves both order and complexity, repetition and variety, redundancy and information" (72), only excess qualifies as a single cause for entropy.

---

25. Paulson, *Noise of Culture*, 56–57. Subsequent citations will indicate the page number in parentheses.
26. Campbell, *Grammatical Man*, 93, 113.

Echoing these ideas, Hayles notes, "Too much information, piling up at too fast a rate, can lead to increasing disorder rather than order."[27] Also, information decreases in proportion to the predictability of a message; if it is too simple and predictable, it tends to become as or more meaningless than a message that is too complex and unpredictable. Hayles argues that the perfect system needs to achieve a balance: "Maximum information is conveyed when there is a mixture of order and surprise, when the message is partly anticipated and partly surprising" (53). Paulson, for his part, stresses surprise and its potential for creating new information. He changes the connotation of "noise" by arguing that in a sense all literature qualifies as noise since it represents a perturbation in our language system, but it is a noise that has the potential to create a maximum amount of new information. For Campbell, on the other hand, the ambiguity forming the essence of literary language qualifies as noise all right, and it is to be avoided (163). Although an advocate for some fairly radical views on information theory, Campbell conveys a mistrust for language use that strays from the syllogistic paradigm.

The logic that Campbell implicitly endorses traces its roots back to the Greeks. They created the syllogism with its triad consisting of thesis, antithesis, and resolution. The syllogism constructs evidence so as to lead to solutions, to closure. Syllogizing strives to resolve contradictions and to gloss over or erase differences. Furthermore, language itself expresses this logic system. Since norms and values become institutionalized in language, the syllogism helps present them as natural laws. Poststructuralists, however, have begun to challenge syllogistic logic.

Along with the tendency toward political decentralization and deauthorization and the scientific recognition of the unpredictability of matter, the new antisyllogistic logic strives for multidirectionality. Whereas syllogistic logic accumulates blocks of evidence and assembles them into imposing edifices that it labels as *truth* or *reality,* antisyllogistic logic attempts to dismantle moral and cognitive structures. To do so, it moves in reverse order; the point of departure often is the conclusion, and the process culminates when the underlying thesis is opened to infinite speculation. It reveals how the speaking subject is simultaneously subject to ideological

27. Hayles, *Chaos Bound,* 49.

forces that determine what he or she speaks: "Subject and object give a poor approximation of thought. Thinking is neither a line drawn between subject and object or a revolving of one around the other."[28] The new logic accepts contradiction and encourages plays of difference. It challenges the concepts of centralized power structures and either/or polarities. It postulates that every margin is also a center, and that logic based on binary opposition tends to negate being. Language cannot lead us to values and ethics, and in offering us definitions of them it merely reveals their absence. In short, the new logic proposes to lay bare the role of language in representing social constructs as universal truths.

In a book on Lacan, Ellie Ragland-Sullivan uses the words *philosophy* and *psychoanalysis* in the title, thereby illustrating how easily two historically distinct disciplines now tend to slip into one another's space. But the slippage does not end there, since linguistics also enters the picture. Lacan himself argues that the human psyche functions like a language. As a result, one theorist boldly proclaims "that psychoanalysis must consequently be understood as a branch of semiotics."[29]

Evolving from this fusion of logic, linguistics, and psychoanalysis is the thesis that the human psyche is not unified and stable, but fragmented and dynamic. The grammatical subject *je* has a prelinguistic counterpart, *moi*. The grammatical subject relies both on others and on an ideal "Other" for its language and identity, while the prelinguistic subject relies both on others and on an "Other" for its sense of being. The connecting lines run horizontally and diagonally, indicating that each cause is also an effect.[30]

---

28. Deleuze and Guattari, *What Is Philosophy?* 85. For her part Susan A. Handelman, *The Slayers of Moses: The Emergence of Rabbinic Interpretation in Modern Literary Theory,* argues that many of the aspects I have noted are characteristic of rabbinic thought, to which she attributes much of what we call "deconstruction" or "poststructuralism."

29. Kaja Silverman, *The Subject of Semiotics,* 194. The previous reference is to Ellie Ragland-Sullivan, *Jacques Lacan and the Philosophy of Psychoanalysis,* and subsequent citations will indicate the page number in parentheses.

30. The cause and effect combination of *je-autre* also obtains for *je-Autre,* just as it does for *moi-autre* and *moi-Autre,* and vice versa:

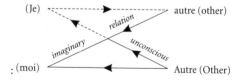

Similar to the linguistic concept that only another sign can respond to a sign, the quest for both subjects (*je* and *moi*) can only lead to further quests; whether speaking of identity or being, each can exist only as a becoming, as process. "The artist is a seer, a becomer."[31] In Lacanian terminology, the real exists only in the interstices between the signifier and the signified.

Postmodernism forms the most obvious bridge connecting literature not only to psychoanalysis and antisyllogistic logic but to politics and science as well.[32] Whether we turn to Jean-François Lyotard, who in *The Postmodern Condition* defines the movement in terms of the demise of master discourses in the service of scientific projects; or to Brian McHale, who in *Postmodernist Fiction* interprets it as a switch in the "dominant" from epistemology to ontology or from problems of knowing to problems of modes of being; or to Linda Hutcheon and her historiographic metafiction explanation in *The Poetics of Postmodernism;* or to Fredric Jameson and his claim that the movement represents consumer society's success in reducing all culture to a pastiche in his *Postmodernism, or, the Cultural Logic of Late Capitalism*—the implicit common denominator for all those mentioned is a move away from any totalizing representations. Since we are in the midst of the postmodern movement, it would be premature to attempt any absolute definition of it. Furthermore, as I turn the focus first to a Spanish novel published during the Franco regime and then to works of fiction published from the year of the dictator's death up to 1989, I will be adding to and refining the schematic explanation above. And by eschewing a detailed explication here, I hope to avoid the trap of allowing any such definition to become prescriptive.

See Ragland-Sullivan's re-creation of Lacan's Schéma L diagram and her explanation of its multidirectional process (*Jacques Lacan*, 2).

31. Deleuze and Guattari, *What Is Philosophy?* 171.

32. These connections should not be taken too literally. One discipline does not serve as an exact mirror image of another. Hayles, for example, explains how deconstruction and chaos theory are fundamentally different. Yet she also sees the general concept of postmodernism serving as the bridge between science and culture. In *Chaos Bound* she offers the following example: "Fractal geometry is emerging as an important area of research because it is one way of conceptualizing and understanding postmodern space" (289). Her study is important because she stresses common denominators rather than exact correspondences. The dangers of literal transference can be seen in John W. Clark's "Views from the Ivory Tower's Basement. A Commentary on 'The Clock and the Cloud: Chaos and Order in *El diablo mundo.*'" Clark, a physicist, criticizes what he considers the Hispanist John Rosenberg's misapplication of chaos theory to Espronceda's text.

Postmodernism, after all, is merely one expression of the multiple discursive practices we will examine in the ensuing pages.[33]

Availing myself of the new scientific discourse, I would like to suggest that politics, science, logic, psychoanalysis, and literature act as strange attractors on one another. Each helps create a loop, a perturbation, that disrupts the linear course the others tend to follow. The sum of those perturbations points to a shift in the episteme or in our way of perceiving reality. The decline of totalitarianism, the advent of chaos and information theories, the move toward antisyllogistic logic and Lacanian psychoanalysis, and the emergence of postmodern fiction form part of an ecological discursive field. Perhaps it is stating the obvious, but the practices on which I focus represent only a small part of a very large whole. Although essentially I followed the signs provided by the fiction itself to arrive at a determined discursive practice, clearly the cultural and intellectual repertoire that I carry with me determines what signs I detect and how I draw the interconnections. Again, at best I have covered only a tiny section of a vast epistemic field. But since "there is no such thing as observing this interactive whole from a frame of reference removed from it,"[34] I can only hope that the partial view I offer is better than no view at all.

33. Ernst van Alphen, "The Heterotopian Space of the Discussions of Postmodernism," offers an extremely lucid critique of Brian McHale's and Linda Hutcheon's theses and adds his own insights to the concept of this phenomenon. In his much more recent *Constructing Postmodernism*, McHale asserts that "there 'is' no such 'thing' as postmodernism" (1), which he goes on to explain is a discursive category rather than a material object.

34. Hayles, *Cosmic Web*, 49.

2

The Year 1962 and the
Spanish Postwar Years

IN A STUDY of myth and history in Spanish postwar fiction a prominent Hispanist argues convincingly that the Franco regime attempted to mythologize Spanish history, to atemporalize it so as to present the nation as morally superior to other countries. Spain's glorious past, so the regime would have had people believe, is written in stone and not subject to reinterpretation. Coinciding with this official discursive campaign was a novelistic movement generally labeled *neo-* or *social realism*. The novelists of this movement set out to subvert the government efforts, not by directly challenging the official historical view, which censorship would have made difficult if not impossible, but by virtually eliminating history from their fiction. These neo- or social realists dedicated themselves to a fictional documentation of the social and moral decadence of the present, thereby undermining, or so they proposed, the official myth that Spain's present is directly linked to its glorious past.[1]

Perhaps because they were intent on subverting the Francoist version of Spanish history, the Spanish neorealists made such a commitment to

---

1. David K. Herzberger, *Narrating the Past: Fiction and Historiography in Postwar Spain.* Other recent studies that place emphasis on the sociopolitical context while maintaining the conventional novelistic divisions for this period are found in Jo Labanyi's *Myth and History in the Contemporary Spanish Novel,* and Barry Jordan's *Writing and Politics in Franco's Spain.* The classic overviews of the Spanish novel of this period are Gonzalo Sobejano's *Novela española de nuestro tiempo (En busca del pueblo perdido),* Ignacio Soldevila Durante's *La novela desde 1936,* and Margaret E. W. Jones's *The Contemporary Spanish Novel, 1939–1975.* My *La novela española de posguerra: Creación artística y experiencia personal* is more limited in scope as it offers detailed analyses of some of the key novels of the period.

mimetic representation that they projected a view of reality that many readers consider excessively provincial, static, and politically disengaged. These novelists' emphases on scenic descriptions echoed an earlier twentieth-century aesthetic advocated by Henry James, Percy Lubbock, and others that privileged "showing" over "telling" or the exclusion of narrative commentary from what Lubbock defined as the "craft of fiction." Serving as principal critical spokesperson for a counternovelistic mode, Wayne Booth responded to those who would make novelistic art synonymous with mimesis by calling for a return to what he labeled the "rhetoric of fiction." As Booth employed the term, *rhetoric* refers to the writer's license to indulge in editorial intrusions, linguistic experimentations, or any kind of verbal excesses. By the 1950s North American, South American, and European writers were already breaking away from the restraints of an aesthetic based so predominantly on showing. Yet in Spain, no doubt in part due to censorship, that decade marks the zenith of mimetic art. Much more than their nineteenth-century predecessors, the twentieth-century Spanish neorealists tended to transform their narrators into cameras, thereby imposing limitations on the expressive arsenal at the novelist's disposal.[2] That is not to imply that their art has no universal themes or values, for it definitely does. Yet it must rely almost exclusively on metaphorical transformations to project universal implications; readers are required to draw the connection between the parochial scene and the global discursive practices inherent in it. That self-imposed limitation on the art of fiction prevailed for most of the 1940s and 1950s in Spain, but with the beginning of the 1960s the forces for social and novelistic change began to manifest themselves within the peninsula.

When *Tiempo de silencio* appeared in 1962, it provided a model for overcoming parochialism by radically breaking from the mimetic mode of the previous two decades. That model served Juan Goytisolo for his 1966 *Señas de identidad* (Signs of identity) and Juan Benet—one of the original contributors to that mouthpiece of the neorealists' movement, *Revista Española*—for *Volverás a Región* (You will return to Región), which was published in 1967. By the decade of the 1970s a whole list of increasingly nonrealist novels by former members of the old guard followed, among

2. Fernando Morán, *Explicación de una limitación: La novela realista de los años cincuenta en España,* was instrumental in pointing out some of the restrictions the novelists imposed on themselves as a result of this extreme commitment to mimetic representation.

them Gonzalo Torrente Ballester, Carmen Martín Gaite, Miguel Delibes, Camilo José Cela, Luis Goytisolo, Juan Marsé, Jesús Fernández Santos, and José Manuel Caballero Bonald. Tragically killed in an automobile accident before he had a chance to assume active leadership of the new movement, Luis Martín-Santos nevertheless deserves credit for changing the direction of postwar Spanish fiction.[3]

In view of what has been stated above, perhaps it should not be so surprising that, in an overview of the Spanish novel from 1976 to 1986, a leading Spanish critic argues that post-Franco fiction represents a continuation of the innovations he identifies in *Tiempo de silencio*. According to this scholar, the essential contributions of Martín-Santos's novel to recent Spanish fiction include more engaged and subjective social commentaries (as opposed to the neorealists' reliance on the scene itself), a more poetic and baroque style (contrasted with the "objective" descriptions of the former mode), and a more self-conscious narrator (as opposed to the camera eye dominating Spanish fiction of the 1950s).[4] In noting these aspects, the critic cited joins a long list of others who have concerned themselves with defining the stylistic and thematic characteristics of Martín-Santos's novel that separate it from its predecessors and identify it with its successors within the peninsula. A few, including Darío Villanueva, have ventured beyond Spanish borders to make comparative studies between this novel and Joyce's *Ulysses* or some of the Spanish American "boom" novels. But even these comparisons have placed the emphasis on structure or theme.

At the risk of parroting Villanueva, I also intend to begin this study with an analysis of *Tiempo de silencio*. Contrary to the exclusively textual or thematic analyses of the novel to date, however, I will be focusing on how it expresses global discursive practices.[5]

3. At his death Luis Martín-Santos was working on a second novel, *Tiempo de destrucción*, which, though obviously incomplete, was published posthumously. The special 1990 issue of *Cuadernos Universitarios* provides a complete list of his publications and also includes Pedro Gorrochategui Gorrochategui's useful "Una bibliografía global de Luis Martín-Santos."

4. Darío Villanueva, "La novela."

5. There are a number of very valuable studies on *Tiempo de silencio*. In addition to the special issue of *Cuadernos Universitarios*, see also William Sherzer's "An Appraisal of Recent Criticism of *Tiempo de silencio*," and Malcom A. Compitello's "Luis Martín-Santos: A Bibliography." Recent studies of the novel also include Carlos Jerez-Farrán's " 'Ansiedad de influencia' versus intertextualidad autoconsciente en *Tiempo de silencio* de Martín-

On the political front, in the mid-1950s Franco began appointing Opus Dei members to key positions in his government, thereby creating the discursive thread connecting Spain with the Cold War powers in the early 1960s. By then, the effects of Opus Dei's more liberal economic philosophy began to surface.[6] Yet those liberating influences manifested themselves at the very culmination of the regime's program to consolidate its power. Martín-Santos's novel, in other words, arrived on the scene when Spain was undergoing a type of sociopolitical schizophrenia.

The contradiction implicit in the reference to "sociopolitical schizophrenia" also applies to the world powers, for this was the time when the Cold War reached its hottest point. The United States and Russia approached the brink of nuclear war twice, first because of construction of the Berlin Wall and then because of the Cuban Missile Crisis. With the threat of not merely another world war, but of a nuclear one at that, even in the democracies the forces for increased central power grew. Those forces became more pervasive as the United States found itself increasingly involved in the war in Vietnam. But the events of 1968 appear to corroborate the principle that "the production of power simultaneously implies the production of that which opposes power."[7] It can be argued that the year 1989, with more dramatic and fundamental effects, represented for the totalitarian states of the Eastern bloc and South America what the year 1968 represented for the Western democracies. The demonstrations in Paris, Mexico City, and Chicago signaled a reversal of some twenty-five years of centripetal movement around the axis of the disciplining state. Throughout the 1970s, 1980s, and thus far in the 1990s, advocates of individual freedoms have increasingly challenged defenders of national interests. Yet a new shift may now be underway, as oppositional forces to the cult of the individual speak with growing authority.

Similar processes occurred in other areas. For example, the modern states' increasing efforts in the decade of the 1960s to centralize scientific research

---

Santos"; Stacey L. Dolgin's *La novela desmitificadora española (1961–1982)*; and Dale F. Knickerbocker's "*Tiempo de silencio* and the Narration of the Abject."

6. This Catholic lay organization was founded by José María Escrivá de Balaguer in 1928. Escrivá, who like Franco died in 1975, was selected for beatification on May 17, 1992, by Pope John Paul II. During the Spanish civil war he supported Franco and the Nationalists. Escrivá and his followers, ultrareligious conservatives opposed to the reforms of Vatican II, advocate science and technology as a means to economic growth.

7. Ross Chambers, *Room for Maneuver: Reading Oppositional Narrative*, xviii.

in the universities by means of economic pressures (such as direct military funding for secret projects, imposed security regulations, and federal influence over the type of experiments eligible for grants), stood in marked contrast to the scientific academic community's growing interest in how matter creates and responds to random, decentralizing patterns. Although these relationships are surely epistemic rather than causal, the university community increasingly began to challenge the central government's role in scientific and other research.

Similar decentralizing theories also appeared in other disciplines. By the mid-1960s such dissenting voices as Foucault, Lacan, and Derrida began publishing their destabilizing theories on social practices, the human psyche, and language. Preceding them by about a decade were Noam Chomsky, who spoke as a major voice for a linguistics severed from the diachronic chain of cause and effect, and Claude Shannon, who developed the new discipline called information theory, which draws its basic premises from entropic theory.

I think it is accurate to say that when *Tiempo de silencio* appeared in 1962 an epistemic shift was underway that began at the turn of the century and manifested itself most dramatically as an aftermath of the bombing of Hiroshima and Nagasaki. That same basic episteme, with gradations that I will analyze, obtains for the post-totalitarian period discussed in Chapters 3, 4, and 5. I have selected Martín-Santos's novel, therefore, as the most effective point of departure from which to experience, by means of selected literary texts, some of the major discursive practices that define the post–World War II episteme.

The Discursive Field of *Tiempo de silencio*

Given the Spanish sociopolitical context of the early 1960s, most observers agree that *Tiempo de silencio* (A time of silence) represents a challenge to the new privileged role of technology and science promulgated by Opus Dei. The novel subverts that program by means of an excessive and hence parodic employment of technical and scientific terminology, neologisms, and foreign words. While the philosophy of Opus Dei may well inform *Tiempo de silencio,* Martín-Santos's novel addresses the role of science and technology in more universal terms. The text also undermines many of the pillars of Western tradition, including syllogistic logic, systems of power and authority, paternalistic hierarchies, and the definitions of "centrality" and "marginality."

The plot centers on Pedro, a young medical scientist who dreams of winning the Nobel Prize by detecting the virus that causes cancer. The project is threatened when the supply of imported laboratory mice runs out and there are no funds to buy more. He discovers that Muecas, a trash collector, has stolen some of the mice and is reproducing them in his shack. Hoping to bargain for the rights to some of the offspring, Pedro visits Muecas in the slum area where he lives with his wife and two daughters. They fail to reach an accord on that occasion, and later Muecas appears at Pedro's boardinghouse in the early hours of the morning and begs the young doctor to help one of his daughters, Florita, who is suffering a miscarriage. Pedro does not know that Muecas, who is responsible for the pregnancy, induced the abortion. Pedro agrees to help, inspired by the possibility that the girl has been infected by the mice and may provide the key to the virus for which he has been searching. He arrives too late, for apparently Florita is already dead. Yet that unfortunate turn of events does not deter him from performing a surgical intervention, and when the police are informed they arrest him as the person responsible for the young woman's death. The victim's mother then confesses that her husband is to blame, and the young scientist is given his freedom. He is dismissed, however, from the laboratory where he works, and shortly thereafter his fiancée is murdered by Florita's boyfriend, who believes Pedro was responsible for the pregnancy. The novel ends as Pedro heads for a remote village where he plans to set up a medical practice.

In the early part of *Tiempo de silencio* the reader is introduced to the slum area where Muecas and his family live. As the narrator adjusts his lens, the focus falls first on the city proper, then widens to encompass the nation-state, and finally pans to the extrageopolitical region of poverty and hunger: "the neighboring city still not destroyed by the bomb . . . the state not destroyed by the bomb, . . . and the land of hunger which—for certain—was absolutely indestructible by the bomb."[8] This passage, which ironically underscores the power of the atomic bomb to eradicate everything

---

8. Luis Martín-Santos, *Tiempo de silencio*, 70. Subsequent citations will indicate the page number in parentheses.

but poverty, also points to a dramatic change in attitude toward scientific and technological progress. Although much literature of the 1920s and 1930s satirized and ridiculed technological progress, writers in those years could not cite anything as concrete as the atomic bomb as proof that the applied sciences had betrayed rather than created the promised social utopia.[9] With the projection around the world of the photographs of Hiroshima and Nagasaki, however, Utopia suddenly became Armageddon, and a new and broader discursive field emerged. The bomb hastened a growing conviction that the time had come to question the authority behind some basic social, religious, and political assumptions; perhaps people should begin to contemplate alternative ways of thinking and being.

Many now argue that since the nineteenth century science, technology, and capitalism have been inexorably united in the Western world.[10] The social philosophy of Opus Dei stresses such a union; their thesis is that scientific and technological progress will pave the road to economic development for Spain. Yet *Tiempo de silencio* represents progress as a mere exacerbation of poverty, for it juxtaposes scenes of squalor from life in the Madrid slums with signifiers of advancement in the applied sciences. The problem is even more complicated, because the young scientist, Pedro, lacks adequate funds to maintain the supply of laboratory mice for his study of a cancer-causing virus. Scientific research, therefore, also falls victim to national poverty. It is a question neither of science eradicating economic needs, as the technocrats claim, nor of a simple polarity between technology and penury. Technology and totalitarianism, progress and poverty, power and paternalism: all are

9. For an assessment of how Spanish literature from the turn of the century up to the 1930s satirized science and technology, see Juan Cano Ballesta, *Literatura y tecnología (Las letras españolas ante la revolución industrial 1900–1933)*. Michel Foucault in *Power/Knowledge: Selected Interviews and Other Writings 1972–1977*, points out the importance of the atomic bomb in changing our discursive practices. He argues that the bomb marked a change from the "universal" intellectual (the writer) to the "specific" intellectual (the scientist, and he cites Oppenheimer as the prime example). Foucault argues that with the development of the bomb, "for the first time the intellectual was hounded by political powers, no longer on account of a general discourse which he conducted, but because of the knowledge at his disposal: it was at this level that he constituted a political threat" (128). Foucault's theory may apply to my comments on governmental interference in scientific research conducted by universities in this country—an interference that many feel peaked in the 1960s.

10. Jean-François Lyotard, *The Postmodern Condition: A Report on Knowledge,* and Fredric Jameson, *Postmodernism, or, the Cultural Logic of Late Capitalism.*

implicated to one another, though not in a linear, syllogistic pattern. The lines run forward and backward, upward and downward, with each cause also constituting an effect.

A subtle undermining of the linear, syllogistic approach to reality takes place on a syntactical level. The challenge to linearity occurs in the first words of the novel as Pedro, working with his assistant, Amador, in his laboratory, narrates: "The phone was ringing and I have heard the bell. I have grabbed the device. I have not understood very well. I have put the phone down" (7). Acting as both speaker and focalizer, Pedro utters verbal constructions that are more paratactic (based on caesuras) than syntactic (based on linking words). Listeners depend on the logic of speech acts to span the gaps. The logical sequence in this case would be "the phone rang and I answered it." But the speaker unnecessarily fills in the gaps and provides an excess of information, thus paradoxically producing a sensation of cacophonous fragmentation or noise: "He dicho: 'Amador.' Ha venido con sus gruesos labios y ha cogido el teléfono. . . . Está hablando por teléfono. . . . Habla despacio, mira, me ve" (I said: "Amador." He came over with his fat lips and took the phone. . . . He is talking on the phone. . . . He speaks slowly, he looks, he sees me, 7). In communication theory, *noise* is the term used to indicate the part of a message lost in transmission. In addition to mechanical or audio interference, noise may result from too much or too little information or from information that is too surprising or too predictable. Excess in any form could be cited as one of the principal producers of noise.[11] In the examples just cited, Pedro negates the readers' inclination to form logical connections, to anticipate deductively the effect of a given cause, and leaves them with the sensation of a world of detached parts, separated into individual slides observed through his microscope. Pedro apparently tries to live in a Newtonian universe of perfect succession; by unwittingly exaggerating the Newtonian paradigm, he effects a reorientation of cognitive processes. Pedro's parataxis forces readers to diminish their reliance on linear cause-and-effect correspondences; contiguity replaces continuity as the key to logic and meaning.

Following this initial section of the novel, in which Pedro as speaker subverts linear reasoning by carrying it to an extreme, an extradiegetic

---

11. See Campbell, *Grammatical Man,* Hayles, *Chaos Bound,* and Paulson, *Noise of Culture,* for more on the concept of noise.

narrator intervenes to demonstrate equally nonlinear relationships among power hierarchies. Convention represents power alliances in the form of a vertical line, with the source at the top and a diminution of power at each descending step: at the top, the politically and economically powerful; at the bottom, the politically and economically powerless. Martín-Santos modifies that vertical paradigm in three fundamental ways. Rather than a single vertical line, the text suggests a horizontal dispersal of brief but interconnected lines. Whereas power is usually presumed to flow downward, here there is a capillary effect, as it runs upward and downward. Furthermore, if politics and economics offer the outward trappings of power structures, the novel points at paternalism as their very foundation. This revisionist view of power hierarchies emerges when the narrative focus turns to the infrastructure of the slums, specifically to Muecas, his wife, and their two daughters.

With the hope of selling them back to the young scientist, Muecas has stolen the laboratory mice (ironically, they had been imported from Illinois) essential for Pedro's research. Although Muecas subsists at the very bottom of the macrosocioeconomic order, possession of the Illinois mice bestows on him a privileged social status within the slum world:

> Gentleman-farmer Muecasthone visitaba sus criaderos por la mañana donde sus yeguas de vientre de raza selecta, refinada por sapientísimos cruces endogámicos, daban el codiciado fruto purasangre. Emitía órdenes con gruñidos breves que personal especializado comprendía sin esfuerzo y cumplimentaba en el ipso facto . . .

> (Gentleman-farmer Muecasthone visited during the morning the breeding stables where his select breeding mares, thanks to a refining process of highly sophisticated endogtamic crossings, produced prized pureblood offspring. He issued orders by means of brief grunts, which a highly specialized staff easily understood and carried out in an ipso facto . . .) (67–68)

This passage parodically echoes English feudalism and colonialism and suggests an infinite number of lines running horizontally and vertically rather than a single hierarchical line descending from above (the British throne) to below (the Madrid slums). Indeed, a few pages later another metaphor underscores the similarity between power structures that occur at points totally removed in time, space, culture, and social level:

> Príncipe negro y dignatario Muecas paseaba su chistera gris perla y su chaleco rojo con una pluma de gallo macho en el ojal orgullosamente,

entre los negritos de barriga prominente y entre las pobres negras de oscilantes caderas que apenas para taparrabos tenían.

(A Negro prince and dignitary, Muecas paraded proudly, in pearl-grey top hat and red vest with a rooster feather in the lapel, among the pot-bellied pygmies and their poor women with swinging hips who hardly had a g-string to cover themselves.) (71)

Muecas serves as the focal point in a discursive field that comprehends the family structure of a contemporary Madrid slum, a colonial English manor, and a sempiternal African tribe. The interconnections for this field are multi- rather than unidirectional.

Despite the cultural, geographical, and generational differences high-lighted in the two previous examples, Muecas reveals the common denom-inator by beating his wife and daughters each night, "thus reaffirming his seigniorial status" (72). Although writing from within a dictatorship where power seems to flow vertically from the top down, Martín-Santos challenges that unidirectional concept. The textual strategy signals that dictatorships are merely larger and more dramatic examples of a vast horizontal network of power structures anchored by the family unit. The family (citizens, vassals, or tribal members) grants the power that the father (executive, lord, or chieftain) exercises over it. Franco often referred to the Spanish citizens as his children and began many of his public addresses with the salutation "My children." The dictator's use of the word *children* when referring to the people may serve as an unconscious register that the system he helped create also created him. *Tiempo de silencio* points to the conclusion that paternalistic attitudes are the source of democratic as well as totalitarian political and economic structures.[12]

Just as the novel points to the conclusion that political hierarchies are founded on paternalistic principles so does it imply that the patriarchal right and obligation of the state is to control and punish its subjects. Society must discipline itself, and to that end the state must classify and segregate its citizens:

que el hombre nunca está perdido porque para eso está la ciudad (para que el hombre no esté nunca perdido), que el hombre puede sufrir o

12. In his analysis of the novel, Stephen M. Hart, *The Other Scene: Psychoanalytic Readings in Modern Spanish and Latin-American Literature,* has suggested the neologism "phallocracy" to characterize the Franco regime (46).

morir pero no perderse en esta ciudad, cada uno de cuyos rincones es un recogeperdidos perfeccionado, donde el hombre no puede perderse aunque lo quiera porque mil, diez mil, cien mil pares de ojos lo clasifican y disponen, lo reconocen y abrazan, lo identifican y salvan, le permiten encontrarse cuando más perdido se creía en su lugar natural: en la cárcel, en el orfelinato, en la comisaría, en el manicomio, en el quirófano de urgencia, que el hombre—aquí—ya no es de pueblo. . . .

(for a man is never lost because that is what the city is for [so that a man will never become lost], for a man can suffer or die but not be lost in this city—each of whose nooks and crannies is a perfect lost-and-found souls department—where a man cannot become lost even if he tries because a thousand, ten thousand, a hundred thousand pairs of eyes classify and catalogue him, recognize and embrace him, identify and save him, thereby allowing him to find himself when he feels most lost in his natural setting: in prison, in an orphanage, in the police station, in the insane asylum, in the emergency room, because a man—here in this place—no longer forms a part of the pueblo. . . .) (19)

Some thirteen years after *Tiempo de silencio* appeared, Foucault published *Discipline and Punish,* in which he argues that the contemporary disciplining society tries to act as a gigantic panopticon and devotes much of its efforts to classifying its citizens. With the references in this passage to state apparatuses for finding, identifying, classifying, and segregating its citizens, Martín-Santos anticipates Foucault. The state is intent on developing classificatory systems whose primary purpose, the narrator states (and Foucault no doubt would echo), is to account for every citizen. When at the end of the passage the narrator employs the word *pueblo,* he contrasts it with the repetition of *ciudad* (city) at the beginning—"pueblo," or "populus," connotes humans, while *ciudad,* or *civitas,* connotes institutions—thereby adding dehumanization to his implicit definition of the disciplining state.

As the previous example indicates, the state uses its institutions—prisons, jails, orphanages, hospitals, asylums—to force threatening nonconformists into physical isolation. Difference must be punished—and in more severe cases, erased—and the offenders ostracized or eliminated. The punishment depends on the degree to which society feels menaced by the offenders. This concept of social polarization arbitrarily defines centers and margins: nonconformity as opposed to disobedience, peccadillo as opposed to crime, eccentricity as opposed to insanity. The capriciousness of the system emerges when Pedro, out for a Saturday night on the town and walking along Calle de Cervantes in the old section of the city, begins to contemplate some of the implications of *Don Quixote* and its creator: "What does it signify that the person who knew that insanity merely means nothingness, empty space, a vacuum, should have affirmed that only in insanity does man's moral being reside?" (75). This association of madness with morality underscores the difference between social and medical definitions of insanity, between being and nonbeing. And whereas Don Quixote passes as a comically eccentric character intent on righting imagined wrongs, Pedro finds something tragically serious in this Cervantine farce:

> Lo que Cervantes está gritando a voces es que su loco no estaba realmente loco, sino que hacía lo que hacía para poder reírse del cura y del barbero, ya que si se hubiera reído de ellos sin haberse mostrado previamente loco, no se lo habrían tolerado y hubieran tomado sus medidas montando, por ejemplo, su pequeña inquisición local, su pequeño potro de tormento y su pequeña obra caritativa para el socorro de los pobres de la parroquia. Y el loco, manifiesto como no-loco, hubiera tenido en lugar de jaula de palo, su buena camisa de fuerza de lino reforzado con panoplias y sus veintidós sesiones de electroshockterapia.

> (What Cervantes is shrilly shouting is that his madman was not really mad but rather that he was doing what he was doing so that he could laugh at the priest and the barber, for if he had laughed at them without having previously demonstrated his madness, it would not have been tolerated and they would have taken measures, such as creating their own little local inquisition, their little torture chamber, and their little charitable society for helping the poor of the parish. And the madman, clearly not a madman, would have had, in place of a portable cage, his nice straitjacket and his twenty-two sessions of electroshock therapy.) (76)

The lesson of Pedro's meditations is all too clear. Society tolerates insane people much more readily than it does the sane who are guilty of subversive behavior. Indeed, in Cervantes's days the asylum was a fairly recent institution; previously, the mentally ill had been tolerated in society. For Martín-Santos, however, the issue is not unique to seventeenth-century Spain, since the words *electroshock therapy* extend the discursive field to modern times. As Foucault was to argue, the state did not create insane asylums out of a desire to cure the mentally ill but to control and discipline social nonconformity—that is, to curb behavior that the disciplining society might label *public nuisance*. Thus sociopolitical ideologies define madness every bit as much as do medical abnormalities. The terms *sane* and *insane,* in fact, are not common in modern medical discourse. They have been appropriated by an inquisitional discourse devoted to order and obedience.

As Pedro's ruminations on Cervantes's legacy near their end, he decides that Don Miguel had no recourse but to base his farce on contradictions in order not to go insane himself. Insanity renders ethical behavior possible and serves as the ultimate threat for those who fail to act ethically. Or, to reverse the equation, the reward for ethical behavior is sanity, yet sanity impedes one from acting ethically. This paradox emerging from polarities somewhat resembles a "strange loop" in logic, as when on one side of a paper is written "the statement on the other side is true" and on the reverse is written "the statement on the other side is false."[13] Each statement cancels the other, and therefore the question of truth and falsehood is undecidable. The center of authority and truth, the sense of unity provided by belief in such a center, shatters. Of course, if no center exists or if the traditional center proves to be a myth, there are no margins. This expression of what is popularly labeled *situational ethics* indicates that moral behavior cannot be reduced to the binaries good and bad, right and wrong, virtue and sin. Human beings will probably always need to rely on opposites to determine morality, but the definitions of those opposites are or should be dependent on context, according to the novel. The reference to Cervantes and his masterpiece challenges the validity of fixed centers and margins, of stability and unity, of absolute moral and ethical authority.

In addition to making arbitrary the distinction between sane and insane, prevailing practice draws an equally arbitrary separation between the self and the other. The opening laboratory scene of *Tiempo de silencio* brings into question the social myth of clearly differentiated selves. The phone rings, and as Amador answers it that neatly binary division also seems to break down:

> "No hay más." "Ya no hay más." ¡Se acabaron los ratones! El retrato del hombre de la barba, frente a mí, que lo vio todo y que libró al pueblo

13. Hayles, *Cosmic Web*, 34. At least as I understand what is meant by polarities, the idea is not to deny opposites, for it is difficult to imagine the concept "good" without having in mind something to represent its opposite, "bad." But if we limit our understanding of these two concepts to polarized definitions, we do ourselves and others a disservice. Univocal meaning, which was precisely the goal of Franco's discursive campaign, tends to have a dehumanizing effect.

ibero de su inferioridad nativa ante la ciencia, escrutador e inmóvil, presidiendo la falta de cobayas. Su sonrisa comprensiva y liberadora de la inferioridad explica—comprende—la falta de créditos.

("There are no more." "There aren't any more." The mice are gone! Facing me, the portrait of the bearded man who saw it all and who freed the Iberian people from their innate inferiority in science, scrutinizing and immobile as he presides over the lack of specimens. His comprehending and inferiority-liberating smile explains—comprehends—the lack of funding.) (7)

The bearded man of the picture is Santiago Ramón y Cajal, who as of 1962 was the only Spanish scientist to have won the Nobel Prize. Under the influence of Opus Dei, the regime incorporated him into its discursive campaign by hanging his picture in virtually every science laboratory. Apparently the idea was to make him the "object of desire" for the new scientific generation. Since Pedro functions as the narrator and focalizer of this scene, it seems reasonable to assume that the telephone message concerning the lack of mice for his experiments triggers a psychological bifurcation in which he projects himself into the picture on the wall. Before the call, Pedro's paratactic or choppy narration and magnified perspective suggest a scientific, or microscopic, approach to reality. The picture almost certainly represents his ideal "Other." After hearing the telephone message, however, Pedro assumes the perspective of the photo on the wall and views himself as a failed and alienated "other." In this scene Pedro is simultaneously the focalizing subject and the focalized object. As focalizing subject, he is the ambitious young scientist who aspires to become another Ramón y Cajal and win the Nobel Prize. As the focalized object (that is, the Pedro under observation by his bifurcated Ramón y Cajal self), he is subjected to judgment of a sociopolitical system that encourages vainglorious dreams but refuses to provide the economic support to make the dreams even remotely possible. Rather than a unified self, the text posits two Pedros, one of whom views the other with condescending scorn in his futile attempts to achieve scientific glory. In effect, by referring to himself in the third person he has negated his own being: "the 'third person' is not a 'person'; it is really the verbal form whose function is to express the *non-person.*"[14] The passage suggests, therefore, that Pedro, the aspiring Nobel

14. Emil Benveniste, *Problems in General Linguistics,* 198. Subsequent citations will indicate the page number in parentheses.

Prize winner, is not a person at all. He is a product of the regime's official discursive campaign to champion science and technology, which in turn is the product of what Lyotard has labeled Western society's scientific master discourse.

Whereas in the early part of the novel Pedro transforms himself into a nonperson by virtue of his third-person self-focalization, he begins to refer to himself in the second person as the events unfold. Emil Benveniste further explains that the first two persons are on a totally different plane from that of the third nonperson: " 'I' and 'you' are reversible: the one whom 'I' defines by 'you' thinks of himself as 'I' and can be inverted into 'I,' and 'I' becomes a 'you' " (199). The novel offers an example of this reversible self-focalization as Pedro contemplates his fate in the jail cell where he has been confined. He was arrested for his role in the fatal miscarriage of Muecas's daughter Florita. The police charged him with practicing medicine illegally when he responded to Muecas's pleas to help Florita, who, as noted, apparently had died before Pedro arrived (the text creates a certain ambiguity concerning the time of death). The young medical student had just returned from a drunken Saturday night on the town when Muecas awakened him, and Pedro responded to the solicitation with entirely self-serving motives.

The incarcerated Pedro undergoes a crisis of identity while staring at a stain on the wall that he imagines to be a siren: "From here, if I lie down, the siren can look at me. You are fine, you are fine. Nothing can happen to you because you have not done anything. . . . It is clear that you have not done anything" (216). The object with which he identifies in this case is not an icon sponsored by the state but a blemish he anthropomorphizes into a young woman. That change is fundamental. The Ramón y Cajal photograph is a visual sign placed on the laboratory wall for an official ideological purpose; the stain on the jail wall that Pedro gradually transforms into the dead Florita's image suggests the power of human values that transcend governmental discursive policies. That transcendence helps explain the narrative switch from the third nonperson in the initial section of the novel to the second person in the middle.

Human values notwithstanding, the switch to the second person indicates Pedro's attempt to deny responsibility for any part in the tragedy of Muecas's daughter. He soon discovers, however, that "you" and "I" are reversible, as Benveniste has explained: "You didn't kill her. She was dead. She wasn't dead. You killed her. Why do you say you? —I" (217). The fusion of past and present, "you" and "I," is in turn erased: "No pensar. No pensar. No pensar. No pensar tanto" (No thinking. No thinking. No thinking. No thinking so much, 217). The negatives along with the Spanish infinitives convey a denial of everything, a retreat into total nonresponsibility, nonidentity, and nonbeing. But the spot on the wall refuses to disappear, and the anthropomorphism intensifies:

> va tomando forma semihumana y que acompaña porque llega un momento en que toma expresión, va llegando un momento en que toma forma y llega por fin un momento en que efectivamente mira y clava sobre ti—la sirena mal dibujada—sus grandes, húmedos ojos de muchacha y mira y parece que acompaña.

> (it is taking on a semihuman form and it stays by your side because the time comes when it takes on an expression, the time finally comes when it assumes a form and it fixes its gaze on you—this poorly drawn siren—its large, teary child's eyes and it looks and it seems to stay by your side.) (217–18)

Pedro's bifurcated self will not let him ignore the victim ("que acompaña") or the circumstances: "Why did you have to do it drunk, completely drunk?" (216). Finally, the struggle between accepting and denying guilt, between bifurcation and unification of self, culminates in a momentary first-person acceptance of responsibility: "You didn't kill her. She was dead. I killed her. Why? Why? You didn't kill her. She was dead. I didn't kill her. She was already dead. It wasn't I" (220). Not only is the fusion of self by means of the first-person verb form tentative, but the confession of guilt is misguided and finally denied as well. The only guilt Pedro seems to recognize concerns his intoxicated state when he operated on the unfortunate young woman. But if she was already dead his drunkenness is not an issue, and he is not guilty of anything. Never does his other self confront him with his motives. The sense of psychic unity ("It wasn't I") is false, and the section ends appropriately with "Imbécil" (221), an apparent self-indictment, though it lacks any verbal markers specifying who is the speaking subject and who is the indicted object.

The disciplining state prevails, and at the end of the novel Pedro has been exiled to a village where he decides to blend into the social order to which he is now totally subjected. Any hint of unity of self is destroyed by the emergence of an authoritative voice with biblical overtones: "Podrás cazar perdices, podrás cazar perdices muy gordas cuando los sembrados estén ya . . . podrás jugar al ajedrez en el casino. . . . Estarás así un tiempo esperando en silencio, sin hablar mal de nadie" (You will be able to hunt partridges, very fat partridges when the fields are sown . . . you will be able to play chess in the casino. . . . You will spend a time waiting in silence, without speaking badly of anyone, 293). The reiteration of future imperatives echoes the biblical phrase "Thou shalt," in turn underscoring the cosmic implications of Pedro's moral decay. Rather than a true speaking and acting subject, he is the conduit for a discourse of which he is really the object. The imperatives suggest that Pedro must assume responsibility for allowing his socially imposed ambitions to transform him into a product of that society. The novel implies that, in an emerging consumer society fueled by science and technology and controlled by a panoptic and paternal system, the individual must nevertheless find a means for making ethical choices.

If Pedro emerges as the tragic product of a scientific imperative that is willing to sacrifice ethics for comfort and conformity, *Tiempo de silencio* offers one character who refuses to make that ethical compromise. Ricarda, Muecas's wife and a woman whose physical description connotes both subhuman status and religious avocation (61), represents an innate sense of morality. Because Ricarda witnessed Pedro's intervention in her daughter's miscarriage, she tells the police that the young scientist is innocent and thereby gains his freedom. As the narrator begins to penetrate Ricarda's consciousness, the grieving mother seems incapable of dealing with the sophisticated medical and legal nuances of the case:

> No saber nada. No saber que la tierra es redonda. No saber que el sol está inmóvil, aunque parece que sube y baja. No saber que son tres Personas distintas. No saber lo que es la luz eléctrica. No saber por qué caen las piedras hacia la tierra. No saber leer la hora. No saber que el espermatozoide y el óvulo son dos células individuales que fusionan sus núcleos. No saber nada. No saber alternar con las personas, no saber decir: "Cuánto bueno por aquí," no saber decir: "Buenos días tenga usted, señor doctor." Y sin embargo, haberle dicho: "Usted hizo todo lo que pudo."

> (To be totally ignorant. To be ignorant of the roundness of the earth. To be ignorant of the sun's immobility, because it seems to rise and fall. To be ignorant of the three distinct persons of the verb. To be ignorant of an electric light. To be ignorant of why rocks fall toward the earth. To be ignorant of how to tell time. To be ignorant of the fusion of the

nucleus of the two individual cells named the sperm and the ovum. To be ignorant of everything. To be ignorant of how to interact socially with people, to be ignorant of how to say: "What nice things you have," to be ignorant of how to say: "May you have a nice day, Doctor." And yet, to have said: "You did everything you could.") (248)

The repetition of the words "to be ignorant" *(no saber)* reinforces the implicit protest against the dehumanizing effect of reinforcing scientific and technological knowledge as the master discourse of modern society. Language contributes to that effect as it obfuscates rather than clarifies human sentiments.[15]

Ricarda represents a precivilized and almost presymbolic (or prelinguistic) stage of development. She does not understand scientific explanations of human life or possess the linguistic sophistication for effective social interaction, but she somehow manages to say and do the right thing:[16] " 'El no fue.' No por amor a la verdad, ni por amor a la decencia, ni porque pensara que al hablar así cumplía con su deber, . . . sin ser capaz nunca de llegar a hablar propiamente, sino sólo a emitir gemidos y algunas palabras aproximadamente interpretables . . ." ("It wasn't him." Not for the love of truth or decency, nor because she thought that by speaking this way she fulfilled her duty, . . . without ever becoming capable of speaking adequately, only able to emit groans and a few words that were barely interpretable . . . , 248–49). Ricarda negates science, logic, social discipline, and paternal authority with her act of righting the wrong done to Pedro. She even defies the laws of the symbolic order with her use of words that are only "approximately interpretable." But somehow her primitive "It wasn't him" suffices to negate the lies, political maneuvering, bureaucratic red tape, and legal complexities of a civilized Western society. How, then, do we explain this marginalized being's need to say and do the right thing when, according to the narrator, she has no ethical motive? Perhaps the relationship between ethics and marginality can be explained by reference to the earlier section

15. The repetition also radically separates this woman from the intellectual "groupies" who hold a cocktail party in honor of an Ortega y Gasset caricature—the narrator builds the scene around Goya's "El Gran Buco," a painting in which a group of mesmerized women offer their infants as sacrifice to a he-goat. See Betty Jean Craig's article, "*Tiempo de silencio:* Le grand bouc, and the maestro," for a detailed analysis of this scene.

16. I have opted for the expression "right thing" since it and its implied opposite, "wrong thing," depend totally on context for meaning.

on *Don Quixote,* whose hero can express his sense of ethics only by being *ex-céntrico.* Martín-Santos carries the Cervantine model one step further by offering a female character who does not inhabit the margin by choice but is forced there by society, yet who, like Don Quixote, expresses from the margin a sense of ethics that those in the center seem incapable of duplicating.

Pedro obsessively aspires to reach that center. Although he is innocent of the crime with which they have charged him, he is guilty of offering his help in the vainglorious hope of winning the Nobel Prize. In his ruminations on Cervantes he addresses the problem of ethical behavior, and briefly in the jail cell he approaches recognition of his own moral responsibility. Finally, however, Pedro opts for the comfortable role of passivity and apparently will reap divine punishment. There is little evidence that his actions, in or out of the laboratory, are motivated by human compassion or moral awareness. As he reveals in the opening scene of the novel, he serves as a register of irrational rationality and of the dehumanization wrought by the modern nation-state. The juxtaposition of Pedro, the socially integrated character, and the socially marginalized Ricarda allows the focus to fall on their respective expressions of ethics. In his efforts to position himself in the center Pedro becomes enslaved by unethical behavior, while the margin provides Ricarda with the freedom to act ethically. The strategy of presenting Muecas's wife, the pariah, as the moral heroine of the novel can also be seen as a challenge to logocentralism. The novel denies the possibility of reifying a code of ethics or of centralizing its area of operation. The definition and location of ethical codes lie somewhere between the signifier and the signified, in the silent zone where meaning must be created by context rather than by custom or decree.

Standing in judgment of the choices made or avoided by each individual is the discursive practice labeled *Christianity,* which transcends those of the Franco regime, the Industrial Revolution, and the scientific episteme that comprehends Newton, Galileo, Ptolemy, and finally Plato and Aristotle.

Many argue that all works of literature lead readers to the open space between words and meanings. Yet the textual strategies of *Tiempo de silencio,* as opposed to those of its immediate Spanish neorealistic predecessors, are *consciously* designed to lead us to open spaces. In effect, the novel forces readers to assume a different viewing perspective, to experience other systems of logic, to resist closure, to contemplate being otherwise. Furthermore, the discourse of *Tiempo de silencio* projects the novel beyond the Spain of 1962. Unlike the neorealistic school that preceded it, Martín-Santos's novel voices international, postmodernist currents of thought that only fairly recently have become the center of discourse in literary criticism.

Finally, Martín-Santos's novel was selected with the intention that it serve as a means for experiencing many of the basic epistemic elements for the analyses to follow. As Foucault stated, "the episteme makes it possible to grasp the set of constraints and limitations which, at a given moment, are imposed on discourse."[17] Much like Saussure's "sign," Lacan's "real," and Derrida's "trace," if the episteme could be reduced to a univocal definition it would lose its reason for being. Since a work of art also resists reification and relies on narrative expansion as opposed to formulaic compression, *Tiempo de silencio* serves as a display text rebelling against the constraints and limitations that were imposed on discourse during the Francoist totalitarian period and that continued to some degree even years after his death.

Franco's death in 1975, thirteen years after Martín-Santos's novel was published, and the Spanish elections of 1977 can be seen as two key moments within a network of similar sociopolitical global events. The move away from political centrality and totalitarianism that the intertextual complexities of *Tiempo de silencio* adumbrate is later expressed in the new Spanish democracy and ultimately in the changes in dictatorial regimes all over the world. But the interconnections do not stop there. The global breakdown of geopolitical centers and the shift to ethnic margins have correlations in the physical and social sciences as well as the arts. Each of these centrifugal movements belongs to a larger web of allusive interrelationships; each constitutes an event that cannot be detached from the much larger network in which it occurs. Like the textual strategies in *Tiempo de silencio*, these connections form part of a new nonlinear discursive field in which speaking subjects are also subjects of other speakers, in which hegemony cedes to heterogeneity, in which power, paternalism, and the panopticon become one, creating horizontal as well as vertical hierarchies that extend beyond geographical, cultural, and temporal divisions. *Tiempo de silencio* ushered into the Spain of 1962 a new discursive field whose borders extend at least to the 1990s.

As we now move to the 1975–1979 period and the end of totalitarian government in Spain, we will see how four novels function as registers of

17. Foucault, *Archaeology of Knowledge,* 192.

many of the same elements, but each emphasizes certain dimensions that foretell a further shift in the global as well as Spanish episteme. In the case of Juan Goytisolo's *Juan sin Tierra,* the emphasis falls on mode, genre, and heteroglossia, while Carmen Martín Gaite's *El cuarto de atrás* points to the realm of state and social apparatuses vis-à-vis gender roles. Eduardo Mendoza's *La verdad sobre el caso Savolta* (The truth about the Savolta case) addresses the dual but related issues of subject position and truth, followed by Juan José Millás's *Visión del ahogado* (A drowned man's vision) and its probe into the interconnecting lines linking the instruments of popular culture with a panoptic system.

3

The Years 1975–1979

IF THE DECADE of the 1960s, with an influx of tourism and foreign investments, marked what many consider the beginning of modern Spain, the second half of the decade of the 1970s bore witness to Spain being cast in the leadership role of a global change.[1] Franco's death in 1975, along with the elections of 1977, set in motion what was destined to become a worldwide trend away from dictatorship and centralized power.

In the United States, 1975 was significant because of Watergate, which seemed to underscore the corruption of centralized power, and primarily because by early May the government withdrew the last five thousand U.S. troops from Saigon. That decision can be considered a part of the discursive field under examination. The boast that the United States had never lost a war formed one of the cornerstones of American nationalism up until the Vietnam fiasco. Yet when the United States pulled its troops out of Southeast Asia, which was tantamount to admitting that we had lost the war, the government responded to public opinion. Obviously, Americans of that time had experienced a radical change of mood that emerged in consonance with other discursive events. Nationalism, with its inherent unqualified allegiance to the central government, was on the wane by the mid-1970s. What would have been unthinkable a decade earlier—capitulation not only to a rival but also to one that was not even a superpower—by 1975 seemed like a reasonable price to pay for extricating the United States from its central

---

1. This was also a period of significant economic growth in Spain. Gallagher, "Culture and Education," reports that between 1960 and 1971, "real per capita income had tripled, annual growth rates of about 7 percent were attained, and the bases of a broadly industrialized consumer society had been prepared" (8–9).

role in global military ventures. The idea of sacrifice for the good of the international community or of the nation increasingly lost its appeal, and in its place were heard demands that efforts and resources be directed to meeting the needs and desires of the individual citizens, states, and regions. In the decade of the 1990s that anti-international attitude has intensified, and many are calling for the United States to withdraw from the United Nations.

Whereas at home the mood favored anticentralized power (Carter won the 1976 presidential election on the platform that he was a Washington outsider), the pressure to maintain the status quo increased on the international front—as opposed to the open competition for areas of influence that helped draw us into Vietnam. In his last days as secretary of state, Henry Kissinger stressed the need within the North Atlantic Pact for power, equilibrium, and hegemony rather than aggression to neutralize the Soviet threat. Another political observer echoed that general philosophy, particularly in reference to equilibrium, in a 1976 article in which he argued the West should refrain from any policy designed to encourage defections among the members of the Warsaw Pact.[2] The suggestion that the West should help maintain the status quo within the Soviet bloc demonstrates how radically foreign policy had changed in a ten-year span. The West had entered a period of retrenchment rather than expansion. The key words of the decade were *détente* and *SALT* (Strategic Arms Limitation Talks) as the world powers tried to minimize major international conflicts while confronting the decentralizing forces from within.

In political parlance, the type of changes outlined tends to be labeled *conservative*. Yet in the intellectual sphere, this was a period of not just liberal but also radical theories. Of course, language or labels assigned to theoretical positions creates the problem here. Despite the dichotomy implicit in the terms *conservative* and *radical*, the political and intellectual events of the decade of the 1970s were very much interconnected. For example, Foucault published *Surveiller et Plenir: Naissance de la prison* (Discipline and punish: The birth of the prison) in 1975, followed the next year by *La Volonté de savoir* (The will to knowledge). Both works unmasked as social

2. For interesting perspectives on U.S. foreign policy at this time, see J. L. S. Girling, " 'Kissingerism': The Enduring Problems," and Humphrey Trevelyan, "Reflection on Soviet and Western Policy."

constructs attitudes that had passed as natural laws. Lacan published *Livres 20–24* (Books 20–24) between 1973 and 1977, key volumes of his opus deconstructing the myth of psychic unity and the stability of consciousness. The 1970s also saw an increased flow of papers, articles, and books on chaos theory, fractal geometry, entropy, and information theory. All these scientific movements tended to challenge the concept of absolute laws. By juxtaposing these political, philosophical, and scientific fields, lines can be drawn interconnecting the events and thereby helping to define the context in the second half of the decade of the 1970s in which appeared the Spanish novels *Juan sin Tierra, El cuarto de atrás, La verdad sobre el caso Savolta,* and *Visión del ahogado.*[3]

Heteroglossia in *Juan sin Tierra*

Juan Goytisolo's *Juan sin Tierra* (Juan the Landless) falls within the epistemic boundaries staked out in *Tiempo de silencio.*[4] But Goytisolo's novel was of course temporally much closer to the key geopolitical events of the discursive field under examination than was Martín-Santos's. Indeed, *Juan sin Tierra* represents one of the more revolutionary novels to appear on the scene in the mid-1970s, and over the years it has become identified with the 1975 change from a totalitarian to a democratic government in Spain.

---

3. Miguel Delibes's *Las guerras de nuestros antepasados* (The wars of our ancestors), published in 1975, and Javier Tomeo's *El castillo de la carta cifrada* (The castle of the coded letter), published in 1979, are two other novels appearing during these years that also serve as effective registers of the processes being discussed. A great deal has been written about Spanish fiction since the dictatorship, but I have found most influential in my own thinking the essays by Gonzalo Sobejano, "La novela poemática y sus alrededores," and by Villanueva, "La novela." In general I do not refer to interviews conducted with the individual novelists, but exceptions should be made in the case of Marie-Lise Gautier Gazarián's *Interviews with Spanish Writers* and Geraldine C. Nichols's *Escribir, espacio propio: Laforet, Matute, Moix, Tusquets, Riera y Roig por sí mismas.*

4. The other two works of the trilogy, *Señas de identidad,* 1966, and *La reivindicación del Conde don Julián* (The vindication of Count Don Julian), published in 1970, were both published in Mexico. Although *Juan sin Tierra* was published in Spain, it was banned until after Franco's death. For a complete list and discussion of Juan Goytisolo's works and a current bibliography on scholarship dedicated to *Juan sin Tierra,* see Abigail Lee Six's *Juan Goytisolo: The Case for Chaos,* and also the chapter on this novel in Dolgin's *La novela desmitificadora española.* Both studies appeared before Goytisolo published *La cuarentena* and *La saga de los Marx* in 1993.

As noted in the previous chapter, *Tiempo de silencio* heralds a change of emphasis from focalized scenes to rhetorical narration; the camera eye gives way to the commenting voice. Following Martín-Santos's model are Juan Goytisolo's 1966 *Señas de identidad* (Signs of identity), Miguel Delibes's 1966 *Cinco horas con Mario* (Five hours with Mario), and Juan Benet's *Volverás a Región* and *Una meditación* (A meditation), published in 1967 and 1970 respectively.[5] But whereas Martín-Santos's novel also restored story in its more conventional sense, the immediate school that formed around *Tiempo de silencio* eschewed that particular element. Benet is a good example of this group that combined rhetoric with an antistory bias. Starting with his very first novel, *Volverás a Región*, the story lines work against each other; generally there is little or no dialogue, and the narrator not only changes the names of the characters but contradicts what he himself narrated earlier concerning their words and actions as well. Luis Goytisolo, author of *Antagonía* (Opposing death struggle), and Juan Marsé, author of *Si te dicen que caí* (If they tell you I fell in battle), employed similar strategies to undermine the conventionally stabilizing effect of the narrated story. But Juan Goytisolo deserves major credit (or blame) for redefining the very concept of a novel. Particularly with his *Juan sin Tierra*, he served as standard-bearer for a new poetics that privileged the act of narrating *(récit)* over what is narrated *(histoire)*.[6]

In effect, Goytisolo's novel inverts the *récit/histoire* model. In modernist texts, the *récit* typically fragments the *histoire* and presents it in nonsequential order (Faulkner's *As I Lay Dying* and Cela's *La colmena* [The beehive] offer contrasting examples of this technique). By reconstructing the *histoire*, critics not only discover the chronological order of the narrated events (or at

5. The general term applied to this group of works is *Spanish new novel*. See Jones, *Contemporary Spanish Novel*, for a lucid definition of this term.

6. In presentations at the University of Colorado, "Reading and Rereading," and in Madrid, "Texto literario y producto editorial," Goytisolo stated that his goal is to write novels that require multiple readings. At both presentations he insisted that if people tell him that they have read and enjoyed one of his novels, he always asks them how many times they read it. If the answer is only once, he feels that either he has failed as a novelist or they did not understand what they read. In his remarks, Goytisolo does not distinguish between a work that invites multiple readings and one that requires them. That attitude may help explain why the influence of writers such as Benet and Juan Goytisolo himself has diminished among the new generation of Spanish writers (with the possible exception of a Benet–Javier Marías connection). It is interesting that in their latest efforts, both Luis Goytisolo *(Estatua con palomas)* (Statue with pigeons) and Juan Marsé *(El embrujo de Shanghai)* (The sorcerer) have resorted to more "readerly" novels.

least their approximate order) but also are able to interpret more clearly the effect created by the *récit*, or narrating process. Since *Juan sin Tierra* is about its own coming-into-being, it is fair to say that its *histoire* is its *récit* and vice versa. By the same token, the speaker within the text is not only the creator but also the creation of his own writing process: "te has transformado y has transformado el instrumento en que te expresas abandonando en cada hoja de papel blanco jirones y andrajos de tu antigua personalidad . . ." (you have transformed yourself and you have transformed the instrument with which you express yourself as you abandon with each sheet of white paper shreds and pieces of your old personality . . .).[7] In addition to the fictional author becoming a product of his own writing process, the reader is also embedded in the fictional world: "you will follow the example of the anonymous architect and you will disorient your future reader in the twists and artifices of your written text" (145). Such textual strategies suggest an interconnectedness with recent scientific approaches claiming that every cause is also an effect and the idea that observers can never divorce themselves from what they observe.

Although the fusion of the act of narrating with the narrated product explains the structural contribution of Goytisolo's novel, his text also serves as a benchmark for challenging prevailing discursive practices. By introducing into the fictional world marginalized expressions and ideas, the novel undermines many of our centralized linguistic and conceptual patterns. Perhaps in a more obvious way than any other work included in this study, Juan Goytisolo's novel showcases Bakhtin's thesis of how heteroglossia challenges and subverts authoritative discourse.[8]

According to the Russian theorist, in every literary work there are representations of "forces that serve to unify and centralize the verbal-ideological world" (270). These linguistic and ideological forces constitute the work's authoritative discourse, and they exert a centripetal force. In that sense they

7. See Gérard Genette, *Narrative Discourse: An Essay in Method,* for a detailed analysis of *récit* and *histoire*. I discuss specifics of this aspect of the novel in *Beyond the Metafictional Mode: Directions in the Modern Spanish Novel*. The passage quoted comes from Juan Goytisolo, *Juan sin Tierra*, 318. Subsequent citations will indicate the page number in parentheses.

8. M. M. Bakhtin, *The Dialogic Imagination: Four Essays*. Subsequent citations will indicate the page number in parentheses. Of course Bakhtin's context also informed his theoretical work. Since it is beyond the scope of this work to examine the context of the theorists from whom I draw, I might signal as a point of departure for defining Bakhtin's context the introduction of the book cited (xv–xxxiv).

serve as a register of the disciplinary regime that attempts to contain diversity and nonconformity by means of laws and to reduce language to univocal ideological statements by means of political slogans, official pronouncements, and censorship. Of course what literature offers is not really authoritative discourse but rather its representation or fictional transmission.

Opposing the centripetal force of transmitted authoritative discourse is heteroglossia, an alien language whose effect is centrifugal. Heteroglossia appears in the forms of parody, comic style, common language, indirect reported speech, "hybrid constructions," and refracted and double-voiced discourse (301–31). Heteroglossia serves to subvert linguistic and ideological centralization and stratification and replace them with decentralization and disunification.

Both authoritative discourse and heteroglossia are realities of the extra-textual, sociopolitical world. The act itself of transmitting authoritative discourse to a literary text functions as a type of subversion, a deauthorization. Indeed, fiction itself can be considered an expression of heteroglossia.[9] But subversion does not end with merely transmitting authoritative discourse to the fictional text. As noted above, parody, comic style, common language, and so forth also serve, consciously or unconsciously, to deauthorize. In *Juan sin Tierra* the speaker resorts consciously to textual strategies designed to subvert the transmitted authoritative discourse, which has already been deauthorized. Perhaps as a result of this conscious effort to subvert the always already subverted, a fictional reauthorization takes place; the linguistic and ideological authority that was lost in the act of transmission is restored by the protesting act of representation. Stated in another way, not only does resistance sustain power but resistance to a force that no longer exists also acts to resurrect, albeit in a different form, that very force.[10] By examining Goytisolo's novel as a register of a particular and global political system on the brink of collapse, I propose to demonstrate how poetics and politics fuse in *Juan sin Tierra*.

Imperial Spain is an example in *Juan sin Tierra* of a resurrected force. The action of the first chapter takes place on a Cuban sugar plantation owned

---

9. According to Bakhtin, "authoritative discourse cannot be represented—it is only transmitted" (344). I take this to mean that the transmission to the text changes and deauthorizes it, and therefore the representation has to be of a discourse already stripped of its authority.

10. I am suggesting a power/resistance relationship similar to what Nina Molinaro, *Foucault, Feminism, and Power: Reading Esther Tusquets,* posits in her introduction.

by Spanish immigrants, a setting that contributes to a conflict between new- and old-world values. The speaker knows that European tradition undergirds his opponent's centralized power base. For that reason he strives to assert a new discursive practice:

> antes de que la vieja predisposición de la estirpe a suprimir la libertad viva de hoy en nombre de la imaginaria libertad de mañana sometiese la invención creadora a los imperativos de la producción, sacrificara el país a la plantación y triturara otra vez a sus hijos como cañas en molino, devolviendo a la Isla siempre Fiel su aborrecida y sempiterna condición de latifundio azucarero.

> (before the old predisposition of our lineage to suppress today's vital liberty in the name of tomorrow's imaginary brand and surrender creative invention to the imperatives of production, and to sacrifice the country for the sake of the plantation and grind up its children like sugar cane once again, thus returning the always Faithful Island to its hated and eternal condition of sugar estate.) (14)

The Spanish empire represents the old order here, an empire that since the time of Columbus's voyage through the nineteenth century dedicated itself to reducing the new world to a "sugar estate." Although that imperial order no longer exists, the speaker sees it as part of a capitalist system still very much in evidence, a system all too eager to sacrifice creativity for productivity. Yet in spite of pointing to an imperialist and capitalist discursive practice that is very much in evidence today, the speaker also resurrects a political order that was finally put to rest in 1898. In that sense he both works within the boundaries of the episteme outlined in *Tiempo de silencio* and, by textually recreating a distinctly Spanish institution that has ceased to exist, narrows those boundaries or shifts the focus from the universal to the parochial.[11]

11. Louis Althusser, *Lenin and Philosophy and Other Essays,* distinguishes between what he calls "repressive apparatuses" that totalitarian regimes create to control their citizens and the ideological apparatuses of every regime, democratic and totalitarian, that also exert control. Whereas European imperialism is one of the trademarks of the nineteenth century, it was also a period when Spain lost its empire. And Herbert Rutledge Southworth, "The Falange: An Analysis of Spain's Fascist Heritage," insists that though the underlying ideology of twentieth-century Spanish fascism was imperial expansion, fanned by nostalgia for past glories, it was never really translated into action (3–4). If indeed Spain's imperialistic ambitions explain why it toyed with the idea of joining forces with Italy and Germany, the sociomilitary reality in the aftermath of its own civil war easily counteracted any dreams of conquest. In fact, those ambitions now strike us as

Whereas Spanish imperialism is an anachronism whose only current centripetal force results from the very attacks against it, the speaker also criticizes Christianity, a discursive practice that is not nation-specific and that for centuries has exerted enormous centralizing power over our modern world. To launch his attack, he avails himself of another of the strategies Bakhtin lists for subverting authoritative discourse: comic style.

The most dramatic comic subversion occurs in the first chapter of the novel. Again, the action takes place on a Cuban sugar plantation, where the black African slaves serve their Spanish masters. The Spaniards feel that it is their Christian obligation to convert the slaves, and the priest assumes the responsibility of monitoring their activities. When one day the grandfather orders his granddaughter to check on the slaves' activities, she asks the priest, who is observing them with binoculars, to describe what they are doing. He replies that he does not dare say the words, to which she answers, "then say it in Latin." The priest then recites:

> membrum erectum in os feminae immissint!
> socios concumbentes tangere et masturbationem
> mutuam adsequi!
> penis vehementis se erixet tum maxime cum
> crura
> puerorum tetigent!
> anus feminarum amant lambere!
> sanguinis menstruationis devorant!
> coitus a posterioris factitant!
> ejaculatio praematura!
> receptaculum seminis! (32)

The priest attempts to temper the narrated transgression by means of the Latin, a symbol of sacred authority. This liturgical expression forms part of a discourse that since the beginning of Christianity has tended to condemn sensuality. The goal of sexual intercourse is to fulfill the biblical imperative to "Be fruitful and multiply" (Gen. 2:28). The act of seeking pleasure in such an act signals paganism, and clearly paganism indicates inferiority. Thanks to this Christian discursive practice, the faithful have a weapon that enables them to transcend the carnal world and proclaim their position

---

almost comical. For Goytisolo, therefore, to attack Spanish imperialism in Latin America seems to be an example of "beating a dead horse."

of superiority in the human hierarchy. But in this example from *Juan sin Tierra,* that very authority becomes impotent in the face of a life force that refuses to be erased by a dead language. Carnal reality cannot be negated by political, religious, or linguistic abstractions.

Christian discipline attempts to negate not only sexual appetites but physiological needs as well. For example, the plantation priest insists that there is a direct relationship between sainthood and the suppression of bodily functions. He notes that since the Bible never mentions the physiological needs of the saints, clearly the true Christian seeking his or her road to perfection must imitate plants, whose "secretions are delightful and pleasing" (22).[12] In addition to heavenly rewards, the members of the Spanish manor feel confident that their celestial state will serve as a means of affirming their superiority over the hedonistic pagans.

Yet the denial of physiological functions proves to be difficult at best, and as a result the Europeans depend on technology to aid and abet them. One such technological device is the flush toilet. Thanks to it, the grandmother of the household declares to herself as she pulls the chain, "I have shit like a queen" (20). Although she attempts to affirm her superior hierarchical position by employing the noun "queen," the regal value of this noun is comically undermined by the scatological verb. As a result of the juxtaposition, this woman who strives to hide her corporal essence by means of a technological device (the flush toilet) instead draws attention to it. By way of contrast the slaves, who have only a public latrine at their disposal, proclaim their earthy essence, according to the speaker, by means of "the nonsublime, nonhidden, nonperfumed, nonaseptic visceral explosion that will not vanish from sight, smell, and sound by means of any safe deposit box, sacristy or toilet" (46).

Comic style is merely one of many means for subverting the centripetal force of Christian discourse. The speaker seeks to undermine language itself as he shifts the emphasis to lexicon. For example, convention has tended to reduce the colors white and black to polarized symbols: purity and sin, respectively. But the same colors change meaning radically in reference to

---

12. The character named Vosk acts as the principal spokesperson within the novel for the authoritative discourse of the regime. Indeed, one of his favorite means of addressing his parishioners, "hijitos míos" (195), has a clear Francoist ring to it. For an analysis of the themes presented by Vosk, see the article by Sonja Herpoel, "El Vosk de Goytisolo, ¿Prisionero de su presunción?"

literary creation: "la página virgen te brinda posibilidades de redención exquisitas junto al gozo de profanar su blancura : basta un simple trazo de pluma : volverás a tentar la suerte" (the virgin page offers you possibilities for exquisite redemption along with the joy of profaning its whiteness : a simple pen stroke suffices : you will try your luck again, 51). In this case the subversion occurs by means of a sacrilege. Although the syntaxis has a biblical ring to it, the message appears to be diabolical; it seems to glorify sin. But the very concept of sin is inverted. By calling attention to the process of creating at the expense of the created product, the connotation of the binary, white and black, is reversed. The violation of the white page with the black ink signifies a purifying profanation, a creative defoliation. In this way the speaker has fused and undermined lexicality and morality. By placing them in the context of novelistic creation, he has subverted their claim of absolute authority.

In fiction readers tend to consider the words *authority* and *author* synonymous. The story of *Juan sin Tierra* concerns a fictional novelist writing the novel as we read. But by virtue of the transformation of a conventional first-person "I" into a second-person "you," the fictional author suffers deauthorization. Rather than being the controlling force, he is a controlled object. As a result of such a narrative reversal, what normally would be the speaking subject becomes the subject of another's voice, the submissive object of an unseen authority:[13] "míralos bien : sus rostros te resultarán conocidos" (look at them carefully : their faces will be familiar to you, 15).

The authority behind such a voice is implicit not only in the imperative mood but also in the future tense. Indeed, the future serves not only as another form of imperative but as an imperative with biblical force as well ("Thou shalt not . . ."). But Juan Goytisolo transforms the function of the voice from prophet to pedagogue: "dividirás la imaginaria escena en dos partes : mejor dicho : en dos bloques opuestos de palabras : a un lado substantivos, adjetivos, verbos que denotan blancor, claridad, virtud : al

---

13. As noted earlier, Foucault in *Discipline and Punish* argues that the disciplinary state objectifies citizens by turning them into submissive subjects of a hidden gaze, as a result of which they become self-disciplinary. One could speculate that Goytisolo, recognizing the strategy of the state for making its citizens submissive, has opted for a novelistic strategy of subverting the type of discursive authority that subjects people. The goal, then, is to reconstitute his readers as the subjects of his discourse by changing the nature of the discourse. Goytisolo's project constitutes a radical expression of the "writerly text" concept, which in turn can also be interpreted as a strategy to reassert the reader as agent.

otro, un léxico de tinieblas, negrura, pecado" (you will divide the imaginary scene into two parts : more accurately : into two opposing groups of words : to one side nouns, adjectives, verbs that denote whiteness, clarity, virtue : to the other side, a vocabulary of shadows, blackness, sin, 30). By virtue of having been "textualized," the speaking voice is stripped of its connotation of divine authority. In effect, the novel strives to authorize novelistic creation as a new divinity. In this way it subverts a discursive tradition that has served as a foundation of Western civilization.

But the discursive project undertaken by the speaker of *Juan sin Tierra* ultimately entangles him in its web. Although his project has been to substitute novelistic for Christian authority, at a certain point he announces that "from now on you will learn to think against your own language" (83). As opposed to the earlier admonition with its aesthetic emphasis ("you will divide the imaginary scene into two parts"), the command to think against his own language imposes an ontological implication, and as a result the tone acquires a nonparodic biblical ring. The speaker has been subverted by his own subversive project. In an attempt to go beyond poetics, he has had to resort to and reaffirm the very discursive practice that he has up to this point discredited. He has now defined himself as the new centripetal force, and he has resorted to biblical discursive practices to assert his authority.

Even in the area of linguistics the speaker falls victim to the very system he is trying to displace. In the final chapter he announces that "if in the future you write, it will be in another language" (319). The novel then ends with a page written in Arabic preceded by a blank page, thus corroborating the announcement that Spanish would no longer serve as the fictional novelist's linguistic code. Yet Arabic in a novel otherwise written in Spanish conveys meaning even for those who do not know Arabic, just as does a blank page preceding it. In each case meaning is tied directly to and determined by novelistic context. No matter how staunchly he fights against linguistic and ideological stratification, the speaker has no recourse but to impose his own version of each. Just as there is no point from which to observe the interconnected universe that is removed from the whole, so there is no way to subvert a discursive practice without imitating that same practice.[14] In effect discourse is the interconnecting force of the universe.

14. Near the end of the novel the speaker underscores the autonomy of the text and insists that it is governed by an internal system of signs. Many would contest such a claim, pointing out that no work is autonomous from the context in which it is created. As

With *Juan sin Tierra*, Goytisolo attempts to extend the boundaries of what we label a *novel*. His is a bewildering textual complex in which he juxtaposes the flush toilet and the open-air latrine, the Virgin Mary and Changó, Shirley Temple and King Kong, Pére Foucault and Lawrence of Arabia as signs pointing at technology versus corporeality, social propriety versus primordial satiation, mimetic representation versus creative imagination, and extrinsic versus intrinsic meaning. This work of fiction is structured around polarities, and in this sense it functions truly as a register of a dying and desperate totalitarian regime.

I noted at the beginning of this analysis that *Juan sin Tierra* can be considered a standard-bearer for the Spanish self-referential novel. It can also be considered one of the clearest Spanish expressions of postmodernism. Whether referring to Hutcheon's historiographic metafiction or McHale's ontological as opposed to epistemological dominant, by these two definitions Juan Goytisolo's novel certainly qualifies as postmodern.[15] But perhaps the word *totalizing* forms the key. Modernist fiction tends to provide the illusion of a totalizing view of reality, while postmodernist fiction tends to eschew such a view. For example, "metafiction," as defined by Hutcheon or McHale, negates totalization by making the fictional author and reader a part of the novelistic world. As the emphasis switches from the question of knowing to that of being, any totalizing effect undermines the ontological project. The character Vosk of *Juan sin Tierra* provides a dramatic expression of antitotalization. In the beginning he is the plantation priest, but later he plays a variety of roles—literary critic, Spanish tourist, war veteran, and psychologist. Near the end of the novel he announces: "he dejado de ser una entidad completa y tridimensional, de densidad sicológica y acciones transitivas para convertirme en V : una inicial, una letra, un número" (I have stopped being a complete and tridimensional entity, with psychological

---

Paulson points out in *Noise of Culture,* both arguments are valid and invalid. A literary text cannot be divorced from its context, and therefore it is an "artificially autonomous object." But Paulson also points out that it can be said "to contain the fiction of its own autonomy as one of its central organizational principles" and further that "it is also an object from which the reader may well derive the most information by treating it as autonomous, by understanding it and interpreting it insofar as possible in accordance with its own unique internal characteristics" (135). Paulson's comments strike me as extremely useful in helping us understand Goytisolo's project in *Juan sin Tierra.*

15. Linda Hutcheon, *A Poetics of Postmodernism: History, Theory, Fiction,* and Brian McHale, *Postmodernist Fiction.*

density and transitive actions, to transform myself into V: an initial, a letter, a number, 306).[16] Even the blank page followed by the page in Arabic with which the novel ends underscores the antitotalizing, postmodernist focus of the novel. If *Tiempo de silencio* represents the Spanish precursor of postmodernism, *Juan sin Tierra* deserves recognition as one of the first and arguably the most successful expressions in Spanish fiction of what is generally understood by the sometimes abused term *postmodernism*.

The discursive field outlined in *Tiempo de silencio* includes the disenchantment with science and technology, a disciplinary state dedicated to control by means of classifications and exclusions, the disunification of self, and the demonstration of how language does not lead us to absolute meanings but rather to plurality. *Juan sin Tierra* adds to those parameters the incorporation of the fictional author and reader into the text, the deauthorization of the speaking subject, and the subversion of particularly Judeo-Christian authoritative discourse. But Juan Goytisolo's novel becomes a victim of its own subversive project as it must resort to the same discursive practices it attacks in an effort to assert its authority. A similar victimization appears in subsequent novels in which the attacks on Francoism serve to perpetuate the ghost of that very regime. The next novel examined, Carmen Martín Gaite's *El cuarto de atrás*, represents another example of this opposing and perpetuating contradiction. But Martín Gaite also demonstrates how the regime fell into that same contradiction as its resistance to freedom of expression inspired expressions of creative freedom.

State and Social Apparatuses and *El cuarto de atrás*

According to one critic, Martín Gaite's *El cuarto de atrás* (The back room), which was published three years after *Juan sin Tierra*, represents one of the more imaginative literary responses that we have to the end of the Franco regime.[17] I agree with that assessment, and I propose to argue that first of

---

16. Hayles, "Virtual Bodies and Flickering Signifiers," discusses how in novels such as *Neuromancer*, by William Gibson, we are offered positional markers labeled "pov" rather than conventional fictional characters (80–91). Vosk's various metamorphoses that culminate when he is reduced to the marker "V" may be considered a precursor to Gibson's textual strategy.

17. Darío Villanueva, "La novela española en 1978," 93. See also the collection of essays edited by Mirella Servodidio and Marcia L. Welles, *From Fiction to Metafiction: Essays in*

all this response signals a significant shift away from the antistory mode of Juan Goytisolo and his school. Although Martín Gaite also offers her readers a self-referential novel involving its own creation, in her case the story of that creation is inseparable from the story of the creator. Whereas *Juan sin Tierra* is about the creative writing process, about how linguistic signs generate other signs (including the one labeled *author*) in a potentially infinite process of supplement and deferral, *El cuarto de atrás* concerns an author attempting to fuse history and fantasy to write about her own life and times as a woman in a male-dominated fascist society. In doing so, this female novelist also strives, as Goytisolo does in *Juan sin Tierra*, to affirm human agency. I employ the verb *strives* because authors, speakers, and readers can never attain a state of agency; they can only proceed toward that state—just as Lacan insists that there can never be union with the Other, only the process toward that union. In Carmen Martín Gaite's case, the process centers on an attempt to free past, present, and future female subjects from their subjection to the various ideological apparatuses fashioned by the modern post-totalitarian state.

The shift of emphasis in *El cuarto de atrás* to institutional apparatuses in part reflects a change of venue from that of *Juan sin Tierra*. Goytisolo chose Cuba and North Africa as the setting for the action of his novel because he wanted to divorce himself and his reader both geographically and linguistically from Spain as the authoritative center. Martín Gaite, on the other hand, chose to operate from the center of Francoist Spain as she focused on the repressive and ideological apparatuses created by the regime to dictate not merely political thinking but gender roles as well.[18] Although these roles had evolved from centuries of discursive practices,

---

Honor of Carmen Martín Gaite, the major overviews of Martín Gaite's fiction are Joan Lipman Brown's *Secrets from the Back Room: The Fiction of Carmen Martín Gaite* and "The Challenge of Martín Gaite's Woman Hero" and Carla Olson Buck's dissertation, "Speaker/Reader: Dialogic Relationships in the Novels of Carmen Martín Gaite." I also found especially insightful the articles by Debra Castillo, "Never-Ending Story: Carmen Martín Gaite's *The Back Room,*" Stephanie Sieburth, "Memory, Metafiction and Mass Culture in *El cuarto de atrás,*" and Brad Epps, "The Space of Sexual History: Reading Positions in *El cuarto de atrás.*" Martín Gaite's most recent novels are *Nubosidad variable,* 1992, and *La reina de las nieves,* 1994. For a complete list of her prior publications, see Servodidio and Welles's *From Fiction to Metafiction.*

18. Again, these are Althusser's terms as defined in *Lenin and Philosophy.* For the sake of simplification, I will use state and social apparatuses to refer respectively to official

the Franco regime made a conscious effort to perfect the apparatuses that would reinforce and perpetuate them. *El cuarto de atrás* represents an attempt to expose and subvert the apparatuses that, three years after the end of the totalitarian regime that had created them, continued to exert their pernicious influence.

Although the Franco dictatorship had ended by the time the novel appeared in 1978, the regime's discursive legacy still asserted itself in the political parties organized to contest the elections. Adolfo Suárez and his Democratic Union Center party won the majority vote in 1977 by appealing for reconciliation and compromise. As the party name suggests, Suárez campaigned as an alternative to the polarities of the Left and Right, though his ties to the former regime proved to be his eventual undoing. In her novel, Martín Gaite also proposed a depolarization or a reconciliation of Spanish (and also Western) political, artistic, and above all gender divisions. To effect a fusion, she created a series of mirrors in which the written text serves as a speculum of the spoken text, which in turn mirrors, primarily in refracted form, the government apparatuses created to dictate gender attitudes.[19] Whereas in Goytisolo's novel the focus was directed at the masculine symbol of domination, Francisco Franco, in Martín Gaite's novel the emphasis falls on the feminine symbol of subordination, Carmencita Franco.

As is the case in nearly all the self-referential novels of this period, *El cuarto de atrás* incorporates the fictional author and reader into the text. The story concerns a woman, at first known only by her initial, "C," who suffers from insomnia. She finally dozes off, only to be awakened by the visit of a mysterious stranger dressed in black. They talk at length about her writing projects until a phone call from someone who turns out to be a character from one of her earlier fictional stories interrupts them. Finally C, or Carmen, falls asleep again and is awakened when her daughter returns in the early hours. Carmen tells the daughter that she spent the evening alone, even though there are two glasses on the coffee table and she has a gold

---

repressive institutions and to unofficial ideological mouthpieces of popular culture and the evolving consumer society.

19. Sandra J. Schumm, "Metaphor, Metonymy, and Mirrors: Female Self-Reflection in Contemporary Spanish Novels by Women," examines in detail the function of mirrors in Martín Gaite's novel (255–99) as well as in several other Spanish novels written by women.

pillbox that the stranger in black gave her. In spite of this evidence, we can never be sure whether the visit was real or a dream.

Dialogue between the protagonist and her real or imagined visitor and flashbacks inspired by the stranger's comments and questions form the core of the narrative. Much of the conversation concerns Carmen's dilemma of whether to write fiction or history. As they talk, she becomes aware of a strange phenomenon on her desk: "At the upper part of the typewriter appears a page with writing on it, which I read out of the corner of my eye: '. . . the barefoot man is now out of sight.' When did I write this?"[20] The passage she reads and does not recognize is identical to one we have already read in the first chapter of the novel. Almost eighty pages later in our text there is another reference: "But come on, these seventy-nine pages, where did they come from and what do they refer to? The stack of those that stayed under the hat also seem to have grown, although I don't dare to verify it" (101). Finally a wind scatters the pile of papers, and the mysterious stranger volunteers to collect them, and as he does so he remarks: " 'But what a lot of pages,' he exclaims incredulously. 'I didn't think you had written so much' " (200). As he puts the pages in order she falls asleep, and when she is awakened by her daughter the stranger has vanished. She notices that the manuscript titled "El cuarto de atrás" is now on her bedside table. She picks it up and begins to read: "Y sin embargo, yo juraría que la postura era la misma, creo que siempre he dormido así, con el brazo derecho debajo de la almohada y el cuerpo levement apoyado contra ese flanco, las piernas buscando la juntura por donde se remete la sábana" (And nevertheless, I would swear that the posture was the same, I believe that I have always slept that way, with my right arm under the pillow and my body slightly supported against that side, and my legs searching for the seam where the sheet is tucked in, 210). These are the identical words with which the novel begins.

The textual strategies described above create the illusion that the protagonist-narrator in effect reads herself into her text; she is at once the reading subject and the subject about whom she reads. By the same token, the stranger with whom she spoke is now dramatically characterized as a verbal construct. Furthermore, as readers we have aesthetically participated

20. Carmen Martín Gaite, *El cuarto de atrás*, 31. Subsequent citations will indicate the page number in parentheses.

in the dialogic creation of the stack of pages that constitute the very novel we hold in our hands and that the protagonist now fictionally holds in hers. Similar to the experience created by *Juan sin Tierra* and other self-referential novels, as readers we realize that we also have been drawn into a dialogic net intertwining our reality with the fiction here titled *El cuarto de atrás*.

Initially participation in the fictional world of the novel centers around the debate over the mode of expression the protagonist should select to write her memoirs. She is inclined to follow institutionalized practice and write with what Benveniste terms "historical narrative," which excludes every autobiographical linguistic form.[21] In her dialogue with the stranger, however, the protagonist admits that at a certain point in the past she indeed tried to write historical narrative, but she now considers those efforts an attempt to escape: "I had begun to take refuge in history, in dates" (59). As she talks she confesses that the act of writing history did not satisfy her because the historical mode forced her to exclude any overt reference to herself as writer. With the help of the stranger, she now realizes that the only solution is to write historiography, not history; she must break from institutional control and deal with history as process, not product. Rather than pretending to convey truth or facts, she must address the question of who or what institutions determine what is true and factual. Her narration reveals that in Francoist Spain, the government created the apparatuses whose function was to assert the truth. To that end, these institutions fostered a discursive campaign of religious, political, and gender polarization.

Carmen's narrative project sets out to challenge institutionalized polarization. For example, she recalls seeing Franco up close, "muy tieso, con sus leggis y su fajín de general, saludando con la mano y tratando de mostrarse arrogante, aunque siempre tuvo un poco de barriga" (very rigid, with his leggings and his general's sash, greeting with his hand and trying to act arrogant, although he always had a bit of a pot belly, 63). What she describes here from a very personal point of view is not a god or a monster, but a man with a pot. When he died, "there were people who made a public spectacle and celebration of it, and also there must have been those who cried" (133). She, on the other hand, experienced neither total joy nor sorrow. She remembers watching the burial on television in a neighborhood bar: "that

---

21. Benveniste, *Problems in General Linguistics,* 205–15.

illness that, notwithstanding his appearance of eternal leader, had ended up sending Franco toward a thick tomb that awaited him and whose headstone was shown there on television next to the empty hole" (134–35). These memories and descriptions undermine the good versus bad polarization created by state and social apparatuses. Abandoning her former polarized position, the speaker now sees Franco as a man whose destiny, like that of all humans, is "an empty hole." Personal narration has created a bond of human commonality between observer and observed. An even stronger bond emerges as Carmen remembers the dictator's daughter, Carmencita Franco.

The protagonist first saw the daughter when the two of them were children. Carmencita was leaving the cathedral with her parents:

> Fue la primera vez que yo pensé cuánto se deben aburrir los hijos de los reyes y de los ministros, porque Carmencita Franco miraba alrededor con unos ojos absolutamente tediosos y tristes, se cruzaron nuestras miradas, llevaba unos calcetines de perlé calados y unos zapatos de charol con trabilla, pensé que a qué jugaría y con quién, se me quedó grabada su imagen para siempre, era más o menos de mi edad, decían que se parecía algo a mí.

> (It was the first time that I considered how bored the children of kings and ministers must be, because Carmencita Franco looked around with eyes that were absolutely irritated and sad, our gazes crossed, and she was wearing stockings with inlaid pearl designs and patten shoes with buckles, I wondered what she played with and with whom, her image remained etched in me forever, she was more or less my age, and people said that she looked a bit like me.) (63)

Perhaps because she was a child and politically disinterested, Carmen identified with this girl her own age and imagined the things they had in common—boredom with adult ritual and fascination with a childhood world of games, playmates, and clothing. Those bonds disappeared during the time the protagonist became politically engaged, but now they re-form as she remembers recently seeing Carmencita as an adult in her fifties at her father the dictator's funeral:

> hemos crecido y vivido en los mismos años, ella era hija de un militar de provincias, hemos sido víctimas de las mismas modas y costumbres, hemos leído las mismas revistas y visto el mismo cine, nuestros hijos puede que sean distintos, pero nuestros sueños seguro que han sido

semejantes, con la seguridad de todo aquello que jamás podrá tener comprobación.

(we have grown and lived during the same time, she was the daughter of a provincial military man, we have been victims of the same styles and customs, we have read the same magazines and seen the same movies, our children may be distinct, but our dreams certainly have been similar, with the certainty of that which can never be proved.) (136–37)

This is a far cry from the Francoists' attempts to define everything in terms of two Spains or from Goytisolo's polar textual strategies. In a binary situation, each polarity tends to see itself as the center and its opponent as the margin. By eschewing the political position of either polarized antagonist, Carmen projects a new set of centers and margins based on gender. She realizes that the apparatuses created by the regime left no space for her, for the dictator's own daughter, or for women in general. She now lays claim to such a space by positioning herself between the two political factions. By virtue of such a shift in position, the question of party agendas becomes subordinate to that of the gender partition practiced by the Left as well as the Right.

The protagonist and Franco's daughter passed through childhood into female adulthood in the same culture and at the same time. Their lives were determined not only by sempiternal conventions but also by transitory fashions. Social apparatuses such as the movies they saw, the music they listened to, and the magazines they read influenced, if not dictated, not merely their clothing styles but their gender awareness and attitudes as well. Whereas Franco was very much a mortal man, the power of his regime to control discourse was felt in all these social apparatuses, "in language, in dress, in music, in human relations, in public functions, in private clubs" (137). Of course the dictatorship also imposed its discipline by means of state apparatuses in the forms of laws, censorship, propaganda, and religious and political indoctrination. The goal was to control the citizenry in general and to recreate the female sex in the image of the Catholic Queen Isabel. Carmen the protagonist and Carmencita the dictator's own daughter are products and therefore victims of this still-current discursive network firmly rooted in a mythical past.[22]

22. Again I am referring to Herzberger's thesis, *Narrating the Past,* that the regime attempted to mythologize Spain's sacred past and thereby remove it from temporal flow.

Aphorisms are one means by which a legacy of female subordination achieves atemporal credibility. As a young girl, the protagonist remembers a woman saying to her mother in reference to Carmen, "a woman who knows Latin will come to no good end" (93). The brief years of the First Republic marked significant strides toward changing the attitude expressed in the maxim, but after the war there was an official campaign to put women back in their place.[23]

It has been claimed that in literature "the plot of woman's curiosity seems to have a special concern with what is contained within closed spaces."[24] In addition to the sexual connotation to which the quote alludes, closed spaces also suggest social roles. We see both implications when the protagonist, for the first of many times, defines "her place": "Con la C. de mi nombre, tres cosas con la C., primero una casa, luego un cuarto y luego una cama" (With the C. of my name, three things with the C., first a house, then a room and then a bed, 11). On an anecdotal level, these three locations merely identify the setting for most of the action of the novel, but in Bakhtinian terminology this type of spatial marker functions as a chronotope.[25] The act of making a proper name synonymous with space, not just any space but gender-coded spaces (house, room, bed), forms a link between Carmen's awareness of her place and of the state and social apparatuses of not just the Franco regime but also Western society in general.

The official Spanish apparatus for defining women's roles was the Feminine Section of the Falange, directed by Pilar Primo de Rivera, the sister of the founder of the Fascist Party. She initiated another official apparatus in 1945 called "Social Service," a program targeting young women between the ages of seventeen and thirty-five. The Social Service program was nothing more than ideological indoctrination designed to create a woman whose role, according to the protagonist, was to serve as a "complement and mirror of the male" (94). Completion of the program was required for any woman

---

The Francoist government launched a discursive campaign aimed at convincing people that its political platform merely followed the timeless values of Spanish history.

23. Even during the First Republic there existed something of a contradiction since many of the liberal and educated women were opposed to granting voting privileges to women in general. Since the vast majority of Spanish women were uneducated and their ideas and attitudes were dictated by fathers and husbands, many female liberals feared the voting power of the typical ultraconservative Spanish woman.

24. Peter Brooks, *Body Work: Objects of Desire in Modern Narrative*, 252.

25. Bakhtin, *The Dialogic Imagination*, 84–258.

wishing to become a member of a social club or professional association or before applying for employment, a passport, a driving permit, or even a fishing license. In reference to the latter, Martín Gaite bitterly remarks: "To fish for a husband was all that a young woman could do without being asked to show on her lapel the precious blue enamel button that accredited her with having completed her Social Service."[26]

This state apparatus adopted a Spanish monarch as its icon and tried to ensure that every young woman enrolled in the program "tenía madera de futura madre y esposa, digna descendiente de Isabel la Católica" (had the mettle of a future mother and wife, that she was a worthy descendent of Isabel the Catholic Queen, 42). The queen served as the model of a Christian wife and housekeeper, and Carmen explains how she and her contemporaries were trained to one day "preparar con nuestras propias manos la canastilla del bebé destinado a venir al mundo para enorgullecerse de la Reina Católica, defenderla de calumnias y engendrar hijos que, a su vez, la alabaran por los siglos de los siglos" (prepare with our own hands the crib for the baby destined to come into the world to feel proud of the Catholic Queen, defend her from accusations and engender more children who, in turn, would praise her through the centuries, 96).

But Queen Isabel did not merely represent a model for the proper Spanish woman; the regime created a whole discursive practice around her, a practice that Carmen finally recognizes as she listens to the stranger insist that everything is ruled by chance: "Le escucho pensando en Isabel la Católica, en la falaz versión que, de su conducta, nos ofrecían aquellos libros y discursos, donde no se daba cabida al azar, donde cada paso, viaje o decisión de la reina parecían marcados por un destino superior e inquebrantable" (I listen to him thinking about Isabel the Catholic Queen, in the fallacious version of her conduct that those books and lectures offered us, in which no role was given to chance, in which the queen's every step, trip or decision seemed to be marked by a superior and unbreakable destiny, 104). The various apparatuses molded Isabel into a symbol of the supremacy of logic and reason over chance, thereby adding this new iconic function to that of devoted wife and mother. In effect, the institutions strove to reinforce

26. Carmen Martín Gaite, *Usos amorosos de la posguerra española*, 60. See also Jean Alsina's article, "Valeurs matrimoniales et roles feminins dans trois publicités espagnoles entre 1973 et 1986," on how matrimonial and gender codes were reinforced by advertisements and commercials during the final Franco years and the first decade of the democracy.

the two roles until they fused into an authoritative discourse. Yet discourse has a way of undermining itself through repetition. The regime's project of creating apparatuses designed to preach rationality, obedience, and family values as symbolized by Queen Isabel, could only subvert itself, a subversion underscored by the protagonist's own rebellion: "Que sí creo en el diablo y en San Cristóbal gigante y en Santa Bárbara bendita, en todos los seres misteriosos, vamos. En Isabel la Católica, no" (I do believe in the devil and in the gigantic Saint Christopher and in the blessed Saint Barbara, okay in all the mysterious beings. But not in the Catholic Queen Isabel, 105). By and large, *El cuarto de atrás* recounts the failure of fascist discourse to create gendered space and to impose on the populace an official, centripetal worldview. That failure resulted to a large degree from the subversive effect of social apparatuses represented by popular art.

Most popular art during the time of the regime was subject to official discursive policies. The magazine *Y,* whose title in the form of an initial refers to Isabel, really represented a state apparatus since it was edited by the Feminine Section. More clearly social apparatuses such as *novelas rosa* (harlequin romances), popular boleros and war songs, and movies (foreign as well as domestic) all contributed, thanks to censorship, to the fascist discourse defining female roles. Yet in spite of the censors, popular culture that has been appropriated for a specific end tends to undermine that end. If nothing else, romance novels, sentimental songs, and whimsical movies provided an escape from the regulated, uniform society of postwar Spain. Therefore, in spite of projecting the official discourse,[27] these social apparatuses' very effort to conform subverts itself; in spite of themselves, they constitute a centrifugal force. Adding to this impetus is the nonconformist voice of people such as Conchita Piquer and her songs about "chicas que no se parecían en nada a las que conocíamos, que nunca iban a gustar las dulzuras del hogar apacible con que nos hacían soñar a las señoritas, gente marginada, a la deriva, desprotegida por la ley" (young women who did not resemble at all the people we knew, who were never going to enjoy the sweetness of the peaceful hearth that they made us young girls dream about, [they were] marginalized people, drifters, outside of the law, 152). Without question, the protagonist expresses her deep anger at the

27. Sieburth, "Memory, Metafiction and Mass Culture," identifies some of the *novelas rosa* that did not toe the line dictated by the regime.

regime for trying to position women into a subordinate role by means of discourse. Yet that anger is tempered by the delight in narrating how the project subverted itself, a subversion facilitated by popular culture's scattered voices of dissent. In its efforts to construct restraining apparatuses around women's space—apparatuses whose walls were mortared by traditional cultural and religious codes—the regime unwittingly undermined those very restraints.

The protagonist herself incarnates an indomitable spirit refusing to submit itself to restraints. As a child Carmen discovered how to use her imagination to transform an enclosure into a limitless space. For example, the protagonist had a back room, a room of her own, where she could express the centrifugal force of nonconformity. It served a carnivalesque function of escape and freedom.[28] There she and her playmates could jump on the furniture and break all the rules governing the rest of the house. Above all, they could give free rein to their imagination:

> me lo imagino también como un desván del cerebro, una especie de recinto secreto lleno de trastos borrosos, separados de las antesalas más limpias y ordenadas de la mente por una cortina que sólo se descorre de vez en cuando; los recuerdos que pueden darnos alguna sorpresa viven agazapados en el cuarto de atrás, siempre salen de allí, y sólo cuando quieren, no sirve hostigarlos.

> (I imagined it also as an attic of the brain, a type of secret enclosure filled with faded old furniture, separated from the cleaner and more orderly front rooms of the brain by a curtain that only so often is pulled open; memories that can surprise us live squatting in the back room, they always come out of there, and only when they want to, it does no good to whip them into action.) (91)

As noted earlier, Bakhtin defines "heteroglossia" in terms not only of "alien" languages but also of ideological belief systems that infiltrate and undermine the dominant discourse of a given time and culture. The authoritative discourse defined a woman's place in terms of enclosure—again, the three Cs: *casa, cuarto, cama.* In Carmen's house the reference to the "cleaner and more orderly front rooms" has a Feminine Section ring to it. A woman not

---

28. For an insightful analysis of the function of the carnivalesque in this novel, see Carla Olson Buck's forthcoming article, "The World Turned Upside Down: The Carnivalesque in Carmen Martín Gaite's *Retahílas* and *El cuarto de atrás*," in *Romance Languages Annual.*

only was assigned her space but also had the obligation to keep it clean and tidy. The back room, on the other hand, provided the protagonist with an alternative, a "hidden enclosure." This compound within a compound paradoxically provided freedom, a subversion of the chronotope sponsored by the state and social apparatuses of Francoist Spain. The back room represented a space for disorder, imagination, and the fantastic to counteract the legacy of Queen Isabel's world, "where there was no room for chance."

On the surface, *El cuarto de atrás* is less radical and subversive than *Juan sin Tierra*. Yet as its complexity unfolds, Martín Gaite's novel rivals the disruptive message of Juan Goytisolo's. For example, when the protagonist at the end of the story picks up the manuscript that apparently has written itself while she and the stranger talked, she foregrounds the conflict between a speaking and a spoken subject. As Carmen reads the written text, as she reads herself, she has to recognize herself as a subject *of* something else, something outside herself. Someone or something else has written the protagonist's story, which is tantamount to indicating that this same someone or something else has written every woman's story; she and other women are the subjects of others' discourses and of those ideologies that have interpellated and positioned them within the social system. But in spite of the disciplining society in which she lived most of her life, she has discovered that she is the product not only of the official totalitarian apparatuses but also of the unofficial programs of resistance. In effect, the protagonist demonstrates her power as speaking subject by narrating her resistance to the official discourse. She then gains additional power as the act of narrating allows her to become aware of the forces that contributed to her opposition. In a word, she has placed herself and her reader in a position to effect a process of resistance to the enslaving state and social apparatuses. Knowledge is power, even if that knowledge involves recognition of one's self as a subject of others.

In my admittedly suspect reading of Foucault, it seems to me that he totally rejects agency. That is, essentially he places all the emphasis on how discursive practices dictate human acts and thoughts. Yet in writing down and publishing his ideas, implicitly he rises to the category of an agent capable of understanding and explaining how discourse operates and offers to readers who can follow his argument a place beside him. Althusser admits that he occupies a similar contradictory position as he argues that humans cannot escape from the influence of ideology, yet he asserts his own ideological freedom when he argues that marxism is superior to capitalism. One theorist attempts to *cern* or free the subject/individual by drawing on Lacanian psychoanalysis to theorize that there can be no predictably deterministic relationship between subjectivity and the symbolic order. Another makes a related case in his thesis on how an author can change the nature of people's object of desire.[29] Both Smith and Chambers argue theoretically for a type of agency that Martín Gaite expressed artistically. Indeed, I find her mode of expression more compelling primarily because it emphasizes how agency is not a state of being but a process of becoming.

Perhaps the need to exercise power by defining the individual subjection and resistance to the regime explains why Franco's ghost continued to haunt long after the dictator's death.[30] Such an exercise, then, entails a paradox: Continued resistance to a dead system serves to resurrect that system. As long as the discourse persists in targeting Francoism, Francoism will be reborn.

El cuarto de atrás adds another dimension to the discursive field outlined in *Tiempo de silencio* and further defined in *Juan sin Tierra*. Martín Gaite's novel encourages us to confront the paradox of a speaking/spoken subject, particularly as that paradox relates to gender roles and attitudes. In an attempt to assert herself as speaking agent, the protagonist must recognize the degree to which she is subjected to the apparatuses perfected by the Franco totalitarian regime. Yet that system proves to be a symptom rather than the source of a gender disease. The problem is universal, not merely Spanish. Whereas an end to totalitarianism may mark the demise of certain pernicious state apparatuses, the social apparatuses reinforcing gender prejudices tend to prevail long after the totalitarian system ends.[31] Particularly in this sense *El cuarto de atrás* claims its position within the interconnected

---

29. Respectively, Paul Smith, *Discerning the Subject*, and Chambers, *Room for Maneuver*.

30. For some insightful discussions on the relationship between power and resistance, see Molinaro, *Foucault, Feminism, and Power*; Bersani, "Subject of Power"; Bové, *Mastering Discourse*; and Nancy Fraser, *Unruly Practices: Power, Discourse and Gender in Contemporary Social Theory*.

31. As a case in point, the very year that *El cuarto de atrás* appeared in print, 1978, the Congress approved, the country ratified, and the king signed into law a series of constitutional amendments granting various equal rights to Spanish women (see especially articles 1, 9.2, 10.1, 14, 18, 23.2, 27.1, 32.1, and 35.1 of the 1985 edition of the Constitution). Obviously the problem for women in Spain did not disappear with the enactment of constitutional amendments.

discursive field under analysis. In addition, Martín Gaite's novel, with its focus centered on gender issues, serves as a precursor to the Spanish fiction appearing during the decade of the 1980s.

As the preceding analysis has demonstrated, *El cuarto de atrás* represents a much less radical antistory position than the one projected by *Juan sin Tierra*. In effect, Martín Gaite lays claim to a middle ground between the polarities of Goytisolo's novel about a novel and Eduardo Mendoza's novel that heralds a return to conventional storytelling about people and events.

The Subject of Truth in *La verdad sobre el caso Savolta*

It is difficult to conceive of more polarized novelistic techniques than those of *La verdad sobre el caso Savolta* (The truth about the Savolta case) on one end of the spectrum and *Juan sin Tierra* on the other. Between them, Mendoza and Goytisolo appropriate the defining signatures of Spanish fiction at the start of the post-Franco era. In effect, *La verdad sobre el caso Savolta* and *Juan sin Tierra* signal binary oppositions. The preposition *sin* (without) of Goytisolo's title negates, while the noun *verdad* (truth) of Mendoza's affirms. Above all, the two novels respectively negate and affirm the conventional concept of a novel, which helps explain the accommodating role represented by *El cuarto de atrás*. *Juan sin Tierra*, as we analyzed earlier, eschews the orthodox emphasis on plot, character, and setting and turns the focus instead to the process of its own creation. On this basis it can be considered a manifesto for the Spanish self-referential novel.[32] *La verdad sobre el caso Savolta*, on the other hand, concerns people enmeshed in an elaborate story of corporate and criminal intrigue during the labor unrest in Barcelona from 1917 to 1919 (the historical referent is really 1909). With his first novel, Mendoza plays a major part in reintroducing the role of story into Spanish fiction.[33]

---

32. I argue this thesis in *Beyond the Metafictional Mode*.

33. In the words of Santos Alonso, "Desperdiciada fabulación," Mendoza "recuperó el gusto de la narración, la creación de personajes y ambientes y abrió tendencias que gozarían de posterior aceptación en la narrativa española, como han sido la novela histórica o la de intriga con estructura policial" (revived the pleasure of narration, the creation of characters and settings and initiated tendencies that would enjoy subsequent acceptance in Spanish narrative, such as the historical novel or the enigma novel with a detective structure, 21). Like much of what has been written to date on Eduardo Mendoza's fiction, this article is

Perhaps the most dramatic expression of the new emphasis on story is the prominence in post-totalitarian Spanish fiction of a postmodern version of the detective genre. Although the commercial success of the novels of Vázquez Montalbán (his first, *Tatuaje* [Tattoo], was published in 1974), may help explain the popularity of this enigma mode, Mendoza's *La verdad sobre el caso Savolta* was instrumental in bestowing artistic credibility on the genre.[34] Given the tradition of novelistic conformity that crystallized with neorealism in the 1950s and continued with the "new novel" of the 1960s and the self-referential fiction of the 1970s, Mendoza deserves major credit for providing an alternative mode of novelistic expression. Furthermore, thanks to the model provided by *El cuarto de atrás*, subsequent novelists did not even have to choose between the two polarities, but could opt for a compromise position.

In spite of the basic differences concerning the role of story in the Goytisolo, Martín Gaite, and Mendoza novels, they share a concern over

general in nature. Focusing on *La verdad sobre el caso Savolta* are Santos Alonso's *Guía de lectura: "La verdad sobre el caso Savolta,"* José María Rodríguez-García's "Gatsby Goes to Barcelona: On the Configuration of the Post-Modern Spanish Novel," and Frederick Luciani's review of *The Truth about the Savolta Case.* Informative also are the comments by José María Marco, "El espacio de la libertad," and "La verdad sobre el caso Mendoza," in Oscar Barrero Pérez, ed., *Historia de la literatura española contemporánea,* 305–8. For other more general studies see Patricia Hart, *Spanish Sleuth: The Detective in Spanish Fiction,* Malcolm A. Compitello, "Spain's 'nueva novela negra' and the Question of Form," José F. Colmeiro, "E. Mendoza y los laberintos de la realidad," and Lynn McGovern, "A 'Private I': The Birth of a Female Sleuth and the Role of Parody in Lourdes Ortiz's *Picadura mortal"* (the latter draws a comparison between the Mendoza and Ortiz novels).

34. Francisco García Pavón's name also deserves mention in reference to this genre, though the humor of his works is in conflict with the general tone of what is known in Spain as the "novela negra." Other titles that subversively follow the "novela negra" model are Marina Mayoral, *Cándida otra vez,* 1979; Lourdes Ortiz, *Picadura mortal,* 1979; Soledad Puértolas, *El bandido doblemente armado,* 1980; Juan Benet, *El aire de un crimen,* 1980; Beatriz Pottecher, *Ciertos tonos del negro,* 1985; Antonio Muñoz Molina, *Beltenebros,* 1989; and Adelaida García Morales's *La lógica del vampiro,* 1989, as well as some of the fictional works we will examine in detail. For analyses of the detective genre in post-Franco fiction, see: José F. Colmeiro, *La novela policíaca española* and "La narrativa policíaca posmodernista de Manuel Vázquez Montalbán"; Salvador Vázquez de Parga, *La novela policíaca en España* and "Viaje por la novela policíaca actual"; Hart, *Spanish Sleuth;* María-Elena Bravo, "Literatura de la distensión: El elemento policíaco"; Francie Cate-Arries, "Lost in the Language of Culture: Manuel Vázquez Montalbán's Novel Detection"; Juan Tébar, "Novela criminal española de la transición"; Claudia Schaefer-Rodríguez, "Realism Meets the Postmodern in Post-Franco Spain's 'novela negra' "; and Samuel Amell, "Literatura e ideología: El caso de la novela negra en la España actual."

an individual's capacity to act as agent of his or her existence. The issue of how a subject both acts and is acted upon has been demonstrated in *Juan sin Tierra* and *El cuarto de atrás*. In the case of Goytisolo's novel, the strategy for transforming an individual from a passive object into an active subject involves second-person narration. When, for example, the protagonist is told as he labors to describe a scene on his ancestor's Cuban plantation "you will divide the imaginary scene into two parts" (30), he is in the process of being constituted into a new writer with a whole new ensemble of socioartistic values. Agency in *El cuarto de atrás* concerns a woman's subject position during and after the Franco regime's reign. The textual strategy of the novel allows the narrator to position herself as both speaking and spoken subject or to serve as the producer of a resisting discourse and also to see herself as the product of gendered discursive practices. Yet in each of these two novels the issue of agency is secondary to heteroglossia and state/social apparatuses, respectively. In the case of *La verdad sobre el caso Savolta,* on the other hand, the emphasis falls directly on the maneuverability involved in assuming multiple ideological positions. By virtue of this multiplicity, the protagonists pluralize the word *truth* announced in the title.[35]

Mendoza's novel concerns the murder on December 31, 1917, of the wealthy industrialist Savolta. The *récit* begins in 1927 with the testimony of the primary first-person narrator, Javier Miranda Lugarte, before a New York judge (only near the end of the novel do we learn that the testimony is a part of Javier's attempt to collect an insurance claim for a friend). In addition to Javier's declarations, evidence is presented in the form of excerpts of a newspaper article written in 1917 by Pajarito de Soto and an affidavit dated November 21, 1926, and sworn by the police inspector in charge of the Savolta case, Alejandro Vázquez Ríos. These documents help explain the murder not only of the industrialist Savolta but also of the newspaper reporter Pajarito. Vázquez, Javier notes, died under mysterious circumstances just a few days before the court hearing began.

The *histoire* comes to us in nonsequential fragments, with some incidents narrated twice. If initially such a technique suggests neorealist models (such

---

35. I am drawing from a large body of theoretical works that addresses the inseparable issues of the subject and agency. Most influential on my own approach are: Smith, *Discerning the Subject;* Steven Cohan and Linda M. Shires, *Telling Stories: A Theoretical Analysis of Narrative Fiction;* Althusser, *Lenin and Philosophy;* Silverman, *Subject of Semiotics;* Benveniste, *Problems in General Linguistics;* and especially Chambers, *Room for Maneuver.*

as *La colmena, El Jarama,*[36] *Los bravos* [The savages], and others), that analogy is only partially valid. First, this novel—unlike the Cela, Sánchez Ferlosio, and Fernández Santos examples—is narrated primarily by the protagonist Javier in the first person and therefore lacks the implication of a guiding hand standing apart from the action.[37] Indeed, to a degree the fragmentation can be attributed to the judge's requests for clarifications. His questions force Javier to back up or jump ahead of the sequence of events. But the patterns formed by the juxtapositions suggest that not all the fragmentation should be attributed to the judge's questions. Ultimately we must regard the protagonist-narrator in his narrative present—"even today, as I write these lines . . ."[38]—as the one primarily responsible for the *récit.* This protagonist-narrator, at some unspecified time after the testimony of 1927, plays the major role in determining the order in which the events are read. That order serves as a sign pointing to his narrative project.

Most of the action occurs during three years: 1917, 1918, and 1919. One of Javier's friends, Pajarito de Soto, is an anarchist newspaper reporter writing a series of articles exposing the Savolta firm's criminal activities. His stories allege that Savolta's factory is illegally producing armaments and selling them to Germany. The firm's business manager is a Frenchman named Paul-André Lepprince, and since Javier works for the law firm representing the Savolta account, Lepprince and Javier form a professional and personal relationship. In fact, Lepprince coerces Javier into marrying his mistress, a cabaret singer named María Coral, so that the Frenchman can be free to marry his employer's daughter, María Rosa Savolta. Around Christmas in 1917 Pajarito is struck by a car in front of his home and killed. A few days later Savolta is assassinated in his mansion at a New Year's Eve party.

36. The novel takes its name from a river in Spain.

37. There is an introductory note in which the author identifies the sources for the newspaper articles, letters, and documents. Unlike, for example, the "Nota del transcriptor" of *La familia de Pascual Duarte* that forms an integral part of the fiction, I consider the note in Mendoza's novel a nonfictional authorial comment. There are, nevertheless, segments narrated by an unidentified voice (most notably those concerning the activities of the police informer Nemesio) that challenge the conventions of a first-person novel.

38. Mendoza, *La verdad sobre el caso Savolta,* 302. Subsequent citations will indicate the page number in parentheses. To date Mendoza has written seven other novels: *El misterio de la cripta embrujada,* 1979; *El laberinto de las aceitunas,* 1982; *La ciudad de los prodigios,* 1986; *La isla inaudita,* 1989; *Restauración,* 1991 (a Catalan version appeared in 1990); *Sin noticias de Gurb,* 1991; and *El año del diluvio,* 1992.

As 1918 begins, Inspector Vázquez is deeply involved in Savolta's murder. Nemesio, a deranged police informer, comes to the inspector with the claim that he knows who killed Pajarito de Soto. Since Vázquez is totally absorbed by the Savolta murder, he has no interest in information concerning a death he prefers to attribute to an accident. Eventually the inspector begins to realize that there is a connection between the reporter's death and the industrialist's murder and that a mysterious letter Pajarito mailed, which Vázquez has been unable to locate, may provide the key. He decides that Nemesio knows about the letter, but the inspector is transferred to a foreign post before he can track down the informant. Meanwhile, Lepprince now appears everywhere with a German bodyguard he calls "Max." Later we learn that Max's real name is Pratz and that he is Lepprince's partner in the illegal arms sales.

By the beginning of 1919 the Savolta firm is on the verge of bankruptcy, and the labor unions are calling for a general strike. Pratz (alias Max) abducts María Coral and tries to leave the country. Javier, alerted by Lepprince, pursues them to a small town in the Pyrenees, but Pratz eludes him only to be killed by the police deep in the mountains. María Coral survives the shoot-out, but Javier cannot find her. He finally decides to return to Barcelona, but by this time the strikes have paralyzed the country and it takes him days to return. When he arrives he learns that Lepprince died in a fire at the factory. He also runs into Inspector Vázquez who, having recently returned to Barcelona from his foreign assignment, tells Javier that he learned from Nemesio that Pajarito de Soto's letter (documenting the illegal sales by the Savolta firm) was addressed to Javier but sent to the reporter's own wife, Teresa. She fled Barcelona at the death of her husband, taking with her the unopened letter. When Vázquez finally caught up with her and put all the pieces together, he discovered that Pratz killed Pajarito de Soto, and Lepprince, fearing that the reporter's letter had been sent to Savolta, had his boss murdered. Before he died, Lepprince left a letter for Javier revealing that he had taken out an American insurance policy in Javier's name. After waiting a few years, Javier is to collect the money and turn it over to the Frenchman's wife and daughter. Javier and María Coral, who finally are reunited, emigrate to the United States, and in 1927 Javier testifies at the court hearing on his insurance claim. This testimony serves as the novel's beginning.

Greed forms the common denominator for the majority of the characters. Lepprince serves as the most obvious example, and his only saving grace is the insurance policy he took out shortly before his death to provide for the welfare of his family. But that display of moral consciousness hardly compensates for the degree to which he allowed himself to be constituted by the desire for money and power. With the exception of buying the annuity, Lepprince suppresses all other ethical and political forces for the sake of his own material welfare.

Yet his two arch enemies turn out to be subject to the same basic ideological influence as their nemesis. Both Pajarito and Vázquez represent professions advocating truth and justice, the cornerstones of Judeo-Christian ethics, yet both engage in unethical activities in their attempts to achieve personal gain.

Pajarito, for example, is an anarchist reporter who seemingly sacrifices his life for the sake of economic equality. In conversations with Javier he self-righteously expresses his moral indignation with the corruption his investigations uncover. Notwithstanding his professed commitment to ethical conduct, it turns out that Pajarito was murdered not because of what his newspaper articles exposed but because of his attempt to use the information to blackmail the principals involved. He pretends to speak for idealistic social values, only to reveal finally that he is subject to the dream of materialistic personal gains.

Although Vázquez provides the details concerning the murders of Savolta and Pajarito de Soto, he obstructs Javier's attempt to clarify the circumstances surrounding Lepprince's death. Upon returning to Barcelona and learning that the Frenchman died in a fire at the factory, Javier asks himself a series of questions:

> ¿qué hacía Lepprince *solo* en la fábrica? ¿Fue por su propia voluntad o se trataba de un crimen *astutamente* disfrazado de accidente? En tal caso, ¿habría sido Lepprince conducido por la fuerza a la fábrica y encerrado? ¿O tal vez ya estaba muerto cuando el incendio se declaró? ¿Por qué no se había iniciado una investigación policial? Cuestiones todas ellas que jamás hallaron respuesta.

> (what was Lepprince doing *alone* in the factory? Did he go there on his own free will or was it a case of a crime cleverly disguised as an accident? In that case, would Lepprince have been taken to the factory

by force and locked in there? Or perhaps he was already dead when the fire was reported? Why hasn't a police investigation been initiated? All these are questions that will never be answered.) (430)

In the letter he left for Javier, Lepprince notes that Vázquez has just returned from his overseas duties and adds, "That old fox has it in for me and he will not rest until he sees me dead." On reading this statement, Javier asks himself: "Was it a veiled accusation?" (457). With the opportunity at hand, Javier decides to broach the question of Lepprince with the inspector, but Vázquez is evasive. Finally the police officer says: " 'Listen, Miranda, I have always thought that somebody owned Lepprince . . . ,' he pointed up, 'somebody in high places, if you get my meaning. As far as I am concerned somebody got him out of the way, but this is only a theory. Don't tell anyone what I have said to you' " (453). When they finish their conversation and prepare to separate for what is to be the last time, Javier notes in retrospect that Vázquez's "face had turned somber, as if his words were a sure foreshadowing of his own death, which occurred in mysterious circumstances a few days ago" (453). The mystery only deepens if the reader recalls that in his affidavit Vázquez admits leaving the police force in 1920 to take a job in "the sales department of a food-supply company" (38). Later Javier comments on this move:

> Sé que abandonó el cuerpo de Policía en 1920, es decir, según mis cálculos, cuando sus investigaciones debían estar llegando al final. Algo misterioso hay en ello. Pero nunca se sabrá, porque hace pocos meses fue muerto por alguien relacionado con el caso. No me sorprende: muchos cayeron en aquellos años belicosos y Vázquez tenía que ser uno más, aunque tal vez no el último.

> (I know that he left the police force in 1920, or that is, according to my calculations, when his investigations should have been coming to a conclusion. There is something fishy about this. But the reason will never be known, because a few months ago he was killed by someone related to the case. I am not surprised: a lot of people died during those bellicose years and Vázquez must have been one more, although perhaps not the last one.) (46)

Although Vázquez is representative of a social apparatus that supposedly upholds truth and justice, he subverts those ideals. As he solves one enigma, he becomes the subject of yet another; in the process of determining the truth about Savolta, he undermines his own truth. Evidence indicates that this crusader against corruption turns out to be a part of the corruption as both its beneficiary and its victim. Vázquez allows himself to be constituted by the same ideology against which he campaigns.

In the examples examined so far, the characters are subject to various and conflicting ideologies but allow themselves to be dominated by a single one. Javier proves the exception, however, since from the beginning he struggles against the dominant force of self-interests. He functions as an agent rather than merely as a subject.[39] For example, he seduces his friend Pajarito's wife, but she initiates the affair and he experiences moral guilt and remorse. He also agrees to marry Lepprince's mistress, María Coral, and to allow the two lovers to continue their trysts. Yet his motives are not dictated entirely by opportunism, for he is in love with María Coral. If, on the one hand, Javier can be accused in these examples of being more of a moral coward than an immoral conniver, at least his shifting positions allow him the room to withstand a total surrender to material self-interest, the driving force that ultimately destroys most of the other characters. This ability to respond, on both a conscious and an unconscious level, to a sense of moral responsibility becomes most apparent in his relationship with Lepprince.

When the lawyer Cortabanyes hires him to work in his office, Javier is given only menial tasks to perform.[40] Then one day Lepprince appears, and the lawyer assigns Javier to work directly with the Frenchman, making it clear that Lepprince is one of the law firm's most important clients. Even though Pajarito has told Javier about the Savolta fraud and Lepprince's probable role in it, Javier's self-interests seem to erase any ethical qualms as he eagerly accepts the assignment:

> Yo buscaba el éxito a cualquier precio, no tanto por quedar bien ante Cortabanyes como por complacer a Lepprince, cuyo interés en mí me

---

39. I am using these two terms as defined by Smith, *Discerning the Subject*, xxxv.

40. Cortabanyes is a relatively minor character in the novel, yet we discover near the end that he played a key role in Savolta's success in gaining control of the armament factory, a success achieved by means of dishonesty. Cortabanyes apparently withdrew from an active role in the company after the death of his wife, and as a result he survives the 1917–1919 intrigue. Two other Savolta business partners, Claudedeu and Parell, continue to be actively involved in the company and each pays with his life. This interconnected web of corruption even includes María Coral, who negotiates the terms when Lepprince hires two unsavory characters with whom she works in a cabaret to assassinate Savolta. In fact, Javier sees her and her two friends at the New Year's Eve party the night the industrialist is murdered.

abría las puertas a expectativas imprevistas, a las más disparatadas esperanzas. Veía en él una posible vía de salida al marasmo del despacho de Cortabanyes, a las largas tardes monótonas e improductivas y al porvenir mezquino e incierto.

(I was looking for success at any price, not so much to gain favor with Cortabanyes as to please Lepprince, whose interest in me opened doors to unexpected opportunities, to the wildest dreams. I saw in him a possible avenue of escape from the tediousness of Cortabanyes's office, from the long monotonous and unproductive afternoons and a pedestrian and uncertain future.) (77)

Javier's ambitions are well on the road to being realized as he becomes a regular guest in Lepprince's home. Yet contradicting his opportunistic inclinations are his ethical instincts and the guilt he feels concerning his former friend Pajarito. Not only did he and Teresa cheat on Pajarito, but he has remained silent in the face of all the questions concerning the reporter's mysterious death as well. The conflict within him expresses itself when one night, after an elegant meal in his employer's home as he sits before the fireplace with cognac and a cigarette, Javier blurts out: " 'Lepprince,' I heard myself say, 'who killed Pajarito de Soto?' " (97). This passage clearly indicates how Javier allows himself to be subject to plural and conflicting discursive practices. Although the reflexive construction "I heard myself say" is similar in effect to Goytisolo's second-person narration, in Mendoza's version the individual is subject to traditional ethics rather than to postmodern aesthetics. Furthermore, in contrast to his colleagues and friends, he is constituted by both immoral egoism and moral altruism. The plurality of conflicting ideologies allows Javier to achieve the status of an agent by choosing between alternatives and thereby expressing resistance to the one-dimensional opportunism subjecting the other characters of the novel.

What distinguishes Javier, then, is that he fluctuates from being subject to and the subject of conflicting ideological forces. He is not limited to a single subject position. That same multiplicity allows him to see the dangers of polarization so evident in the labor violence, whose participants, he notes, are:

Más unidos por el antagonismo y la angustia que separados por las diferencias ideológicas, los españoles descendíamos en confusa turba-multa una escala de Jacob invertida, cuyos peldaños eran venganzas de venganzas y su trama un ovillo confuso de alianzas, denuncias,

represalias y traiciones que conducían al infierno de la intransigencia
fundada en el miedo y el crimen engendrado por la desesperación.

(More united by antagonisms and anguish than separated by ideological differences, we Spaniards descended in a confused multitude an
inverted Jacob's ladder whose steps were vengeance of other vengeances
and whose extension a confused heap of alliances, betrayals, reprisals
and treasons that led to an inferno of fear and crime engendered by
desperation.) (335)

The explanation applies not only to the fictional context of 1919 but also
to the real context of 1975. This view of revolutionary change looks both
backward and forward in time; it explains Spain's polarized past just as surely
as it predicts its future. Whether operating in the name of revolutionary
politics or institutional pillars of justice, most of the characters are subject
to a single all-consuming materialistic ideology. Yet by virtue of his ability
to recognize and accept the plurality of the discursive practices operating
on him, Javier manages to maneuver into a subject position of resistance to
the dominant materialism of his time. He achieves agency by pitting one
ideology against another, by choosing one over the other.

The final section of the novel dramatizes the connection between agency
and multiple subject positions. A letter appears, written by Lepprince's
widow, María Rosa, and addressed to Javier. In it she asserts that Lepprince
was a great man and makes the following comment in reference to her
daughter: "la pobre ha crecido en un ambiente de clase media, tan distinto
al que por nacimiento le corresponde. La niña, sin embargo, no traiciona
su origen y se quedaría usted sorprendido de su distinción y modales" (the
poor thing has grown up in a middle-class environment, so different from
the one she was born into. The child, nevertheless, is not betraying her
origin and you would be surprised at her bearing and manners, 462). If
the reader accepts the mother's assessment, clearly an aristocratic birthright
counteracts the negative influence of a middle-class environment. Furthermore, since the novel ends with this letter addressed to Javier, the message
could be interpreted to mean that the child is subject to a single, dominant
ideology that cannot be altered by even social evolution.

As the creator of the *récit*, however, Javier assumes responsibility for
ending his story with this letter. Double voicing is involved, then, for
as the message of the letter is decoded not only its contents must be
considered but also the implications inherent in Javier's decision to use

it as a conclusion to his story. With that expanded meaning in mind, it can be argued that rather than affirming polarization, this epistolary device points to multiplicity. First, María Rosa's subject position is radically different from that of Javier and of the reader, which explains why the truth she professes about Lepprince does not correspond to the fictional and real readers'. From where she speaks, as benefactor of an insurance policy safeguarding the future for her and her daughter, her dead husband was a great man. Second, though she insists that her daughter maintains inherited aristocratic attitudes, María Rosa cannot ignore the force of a middle-class environment on her offspring. And so her written words concede what they pretend to deny: "ideology is plural and so is the subject it speaks."[41] Neither the daughter nor the forces influencing her can be one-dimensional, as the mother would have it. The daughter is destined to serve as the speaking subject for proletariat as well as aristocratic values. Since she forms part of a social system in the process of becoming more heterogeneous, clearly the ideological codes underlying that system are also increasingly plural and contradictory.

The speaker's strategy of ending *La verdad sobre el caso Savolta* with this letter addressed to him can be seen, therefore, as yet another demonstration of the plurality of truths, subject positions, and ideologies constituting human subjects and above all as the culmination of the posited author's implicit project to affirm the possibility of human agency. By virtue of maneuvering himself into a position where he can contemplate his own subject position in relation to that of others and in turn the multiple ideologies influencing them and himself, Javier achieves the status of an agent, as does the reader who participates in the process. From this fictional vantage point, speaker and reader should see that there are as many truths as there are subject positions professing something as true.

I would like to propose an oxymoron, "innovative conventionality," as the most appropriate characterization of Mendoza's contribution to contemporary Spanish fiction. He brings the story back in a much more pronounced manner than does Martín Gaite, but at the same time he refuses to let his readers become too comfortable with it. Although his roots run from modernist novelistic modes all the way back to realism,

41. Cohan and Shires, *Telling Stories*, 138.

he displays a postmodernist distrust for the totalizing picture.[42] Without question Mendoza provides readers with an alternative to Juan Goytisolo and his self-referential school, and in this sense the two novelists stand at opposite poles. But after some thirty-nine years of witnessing the attempts by the regime to polarize its citizens by reducing discourse to a univocal function, these novelists seem to share the need to affirm that it is possible for individuals to act as both agents and objects of a vast ideological grid extending far beyond the arbitrary unity that Franco and his ideologues, even in the final year of their regime, still desperately hoped to impose. In spite of the structural polarities evident between *Juan sin Tierra* and *La verdad sobre el caso Savolta* and the more accommodating stance of *El cuarto de atrás*, we should not ignore their common legacy of positing the possibility of human agency. In fact, that thematic commonality is certainly as important as their structural dissimilarities in helping to define the direction of post-totalitarian Spanish fiction. Yet as if to negate the suggestion of a unidirectional course for this period, the next novel we will analyze, *Visión del ahogado,* presents its characters as mere products of discourse.

Panoptic Vision in *Visión del ahogado*

The connection between Eduardo Mendoza's *La verdad sobre el caso Savolta* and Juan José Millás's *Visión del ahogado* (A drowned man's vision) is relatively easy to draw. Like the Mendoza novel, Millás's concerns a crime around which the author creates a story about people and events.[43] Yet

42. In his own polarizing conclusion, Rodríguez-García, "Gatsby Goes to Barcelona," insists that the novel is quintessentially postmodern. Depending on the definition of postmodernism applied, very likely one could make a case for the opposite claim.

43. As of 1994, Millás has published nine novels. In addition to this, his second, they are: *Cerbero son las sombras,* 1975; *El jardín vacío,* 1981; *Papel mojado,* 1983; *Letra muerta,* 1984; *El desorden de tu nombre,* 1988; *La soledad era esto,* 1990; *Volver a casa,* 1990; *Tonto, muerto, bastardo e invisible,* 1995. His collection of stories titled *Ella imagina y otras obsesiones de Vicente Holgado* was published in 1994. Ignacio Javier López, "Novela y realidad: En torno a la estructura de *Visión del ahogado* de Juan José Millás," and Marta Isabel Miranda, "Modos de comunicación en *Visión del ahogado,* de Juan José Millás," have provided useful structural analyses of the novel, while Gonzalo Sobejano, "Juan José Millás, fabulador de la extrañeza," offers an equally valuable overview of the first six novels. Fabián Gutiérrez's *Cómo leer a Juan José Millás* provides a more basic reader's guide to Millás's fiction.

the similarities should not blind us to some basic differences. *La verdad sobre el caso Savolta* addresses the issue of how to create human agency, while *Visión del ahogado* seems to make no concession whatsoever to that possibility. Indeed, Millás's novel concerns itself with a group of people whose existence is defined by others.

Visión del ahogado offers three primary and several secondary characters, each serving as a focalizer of present events that in turn often trigger flashbacks. The present action is limited to a single morning. Jorge, on his way to work, sees a crowd gathered at a subway entrance. He pauses to observe from a distance what has happened. As he watches he sees his former classmate Luis, or Vitaminas, mingling with the crowd. When Vitaminas decided to leave his wife, Julia, he in effect invited Jorge to move in with her. The sight of Julia's estranged husband in the neighborhood prompts Jorge to return home. Vitaminas is also observed at the subway entrance by Jesús Villar, whose wife, Rosario, was Vitaminas's paramour when they were classmates. Jesús, driven by jealousy and aware that Vitaminas's name has been connected with some armed robberies, goes to the police station to file a report.

Meanwhile an inspector has been assigned to watch the building where Julia and Jorge live to ensure that the fugitive does not take refuge there. The officer enlists the building superintendent and janitor, El Ratón, to go to the couple's apartment to make certain that Vitaminas has not already gone there. The inspector then chooses a bar across the street as his surveillance post. After inspecting the rooms, El Ratón informs Julia and Jorge that, in addition to robbing pharmacies, Vitaminas is accused of stabbing a policeman that morning at the subway entrance. He warns them that the officers will likely come later to question them. Jorge, shortly after El Ratón's departure, abandons Julia, explaining that he does not want to be involved with the police.

El Ratón returns to the bar to make his report to the inspector. Vitaminas manages during all this to slip into the building and hide in the furnace room. Jesús Villar, who sees the fugitive enter the building and go down to the cellar, calls the police with a series of false sightings of the wanted man at scattered points in the city. He intends to weave a web that eventually will lead them to the real hideaway. Jesús is arrested, however, before he can play out his little game. Vitaminas is also finally apprehended, not as a result of the organized surveillance but because it is raining and he has left tracks of water that El Ratón, when he returns from the bar, follows to the hiding spot. The fugitive, in a semicoma from an overdose of cold pills, is taken without a struggle.

In *Tiempo de silencio* the narrator declares that every city dweller should know that "a thousand, ten thousand, a hundred thousand pairs of eyes classify and catalog him, recognize and embrace him, identify and save him, thereby allowing him to find himself when he feels most lost in his natural place: in prison, in an orphanage, in the police station, in the insane asylum, in the emergency room . . ." (19). What applies for Martín-Santos's Madrid of the 1950s and 1960s applies equally for Millás's Madrid of 1977 (the same year as the elections). By means of their presentations both authors suggest the existence of a panoptic machine operated by the citizens as well as by the police. As a result, everyone potentially plays the role of both the observing subject and the observed object.

Perhaps the janitor, El Ratón, best exemplifies how the state has created a panoptic system. This man, existing near the bottom of the social hierarchy, is most directly responsible for Vitaminas's arrest. When he appears at Julia's place in search of the fugitive, he is officious and self-aggrandizing, taking care to let Jorge and Julia know that he served in the Civil Guard: "The Mouse, with gestures learned from American movies and practiced to boredom in his doorkeeper's cubbyhole, sniffs around the house."[44] He is not only a "mouse" but also one conditioned by that modern societal laboratory, Hollywood.[45]

In addition to relying on American movies as his model, El Ratón hopes to gain the approval of the police inspector by imitating him. But when El Ratón pompously returns to the bar to report to the inspector that Vitaminas is not in Julia's flat (just like a seasoned detective in the movies, he makes the inspector wait as he urbanely orders a cognac before beginning the account), his dreams of approval and praise are dashed when the inspector almost instantly challenges him to explain why neither Julia nor Jorge has gone to work that day: "Frente a la barra, tras una hilera de botellas, hay un espejo de mala calidad. El Ratón busca sus ojos entre el

---

44. Juan José Millás, *Visión del ahogado*, 95. Subsequent citations will indicate the page number in parentheses.

45. Sobejano, "Juan José Millás," offers some very insightful observations on the significance of movie references in the novel.

cuello de dos botellas; en seguida advierte la diferencia entre su mirada y la del policía, entre su expresión y la expresión del policía" (Facing the bar, behind a row of bottles, there is a broken-down mirror. El Ratón looks for his eyes between the necks of two bottles; immediately he notices the difference between his gaze and that of the policeman, between his expression and the policeman's, 104). The mirror serves as one of the principal metaphors in the novel, signaling a society in which the gaze not only classifies and categorizes individuals but also ultimately authenticates or negates existence itself. Gazing into the mirror allows El Ratón to see himself as an other and from the same position as the inspector, which in turn allows him to determine to what degree his reflected image resembles that of the inspector (the person behind the gaze).[46] Only if his reflection is identical to the inspector's image can El Ratón aspire to the category of true observer or seeing subject, as opposed to his usual status of an observed or seen object. But the mirror confirms that, in the eyes of the inspector, he is a mere janitor and as such an object of scorn.

Yet El Ratón finds momentary consolation in the bartender, Cojo, who, taking advantage of the policeman's brief absence, asks the janitor about the relationship between the subway stabbing and the inspector's activities: "El Ratón comprendió de alguna manera que ser importante estriba en que los demás lo crean, y respondió con vaguedades e insinuaciones que agrandaron su imagen ante el espejo y ante el Cojo" (The Mouse understood that in some mysterious way to be important depended on what others thought, and he answered vaguely and with insinuations that aggrandized his image before the mirror and Cojo, 178). For the moment Cojo serves as an authenticating gaze, but El Ratón knows that a bartender cannot provide him with the assurance he seeks. Since his goal is to enter a higher category of observers, only a member of that category can confirm his membership. As he glances back at the mirror he knows that nothing has changed, that he and the inspector still exist on different levels. Metaphorically, his reflected image defines not only his own nonbeing but also that of the other characters of the novel, all of whose existence depends on the confirmation of others.

46. In addition to their panoptic implications, these references to mirrors—or perhaps more accurately my reading of these references—contain Lacanian overtones. But since Lacan informs so much of the theory and literature written today, it does not strike me as necessary to trace each of the connecting lines between these passages and Lacan's theories. Two basic sources are his *Ecrits: A Selection* and Ragland-Sullivan's *Jacques Lacan.*

Among the observed observers perhaps the most pathetic is Jesús Villar, the current husband of Vitaminas's former classmate and sexual partner. Rosario repeatedly talks of her escapades with Vitaminas, and Jesús is consumed by jealousy. For that reason, he decides to go to police headquarters when he sees his rival in the crowd gathered around the subway entrance where the policeman was stabbed: "He has ended up there after a struggle between a lack of confidence and the attraction of something new, and also urged on to some degree by his office mates, to whom he had told the incident at the subway" (67–68). Whereas his desire for revenge primarily motivates him, he finds almost as much inspiration in the prospect of becoming his colleagues' center of attention. But experience has taught him to be wary. When he appears before the police commissioner he feels more like the accused than the accuser: "Instantly he decides to look at the commissioner at the level of his upper lip or a little above, but avoiding the level of his eyes so that the policeman's gaze would not annul his own" (68). Earlier El Ratón tried to use the mirror to affirm his likeness to that of the inspector and found difference instead. Without that device as a buffer, Jesús does not dare to confront the disapproving glare of this commissioner. He knows that if he looks him in the eye, he will see a negation of his own existence. The poor informer knows without glancing at him that for this police officer, Jesús is not a human being but another specimen to be classified and cataloged.

Jesús's caution proves to be well founded, for what begins as his civic declaration quickly deteriorates into the commissioner's interrogation of him. As chance would have it, the last pharmacy that Vitaminas robbed was the same one in which Rosario, Jesús's wife, used to work. The policeman accordingly begins to question Jesús about his wife's relationship with the wanted man, suggesting that she was an accomplice in the robbery. Then a clerk appears to take Jesús's personal data:

> comenzaba a ver aquellos datos (su profesión, su edad, su estado civil) de manera distinta, a la vez más lúcida y confusa que en las revisiones rutinarias que periódicamente hacía de estos antecedentes, cuya función parecía más compleja y maligna que la de señalar su realidad . . . en Jesús Villar despertaba la sospecha de que los hechos relativos a su estado civil, más que nombrar una realidad, la moldeaban y reducían sus límites de tal manera que cada dato representaba una imposición, una orden.

(he began to see that data [his profession, his age, his marital status] in a different light, clearer and more confusing at the same time, than the routine summaries that he periodically made of his prior existence, whose function seemed more complex and threatening than merely to indicate his reality . . . Jesús began to suspect that the facts relative to his marital status, more than defining his reality, molded him and reduced his options to such a degree that each datum represented an imposition, a command.) (131–32)

As Jesús answers the routine questions he cannot ignore that his responses serve to turn him into an object for future surveillance. By virtue of the data he himself supplies, he now can be, in the words of Michel Foucault, "described, judged, measured, compared with others . . . ," so that in turn he may be "trained or corrected, classified, normalized, excluded, etc."[47] All this is but a preliminary step. With each piece of information he supplies, Jesús provides the materials that others will use to confine him.

Perhaps because he intuits that he has become transformed into a mere object, Jesús makes a desperate attempt to assume agency. After seeing Vitaminas slip into the basement, Jesús begins his calls to the police with bogus sightings of the fugitive. From his make-believe tower, he enjoys the illusionary power of operating the panoptic machine. But of course a phone booth with its glass walls functions more as a watched cell than a watchtower, and in short order the police locate and arrest him. Foucault tells us that in a smooth-running panoptic society there must be an "automatic functioning of power," and "the inmates should be caught up in a power situation of which they are themselves the bearers" (201). Such is certainly the case for Jesús. He is an ideal citizen who bears the power against himself. In this nightmarish self-disciplining machine, the police are merely one of a complex of coordinated gears.

The panoptic machine above all imposes social conformity, and its full force is directed against nonconformists such as political anarchists and of course criminals. As a result Vitaminas feels justifiably threatened by the panoptic society as he walks along the street. When he passes store windows, he has to be concerned not merely with being the object of multiple gazes but also with the possibility that someone will recognize him: "todos miraban

---

47. Foucault, *Discipline and Punish*, 191. Subsequent citations will indicate the page number in parentheses.

con cierta nostalgia a través de los cristales empañados . . . hablaban y reían sin dejar de mirar a la calle (a él tal vez) . . . se movían y gesticulaban en sus puestos de observación" (everyone was looking with a certain nostalgia through the vapor-covered glass . . . they were talking and laughing without removing their eyes from the street [and perhaps also from him] . . . they were moving and gesturing from their observation posts, 106). Like Jesús's pathetic game with the police, Vitaminas's criminal actions also represent futile attempts to defy rather than submit to the automatic functioning of power inherent in a panoptic state.

Linguistic ineptness lies at the core of Vitaminas's efforts to rebel. During his school days he courted Julia, and at the same time he was sexually involved with Rosario: "he sensed that he was in love with Rosario, that he was in love with himself, and that the desire to undress the young woman involved a desire to see in her his own naked body and to touch himself in a misguided search for himself" (193–94). Rather than celebrating the physiological difference of her body, he sees it as an extension of his own. Although he has a narcissistic interest in her, one day in a fit of passion he uttered "Rosario, Rosario," only to sense that he had compromised himself with those words: "No pudo ver entonces en qué medida con aquel error había también trivializado sus relaciones con Julia, pero en adelante tuvo mucho cuidado de no contribuir con las insuficiencias del lenguaje a un proceso de deterioro que se desarrollaba sin embargo a sus expensas" (He could not see then to what degree with that error he had also undermined his relations with Julia, but from then on he was very careful not to contribute with linguistic inadequacy to a process of deterioration that was nevertheless laying claim to him, 128).

In spite of his intentions, the same thing happens with Julia: "en un momento de delirio dice Julia, Julia, haciendo uso de una insuficiencia del lenguaje con la que traza un esquema al que no podrá ya escapar, sino que le servirá en el futuro de modelo. Pero los modelos, entonces no lo sabía, actúan más como limitación que como estímulo" (in a moment of delirious passion he says Julia, Julia, resorting to a linguistic inadequacy with which he traces an outline from which he then will not be able to escape, and that in fact will serve as a future model. But models, something he did not know then, act more as limitations than as stimuli, 130). Discursive practice again forms the connection between his words and the entrapping model. Because of his lack of linguistic sophistication and thanks to "the attractive image learned from the stories of love and war in American movies" (153), he resorts to the strategy of repeating her name, which repetition constitutes a declaration of love. Since he is merely a conduit through which the coded words pass, the text suggests that Vitaminas did not select Julia but rather she was selected for him by the language of pop culture.

Finally frustrated by having his fate decided by a discourse he does not understand and cannot control, Vitaminas makes a fateful decision: "Set phrases surround him and detract from his sense of person, for which reason he finally decides that one has to limit oneself to actions" (204). Feeling himself a victim of language, Vitaminas looks for freedom in actions. He begins to rob pharmacies. But as he sits in his hiding spot in the boiler room swallowing cold pills to alleviate his fever, he realizes that actions themselves are part of the trap: "My life seems to be unreal, my crime an illusion, a poorly written play in which I have to play a role" (203). Even his acts directed against the disciplining society followed a text. He realizes too late that he cannot escape from the world of discourse. Actions as well as utterances are scripted into the human drama called existence, and the novel suggests that individuals lack the capacity to control and integrate their words and deeds. Because he fails to master that integration, Vitaminas is swept away by the flood of discursive practices and can only shout voicelessly as the policeman comes to take him: "can't you see that I am suffering the vision of a drowned man?" (237).

If Vitaminas is a victim of movie scripts he ineptly parrots, Jorge is victimized by the dramatic role that has been scripted for him. He also lives in a panoptic world, and therefore, whether standing on stage or seated in the audience, he feels he must perform. For example, when after an argument Julia begins to display her affection, "he remains expressionless in the sense that the spectator also remains expressionless, in spite of his or her emotional involvement in the drama occurring on the stage" (150). Jorge cannot abandon his role, for it allows him to separate his emotional being from his physical countenance.

Role-playing also allows him to avoid self-scrutiny. Whereas El Ratón relies on a mirror to critique his efforts to imitate the police inspector, Jorge wants no part of such self-assessment: "sale de la bañera y rechaza en seguida el impulso de contemplarse en el espejo, porque una capa de vaho depositada en el cristal le impide tan engañosa comunicación con el exterior" (he comes out of the tub and immediately rejects the impulse to look at himself in the mirror, because a film of steam on the glass impedes such a deceitful communication with exterior reality, 55). The vapor film on the mirror protects him from painful self-contemplation. That protection may be linked to his experiences as a student when he learned to shield himself by ignoring the presence of those for whom he had to perform: "Durante aquella su primera mañana en la academia Jorge actuó de un modo raro y perfecto, como un actor que sabe ignorar la presencia no siempre favorable del público" (During that first morning in the school Jorge comported himself in an odd and perfect manner, like an actor who knows how to ignore the not always favorable presence of the audience, 80). The analogy between Jorge's first day at school and an actor on stage before an audience echoes Foucault's own words on how a panoptic system operates: "By the effect of backlighting, one can observe from the tower, standing out precisely against the light, the small captive shadows in the cells of the periphery. They are like so many cages, so many small theaters, in which each actor is alone, perfectly individualized and constantly visible" (200). Since the whole society serves as a scrutinizing audience, Jorge perfected at an early age the thespian art of losing himself in his role. That strategy of always projecting his persona protects him from others' gazes as well as his own.

Yet if role-playing generally serves as a handy buffer for Jorge against emotional involvement and self-identity, at other times, for example during his initial moment alone with Julia, he finds that the script leads him to areas he would rather avoid: "Pero Julia no hizo intención de encender más luces, lo que en cierta medida molestó a Jorge porque la oscuridad, si bien prometía, tipificaba la situación, la ajustaba a unos modelos y la obligaba por tanto a tomar una dirección determinada" (But Julia made no move to turn on more lights, which to a degree irritated Jorge because the darkness, while it was promising, it made the situation typical, it fit it into established models and obligated it to take a determined course of action, 174). The models, of course, are the products of discourse and serve to dictate how men and women behave in given situations. Once the scene is set, the script takes over and the actors merely play out their roles:

> La cópula no fue ciertamente satisfactoria para ninguno de los dos, y esto no sólo por la posición irreductible de ambos, debida en gran parte a las inhibiciones creadas por la necesidad de dar al otro una imagen sabia y firme de sí mismo, sino también porque aquel encuentro no

era gratuito ni espontáneo, ya que existía en función de dos programas diferentes, de dos búsquedas. Pero los programas, como las búsquedas parecían estar orientados a distintas materias, y ellos carecieron de la habilidad precisa para conciliarlos.

(The copulation certainly was not satisfactory for either one of them, and not only because of the cramped position for both, also because of the inhibitions created by the necessity for each of projecting a wise and confident image of him- or herself, but also because that encounter was not gratuitous and spontaneous, but rather it formed part of two different programs and quests. But programs, like quests, can be oriented to different ends, and they lacked the precise ability to coordinate them.) (207)

Like a play that has been presented too many times, the performances have become mechanical and self-centered. Rather than a cast working toward a common goal, each performer has only his or her own role in mind.

That the role of each performer is both dependent upon and in conflict with that of his or her partner is one of the many ironies presented by the novel. Basic gender roles were written at the dawn of Western civilization, and over time they have been reinforced by various means, a task these days assumed most dramatically by popular art forms. No character in the novel better demonstrates the discursive continuity between the past and the present than Julia. Her role is her birthright, which the movies and "songs . . . with which Julia was identifying herself" (209) reinforce constantly. Ironically Jorge, himself a product of discourse, points out to her that "songs are a lie" (149) and that "movies and songs have provided us with models that have no relation with our circumstances" (211). Although the words themselves may be true, their credibility for her is undermined by the person uttering them.

Julia's enslavement to models perpetuated by popular culture indicates how a whole network of discursive practices has determined her existence. Like the other characters, she is acutely aware of living in a panoptic system, even if she would not attach that label to it. In her case, however, she feels she performs before a voyeur rather than a warden. A blemish in the shape of, significantly, a keyhole in her bathroom mirror creates the analogy of a panopticon. Near the beginning of the novel she stands before the mirror, unties her bathrobe, and watches as it gradually reveals her nakedness: "Julia thought that the blemish over time would end up irritating her, but she also admitted that for now the possibility of imagining an eye on the other side of the mirror excited her" (21). As she continues to observe herself as seen from this symbol of the quintessentially male voyeur peephole, she achieves a state of physical arousal: "a third reflection, barely glimpsed beyond the blemish in the form of a keyhole, produced inside Julia a deep activity that manifested itself on the exterior in a slight hardening of the nipple" (23). All kinds of texts, both ancient and modern, have contributed to defining Julia's position as a female object of beauty.[48] She has been so conditioned by this discursive practice that she experiences sexual arousal from imagining herself performing before a male gaze. Yet her secret pleasures are accompanied by a dual sense of guilt and exasperation:

> Sabe, mientras gira ligeramente el cuello hasta alcanzar a ver con dis-imulo la mancha en forma de cerradura, que determinados fantasmas no son sino la huella de una hábil manipulación efectuada por el miedo sobre su memoria más antigua de las cosas. Pero siente el temor, o la repulsa, de ser depositaria de unos fantasmas que ya tuvo su madre, que se repetirán en su hija, y que a ella le parecen las señales que marcan la distancia entre la corrrupción y el deterioro.

> (She knows, as she turns her neck slightly until she manages to see out of the corner of her eye the blemish in the form of a keyhole, that certain ghosts are merely the aftermath of a skillful manipulation achieved by fear over the oldest memory of things. But she feels the fright, or the repulsion, of being the depository of some ghosts that her mother had, that will be repeated in her daughter, and which seem to her the signs that mark the distance between corruption and deterioration.) (64)

As we have seen, the novel also presents men as products of discourse, but at least they are not burdened with guilt over their basic urges. With women the discursive practice that disciplines even their fantasies passes from generation to generation.

In an act defying her mother's heritage, Julia assumes the role of se-ductress before the mirror: "ella no se sentía vinculada al recuerdo ni a la evocación, sino más bien a su propia imagen, que ahora, en un gesto

---

48. The plastic arts, literature, music, myth, philosophy and, since early in this century, film have contributed to defining the icon that women are supposed to imitate. Two recent studies of both classical and contemporary iconic models are Pilar Pedraza's *La bella, enigma y pesadilla (Esfinge, Medusa, Pantera)* and Brooks's *Body Work*. The latter is a fascinating study of how different representations of the female body determine nineteenth- and twentieth-century narrative. Subsequent citations will indicate the page number in parentheses.

dedicado a un posible espectador, alzaba la mano derecha—tocada ya por la belleza de la sangre caliente—y se apartaba el pelo de la cara" (she did not feel tied to the memory nor to the evocation, but rather to her own image, that now, in a gesture dedicated to a possible spectator, raised its right hand—highlighted now by the beauty of warm blood—and brushed the hair from its face, 23–24). In effect she substitutes one discursive practice for another. Apparently without realizing it, she defines herself here as a mere physical presence.[49]

Yet this young woman's emphasis on her physical being is also highly ironic. Later in the narrative her mind drifts back to the moment when she first met Jorge at a friend's house:

> Se llama Jorge, le dirán en el cuarto de baño de la casa, y esa noche ella recordará sus labios y sus ojos, su expresión descarada, pero no se atreverá a confesar el gusto que tal repaso le produce porque aún necesita—ligada como está a una educación de reflejos cristianos—una justificación teórica para cada recuerdo productor de un movimiento de gozo.

> (His name is Jorge, they will tell her in the bathroom, and that night she will remember his lips and eyes, his defiant expression, but she will not dare to confess the pleasure that such a recollection produces in her because she still needs—tied as she is to an upbringing with Christian resonances—a theoretical justification for each memory that produces a joyful stirring.) (40)

The same discursive tradition that reduces her to a simple physical presence denies her the right to basic physical pleasures. Indeed, later she caresses, in an expression of sensuality compensated by and confused with pain, the bruises and welts Jorge inflicted on her during their lovemaking. In addition to underscoring the centuries-long tradition that women should be punished for any expression of sexual satisfaction, these contusions serve as irrefutable evidence of her role as the always passive recipient: "Thus she would come and go, would educate her daughter and time would teach her new strategies for falsifying everything that she did not dare to fight against" (124). Destiny dictates that Julia perpetuate in her daughter the discursive practice that her mother passed on to her, a practice that ensures the role of woman as victim.

49. López, "Novela y realidad," offers a more Lacanian reading of this scene and connects it to the overall structure he proposes for the novel.

Jorge confirms that role for her when the inspector calls on the phone. Julia answers, and as Jorge listens he contemplates his next part in the drama: "He understands that in a certain sense he has taken stock of the situation because the script calls for a word, a gesture, something that will affirm by him what has already been affirmed by Julia" (220). As a male, one of his options is freedom from responsibility, and so he announces his exit. The narrator then reports her response:

> Julia le mira como si de un desconocido se tratara. Ahora es cuando más te necesito. Tendré que ir a declarar y sentiré pena por Luis. Quédate, aunque sólo sea para ocuparte un poco de la niña. A ti no van a comprometerte para nada. Es normal que en estos momentos esté alguien conmigo.

> (Julia looks at him as if he were a stranger. Now is when I need you. I will have to go to declare a deposition and I am going to feel sorry for Luis. Stay, if it is just to take care of the baby. They are not going to implicate you in anything. In these circumstances I should have someone with me.) (221)

By virtue of appearing as narration rather than as direct dialogue, these statements convey an almost ritual function; they are timeless formulas rather than time-bound appeals.[50] The final sentence reinforces that formulaic sensation. Julia has only one script to work with, and so she can only appeal to the discursive tradition of the defenseless female and the protective male. When Jorge, however, opts for one of his alternative male roles and asserts his freedom, "she merely looks at him with a mixture of astonishment and the disgust of someone who belatedly has discovered a fraud that nevertheless was obvious" (221). Clearly Julia is the product of a discursive system that has taught her to be subject to others and has denied her the right ever to be the true subject of her own actions.

Peter Brooks, echoing to a large degree Foucault, argues that a salient characteristic of the modern world is a compulsion to classify and identify marginalized people and criminals. He adds: "the invention of the detective story in the nineteenth century testifies to this concern to detect, track down, and identify those occult bodies that have purposely sought to avoid

---

50. This is an example of what is generally defined as "direct style of narration." For an exhaustive explanation and examples of the differences among direct, indirect pure, and indirect free style, see the study by Guillermo Verdín Díaz, *Introducción al estilo indirecto libre en español*.

social scrutiny" (26). The recent world revival of the detective-novel format gives it a postmodern twist by sabotaging the epistemological process—all the elements are the same, but the crime generally is not and cannot be solved.[51] Millás adds a new dimension to what in Spain is labeled the *novela negra* by using the mode to subvert the authoritative discourse known as panopticism. His novel mocks and thereby subverts a system dedicated to detecting, tracking down, and identifying criminals. Yet if the disciplining system is inept in preventing and solving crimes, it is very effective in erasing individuality. In this sense the novel is an important register of contemporary reality and an important model for subsequent post-totalitarian Spanish fiction.

Visión del ahogado also deserves credit for connecting panopticism with popular culture. Since each individual performs under the real or imagined watchful gaze of others, he or she relies on familiar roles scripted by pop music, pulp literature, and trite movies to ensure that his or her actions conform to accepted norms. As opposed to *El cuarto de atrás* in which popular art tends to subvert official discursive practices, in *Visión del ahogado* mass culture is an extension of the modern consumer society and serves to impose conformity. These art forms are key contributors to what Foucault calls the "automatic functioning of power" (201) within the panoptic system.

Although *Visión del ahogado*, like *La verdad sobre el caso Savolta*, does not contain any blatant references to Francoist Spain, the regime is an even more palpably absent presence in Millás's novel. Indeed, very indirectly and subtly the novel indicates that the events of the final morning occur at the very end of the dictatorship.[52] Of course we know that the novel was published in 1977, the year of the first democratic elections since

51. William V. Spanos, "The Detective and the Boundary: Some Notes on the Postmodern Literary Imagination."

52. During one of his ruminations, Vitaminas, or Luis, recalls that among the world events occurring the year that he, Jorge, Julia, and Rosario were in school was "el asesinato del presidente Kennedy" (President Kennedy's assassination, 193). In a flashback to the previous summer when, after Vitaminas had left her, Jorge and Julia finally arranged to run into one another on the street, he confesses: "Llevo más de diez años persiguiéndote" (I have been pursuing you for over ten years, 173). Since Kennedy was assassinated in November 1963, the encounter between Jorge and Julia must be in 1973 or 1974, which would indicate that the events of the fateful morning occur in 1974 or 1975, or during the final phase of the Franco regime.

the Second Republic. By forcing the reader to reconstruct the *histoire* to determine the novelistic context, fiction and reality tend to fuse, as does 1975 with 1977. The strategy to blur temporal boundaries suggests that the imprint of a watchtower system is as much in evidence in the infancy of the Spanish democracy as it was during the maturity of the Franco dictatorship. That common denominator places *Visión del ahogado* squarely within the epistemic boundaries mapped out by *Tiempo de silencio*. Also, Millás's novel shares with Martín Gaite's an emphasis on popular culture as a discursive practice influencing gender roles.

Juan sin Tierra and *El cuarto de atrás* (the two self-referential examples) are the most open in their antiregime attacks, yet the themes of revolutionary change and a panoptic system projected respectively in *La verdad sobre el caso Savolta* and *Visión del ahogado* leave little doubt that Francoist discourse is the referent (as it is in the analyst/analysand relationship in Miguel Delibes's *Las guerras de nuestros antepasados* [The wars of our ancestors] of the same year). *El cuarto de atrás* and *Visión del ahogado*, moreover, add a new gender-dimension to the attack. In both novels, but especially in Martín Gaite's, the enemy is not so much fascism as sexism. Her novel demonstrates what a very short step it is from challenging the patriarch of the regime to challenging patriarchy itself. This first and somewhat tentative shift of focus in *El cuarto de atrás* and *Visión del ahogado* from totalitarianism to paternalism was to become one of the dominant characteristics of Spanish fiction in the decade of the 1980s.

Beyond the Spanish borders the world at this time was still divided into sharply defined polarities of totalitarianism (both on the Left and on the Right) versus democracy. But in spite of economic rivalries and polarized ideologies, uncompromising nationalism and centralism were on the wane. The decade of the 1970s began with challenges to authority, and by 1979 there was a clear tendency toward ethnic as opposed to national identity and increasing pressures everywhere to decentralize political power.

The four novels published between 1975 and 1979 that we have examined in this chapter clearly project an attempt to undermine the authoritative discourse championed by the Franco regime, but paradoxically their subversive efforts serve to resurrect an order that is already dead. In this sense they can be seen as registers of a contradictory global situation in which the efforts toward decentralization somehow only exacerbated the existing international polarization. But the shift had begun, and in Spanish fiction as in global politics it gained momentum as the decade of the 1980s unfolded. One of the characteristics of the body of fiction we will examine in the following chapters is an intensifying effort to change the nature of the discourse, to transcend the Franco legacy by eliminating it from the discussion.

4

The Years 1980–1984

THE BEGINNING OF the 1980s became a key period for the new democratic Spanish government. The rate of reforms had increased after the general elections of 1977, and the economy had begun to recover from the 16 percent inflation rates of the late 1970s and a 22 percent devaluation of the peseta in July 1977. Also, by the 1980s the process of entering the European Community was well underway. On the negative side, exports continued to lag, unemployment was running high, factories desperately needed upgrading, and political stability remained very much in doubt.[1] In this socioeconomic context, on February 23, 1981, a group of army officers seized the Cortes. King Juan Carlos appealed to the people, and above all to the armed forces, to remain faithful to the government. To the relief of many and the consternation of a few, his plea was heeded, the leaders of the coup surrendered, and the new democracy passed its severest test.

After the fact, most observers agreed that the February Coup essentially had no chance of success. Yet I think that the ease with which the new democracy squelched the uprising proved to be crucial to the national psyche. Many were convinced prior to 1981 that Spanish democracy would be short-lived and would drift toward civil disorder and chaos sooner rather than later. When the king's call for allegiance at the time of crisis was answered by the majority of the military, it seemed apparent that he had tapped a "deep structure" of unsuspected commitment to a new political order. Evidence indicates it was then that the Spanish populace began to believe an underlying stability supported the new democratic system.

1. Charles F. Gallagher, "Paradoxes and Problems in the Spanish Economy."

Meanwhile, in the United States the end of the war in Vietnam inspired the democratic administration to turn its attention to domestic matters. That endeavor was frustrated when, on November 4, 1979, Iranian radicals seized the American Embassy in Teheran and held its occupants as hostages. President Carter launched an unsuccessful attack in an attempt to rescue the political prisoners on April 24, 1980, and that failure contributed to Reagan's victory in the November presidential election. Reagan, like Carter before him, campaigned as a Washington outsider pledged to less centralized federal government and more states' rights.

On the international front, the first half of the 1980s bore witness to a notable lack of major conflicts. In September 1980 the war between Iraq and Iran began, with the United States and the Soviet Union opting to play behind-the-scenes roles. Then in September 1982 a brief war broke out between England and Argentina over the Falkland Islands. Again the superpowers avoided any direct involvement, and England prevailed. In a provocative assessment of this period, one political commentator noted that by 1982 the United States and the Soviet Union were perhaps more evenly balanced than ever before. But the foreign policies of each country indicated a lack of awareness of the recent appearance of new world powers, and both ignored that the bipolarity, which had obtained since the end of World War II, no longer existed. In addition to the new military strength of China and the economic power of Japan, the emerging European Community began to play a major role in international politics and economics. Viewing it retrospectively, beginning with the early 1980s people should speak in terms of a "multi-polarity."[2] Availing himself of similar terminology, another political scholar referred to what he called international "hyperpluralism" to explain why OPEC failed to control the oil market in the 1980s as it had in the 1970s.[3] Clearly on the global level there was an acceleration of forces challenging the center of influence and power located at the point of conflict between the United States and the Soviet Union. In the fields of science and mathematics, the period 1980–1984 witnessed an increased focus in scholarly papers and books on chaos theory and its subdivisions entropy, information theory, and above all fractals. Mandelbrot published

2. James Joll, "The Ideal and the Real: Changing Concepts of the International System, 1815–1982," 220.

3. Mohammed E. Ahrari, "OPEC and the Hyperpluralism of the Oil Market in the 1980s."

his monumental work on the new geometry in 1982.[4] He presented an earlier French version of his thesis in 1975, but it passed virtually unnoticed. In the English edition, however, he attracted world attention by laying claim to a whole new discipline: "This essay brings together a number of analyses in diverse sciences, and it promotes a new mathematical and philosophical synthesis. Thus, it serves as both a *casebook* and a *manifesto*. Furthermore, it reveals a totally new world of plastic beauty" (2).

As we turn our attention to Spanish fiction, we notice that a pronounced discursive change occurred in the first half of the 1980s. The emphasis switched from totalitarianism itself to its ramifications. In this age of "multi-polarity" and "hyperpluralism," the old dichotomies tended to blend together and lose their individual identity. An unexpected connection appeared between General Franco and gender attitudes, between fascism and phallocentralism, while the old polarities conservatism and communism, suppression and expression, culture and cult gravitated toward one another. Again Spanish fiction serves as a register of these discursive events helping to define the post-totalitarian episteme.

The first half of the decade of the 1980s also heralded something of a renaissance of works published by those who cut their novelistic teeth during the Franco reign. Juan Benet ventured into the *novela negra* mode with his *Aire de un crimen* (The scent of a crime) followed by his signature novels *Saúl ante Samuel* (Saul versus Samuel) and *Herrumbrosas lanzas* (Rusty lances), all three of which were published between 1983 and 1986; Miguel Delibes offered *Los santos inocentes* (The innocent saints) in 1981; Camilo José Cela contributed *Mazurca para dos muertos* (A polka for two dead men) in 1983; and Juan Goytisolo published *Makbara* in 1980. Also appearing in 1980 was José Luis Sampedro's *Octubre, octubre* (October, October), a novel whose staying power has not matched its initial impact. Finally, a new generation of novelists emerged, headed by Alejandro Gándara and his lyrical evocation of the transition from childhood to adulthood in *La media distancia* (The mid-distance runner) (published in 1984), Jesús Ferrero and his exotic world of *Bélver Yin* (published in 1983), and Paloma Díaz-Mas and her ironic treatment of gender roles in *El rapto del Santo Grial* (The abduction of the Holy Grail) (published in 1984).

---

4. Benoit B. Mandelbrot, *The Fractal Geometry of Nature.* Subsequent citations will indicate the page number in parentheses.

Without minimizing the artistic value of the novels just mentioned, I have selected another group that I feel more effectively projects the post-totalitarian discourse of the first half of the 1980s: Luis Goytisolo's *Teoría del conocimiento* (A theory of knowledge) and José María Guelbenzu's *El río de la luna* (Moon river), both of which were published in 1981, Lourdes Ortiz's *Urraca* (Magpie), published in 1982, and Rosa Montero's *Te trataré como a una reina* (I will treat you like a queen), published in 1983. As I propose to demonstrate, each of these works contributes to the expression of a new or, more accurately, different discourse for Spanish fiction, and each also registers a significant shift toward a post-totalitarian episteme. As the analyses progress from the Goytisolo, to the Guelbenzu, to the Ortiz, and finally to the Montero novels, there is a definite move away from Francoism as the authoritative discourse to be subverted. With the demise of the more obvious apparatuses of fascism, these novelists increasingly turned their focus to those ideological forces that facilitated the creation of a fascist state. The first novel to be analyzed in this chapter, *Teoría del conocimiento*, assumes the task of providing a final resting place for the regime's putrescent discursive body.

Colloidal Discourse in *Teoría del conocimiento*

Within the particular focus of this study and as suggested above, *Teoría del conocimiento* (A theory of knowledge) emerges as one of the keys to the 1980s. Luis Goytisolo's final segment to his monumental *Antagonía* directly addresses the issue of a discourse that has reached the point of invalidism.[5] In response, *Teoría del conocimiento* anticipates and offers a solution to Gilles Deleuze and Félix Guattari's lament about our current world: "We do

---

5. This is the last of his tetralogy titled *Antagonía*. Since completing it, Luis Goytisolo has published *Estela del fuego que se aleja*, 1984; *La paradoja del ave migratoria*, 1985; and *Estatua con palomas*, 1992. Of the four novels of the tetralogy, *Teoría del conocimiento* has attracted the least critical attention and in general is only discussed in relation to the other three novels of the set. See Fernando Valls's "Para una biografía completa de Luis Goytisolo." The most detailed and insightful studies of *Teoría del conocimiento* to date are Beckie Gardiner de Arias's unpublished dissertation, "Cosmogonic Myth in *Antagonía* by Luis Goytisolo: A Creation of Creations," and Randolph D. Pope's "Una brecha sobrenatural en *Teoría del conocimiento* de Luis Goytisolo." In April 1994, Luis Goytisolo was named to the Spanish Academy.

not lack communication. On the contrary, we have too much of it. We lack creation."[6]

Goytisolo's novel features three narrators representing conflicting generations and ideologies yet speaking with basically the same voice. This deleterious blending of oppositional personalities and political beliefs creates a colloidal or mucoserous effect that points to a more general sociopolitical-artistic context. Rather than hoping that a group of internalized rules or codes will manage to breathe new life into a diseased system, *Teoría del conocimiento* suggests the need for a surgical procedure to change the discourse itself. The change proposed would switch the focus from philosophy, science, and politics to the creative act itself. And from this new focus emerges a theory of knowledge proposing that iteration is the key to creation.

The emphasis in the novel on iteration as creation responds to a state of inertia. The style of the three narrators of the story tends to blend into a noxious compound that one of them, Ricardo, characterizes as "no less colloidal than the mercury and sulfur that alchemists blend."[7] It strikes me that the connotation of colloids, a gelatinous or mucous substance whose particles never manage to fuse with their dissolvent, can serve as a metaphor for the discursive art of *Teoría del conocimiento* as well as also for past and present Spanish society and, more generally, Western civilization.

The novel projects an interconnection between politics and poetics not only on the metaphoric level suggested above but also on a more literal level within the novel. Several references to the head of state and his failing health serve to join the fictional and Francoist worlds. In addition, one of the narrators, the Old Man, is referred to as a famous *cacique* or political boss, thereby conjuring forth images of the Generalissimo. What we have, then, is a literary text serving as a distorting mirror of the sociopolitical text, which helps to explain one of the basic dimensions of Goytisolo's *Teoría del conocimiento.*

The use of a mirror technique that reflects a distorted image is not new,[8] with Valle-Inclán's *esperpento* serving as a handy referent. Yet it is

6. Deleuze and Guattari, *What Is Philosophy?* 108.

7. Luis Goytisolo, *Teoría del conocimiento,* 153. Subsequent citations will indicate the page number in parentheses.

8. The mirror metaphor extends to the tetralogy itself, in which each novel composing it can be imagined as a distorted mirror image of the other three novels.

viscousness rather than grotesqueness that characterizes Luis Goytisolo's reflections. The mirrored images tend to coagulate into a strange mixture that erases the very concept of origin and speaking subject and obliterates the line between fact and fiction. For example, there are two title pages for the novel. The first one identifies the author as Luis Goytisolo, the title of the novel as *Teoría del conocimiento,* and the publisher as Seix Barral (or Alfaguara or Plaza and Janés, publishers of the two subsequent editions of *Antagonía*). On the next page, however, there is a repetition of the same title and publisher, but with the author listed as Raúl Ferrer Gaminde. Repetition again comes into play, because those who have read the other three novels of the tetralogy know that Raúl is a fictitious character who plays a key role in each. This transformation of a character into an author underscores the inevitable role of fiction as an inverted mirror of reality; every character is, to one degree or another, an image of its creator, and vice versa. Raúl is as real as Luis, and Luis as fictitious as Raúl. In other words, the image we form of Raúl Ferrer Gaminde as author is a product of our reading process. He is a fiction created by a fiction. By the same token, the image we form of Luis Goytisolo is also a product of our reading process. Although a real person, the Goytisolo we come to know in the novel is created by the novel. The Luis and the Raúl of the two title pages are both creations of a creation in which there is no center of origin, identity, or narrative authority.[9]

But the concept of creative mirrors is not limited to the authorial sphere. As noted earlier, there are three narrators within the novel, and each one serves as a creative reflection of the other. Approximately the first third of *Teoría del conocimiento* is narrated by Carlos, a young apolitical cynic who is writing his diary. The next third is narrated by Ricardo, a former communist architect turned novelist who comments upon Carlos's diary, which he has somehow acquired, as he writes notes for his own novel. Finally, the third narrator is an old political boss, on his deathbed or perhaps already dead, who speaks into a tape recorder. Much of his commentary concerns Carlos's diary and Ricardo's notes, documents he possesses because, he claims, those two authors are now dead. His recordings are to be transcribed into written form by a man named Carlos, the father of the young man of the same name who narrates the first part of the novel.

9. I draw the reader's attention to the subtitle of Gardiner de Arias's dissertation, "A Creation of Creations."

As the narrating process passes from one speaker to the next, the style of one tends to become amalgamated but not fused with that of the other, finally forming a colloidal circle. The process begins with young Carlos and ends with the elder Carlos, whose transcription will carry the traces of his son's diary along with those of Ricardo's notes and the Old Man's recordings, all mingled with the transcriber's own mode of expression. For example, without realizing it, Ricardo describes the overall result when he criticizes the style of young Carlos's diary:

> esas largas series de períodos, por ejemplo, esas comparaciones que comienzan con un homérico así como . . . metáforas secundarias que más que centrar y precisar la comparación inicial, la expanden y hasta la invierten en sus términos. . . .

> (those long series of periods, for example, those comparisons that begin with a Homeric just as . . . secondary metaphors that rather than centering and specifying the initial comparison, expand it and even invert its sense. . . .) (153)

In effect, the mode of expression he describes also applies to his own narration. To cite his own words again, the effect created is "no less colloidal than the mercury and sulfur that alchemists blend" (153). But Ricardo notes that there is yet another element contributing to this colloidal amalgamation: "as far as the style is concerned, it is not difficult to detect the traces of Luis Goytisolo" (153). It may be significant that colloids are often associated with diseased or infected tissue. As the narrating process passes from one speaker to another, what results is a circle not only of mirrors but of textual contamination as well. The gelatinous condition that emerges from such a process makes it difficult to distinguish between beginning and end, between creator and creation.[10] In short, these textual mirrors reflect distorted images that, as they are mingled, form a colloid.

Since process has coalesced into mucus, it is even impossible to distinguish between the traditional political polarities, Right and Left. Although Ricardo (the former communist activist) and the Old Man (the ex-*cacique* fascist) seem to define political extremes, in reality they can no longer

---

10. There is a certain echo here of Martín-Santos's use of the word *magma* in *Tiempo de silencio*. For an insightful analysis of how this word functions in Martín-Santos's novel, see Gustavo Pérez Firmat's, "Repetition and Excess in *Tiempo de silencio*."

claim membership to a political entity. Indeed, the old competitors are now unwitting comrades.

As the apolitical cynic, or what in popular parlance is labeled a *pasota*,[11] Carlos most clearly recognizes the process toward fusion between the two antagonists. As for the possibility of a communist revolution in Spain, he opines that if it were to occur it would not change the country's basic social system: "The change of social structures does not prevent the moral principles from continuing to be the same as before the revolution, even reinforced by the fact that, after the revolution, the state acts as a second father and the society as a second mother" (56). Carlos seems to be referring to the modern state's propensity to impose patriarchal discipline on its citizens. A communist revolution, rather than establishing a new social order would, according to him, merely reinforce the prevailing system of discipline. Communist idealism itself, as far as Carlos is concerned, is absurd. He offers as an example one of his militant friends:

> Me hace el efecto, por otra parte, de que cuanto supone cambiar de plano, ir más allá de lo teórico, también le asusta. Así, por ejemplo, a principios de verano, cuando me llamó por teléfono con espanto para anunciarme que Franco estaba grave, poco menos que en estado de coma, noticia que parecía llenarle de temor, cosa que no dejó de chocarme viniendo de un militante comunista.

> (I have the feeling that, on the other hand, anything that implies a change of design, to go beyond the merely theoretical, also frightens him. For example, at the beginning of summer when he phoned terrified to announce to me that Franco was in a grave state, almost in a coma, news that seemed to scare him, something that could not help but shock me since it was coming from a militant communist.) (67)

That a militant leftist is frightened by the prospect of Franco's death has far-reaching implications. Apparently the Spanish Left needed Franco to give meaning to its cause; without an opponent, its struggle would lose its raison d'être. On the other hand, as Carlos notes, "it does not bother him that things around here are not going very well, that for some thirty years we have been unsuccessful in our efforts to end Francoism" (61). Obviously it is

---

11. Manuel Martín Serrano, "Nuestros años jóvenes," argues that the *pasotas* of the early 1980s anticipated the posterior apolitical attitude that seems to prevail among young Spaniards even today (*El País Semanal* [Madrid], February 7, 1993, pp. 16–28).

the struggle and not the solution that sustains this type of political activism. Franco's death is as much a threat to the Left as it is to the Right.[12] In effect, as temporal decay has extracted its toll, the two antagonists have created an alliance of opposition, of one force dependent on the resistance of the other until they have formed the colloid of Spain in 1975 (the context of the narrated story) and 1981 (the context of the published novel).

The colloidal alliance formed between the right-wing force and the left-wing resistance is underscored by the middle-aged Ricardo's anxiety over the impotency of his aging opponents. This former militant leftist expresses his disillusionment by means of caricature as he describes the physical appearance of his enemies:

> la mitología franquista, sus principios, sus símbolos, sus héroes, hoy calvicie y dentadura postiza, mejillas flojas y boca glotona, donde hubo músculo y nervio, la fidelidad al bigote—ya blanco—y a las gafas de sol—que siempre contribuyen a mantener la impasibilidad del ademán—a manera de reliquia cuidadosamente preservada.

> (the Francoist mythology, its principles, its symbols, its heroes, today baldness and false-teeth, sagging jowls and gluttonous mouth, where there used to be muscle and nerves, the fidelity to the mustache—now white—and to sunglasses—which always contribute to maintaining a stoic demeanor—more or less like carefully preserved relics.) (108–9)

Now only the facade of vitality and power remains, a facade that the Francoists strive mightily to preserve in their readiness to live in the past and take possession of or defend a position. What was once a robust generation of warriors and ideologues now resembles the internees of a home for the elderly. Although they try to display the same arrogance, the same gestures of their youth, "una generación esencialmente vertical y afirmativa, . . . gente siempre dispuesta a saltar como un resorte, impasible hasta la crispación" (a generation essentially vertical and affirmative, . . . people always ready to jump like a sling shot, impassive to the point of appearing frozen, 109), their studied posturing is comically pathetic. Indeed, it is difficult to avoid the temptation of substituting some vivid media images for this novelistic one.

---

12. By taking one step further the idea that the resisting force is dependent on its opponent, one arrives at Bersani's thesis in "The Subject of Power" that the power force and its resistance really represent the same thing: "There is no protest against power which does not rejoice in its own capacity to control and to dominate" (6).

First there is the inept coup of February 23, 1981—the same year the novel was published, of course—during which the renegade officers fired their weapons into the ceiling of the Cortes with great bravado, a scene captured live on television and projected around the world. In addition, anyone who has witnessed the annual demonstrations and parades to commemorate Franco's death can likely recognize many of the faces and gestures that Ricardo describes.

From Ricardo's point of view, however, the image of the enemy is also a portrait of himself. If the reigning power is decrepit, the opposition, which for thirty-six years had been unsuccessful in its program for revolutionary change, must be at least as decrepit. And with a merging of images, there is a gravitation from their former polar positions toward a common center of equilibrium. Power and resistance have coalesced into a state of entropy. Paradoxically, then, the former state of disequilibrium or polarization created order since each force occupied a clearly marked territory; the present state of equilibrium or fusion, on the other hand, creates disorder since there is no way to distinguish between force and counterforce, reactionary and visionary, fascist and communist.[13] In such a system, even the ideological rhetoric tends to blend into a commonality of meaningless noise. That is to say, when equilibrium overtakes a system and there is no orderly division, or when the message is totally predictable, the system tends to produce noise rather than information. Accordingly the fictional text suggests that, as Spain crosses the threshold into a new sociopolitical order, entropic equilibrium may be more of a threat to the future than armed insurrection.

Apparently because ideological discourse has coagulated, Ricardo turns to art for a solution to the resulting colloidal state. At any rate that can be seen as one of the implications behind his decision to abandon politics

---

13. Campbell, *Grammatical Man,* uses the image of a glass of ice water to help clarify the concept of entropy. With the ice floating at the top of the glass, an orderly division is created between the colder and warmer molecules. Although they are in a state of disequilibrium, that disequilibrium allows for an orderly distribution. From such a division, it is relatively easy to channel the energy into work and information, the moisture formed at the top of the glass being an example of the latter. When, however, the ice melts and the temperature of the molecules becomes uniform and allows them to merge into equilibrium, the result is disorder; the molecules are no longer separated into an orderly distribution, and it is much more difficult to channel energy in a state of disorderly equilibrium or entropy into work and information (34–35). See also Hayles, *Chaos Bound,* and Paulson, *Noise of Culture,* for more on the concept of entropy and information.

and architecture and to become a novelist. But for him the challenge is how to express in a static medium a dynamic solution to existence. As he muses about this problem, he notes that in the plastic arts Velázquez's "Las Meninas" addresses the issue by metaphorically extending the canvas to infinity. But Ricardo has elected to work with verbal expression, and as a result he strives by that medium to transform a personal experience into a message with universal implications. To that end he recounts a day in his childhood when he was seated beside a reservoir contemplating the reflection not only of his own image but also of the sky. He narrates that it occurred to him in that distant moment

> la posibilidad de que, así como aquella balsa redonda reflejaba igual que una pupila mi figura contra los cielos soleados, mi propia pupila resultase ser, de modo semejante, imagen misma del universo; si una célula cualquiera de mi ojo, una simple célula, no contendría realmente esos cielos reflejados, y los planetas, astros y galaxias que esos cielos encerraban en su pálido azul, así como los cielos de otras galaxias, incluidas las que, debido a su lejanía, ya ni resultaban visibles o calculables desde ninguno de ellos; y si yo, el niño que contemplaba los cielos reflejados en una balsa, si yo, y conmigo esos cielos reflejados y sus planetas, astros y galaxias, no constituiríamos sin saberlo una insignificante célula del ojo de un chico inconcebiblemente superior, un chico igual a mí en aquel momento, un chico que, al igual que yo, se hallaba contemplando el reflejo de su propia figura contra el cielo soleado en las aguas de una balsa.

> (the possibility that the round reservoir reflected as if it were the pupil of an eye my figure against the sunny skies, by the same token my own eye pupil turns out to be the very image of the universe; if any given cell of my eye, a simple cell, might not really contain those reflected skies, and the planets, astros, and galaxies that those skies enclose in their pale blue, just as the skies of other galaxies, including those that, because of their distance, are no longer visible or calculable from any of the former; and whether I, the child that was contemplating the skies reflected in a reservoir, whether I, and with me those reflected skies and their planets, astros and galaxies, without knowing it might not constitute an insignificant cell of the eye of a child inconceivably superior, a child just like me, who is contemplating the reflection of his own figure against the sunny sky in the water of a reservoir.) (215)

Ricardo discovers in a cell and expresses in his own writing style the dynamism of infinite fragments, reflections, and iteration. Although it is impossible to contemplate the universe in its totality, by juxtaposing fragments of distinct objects it is possible to create an idea of how a particle is the reflection of something larger and this something the reflection of yet another something even larger and in this way project an image, or perhaps only an illusion, of totality. The suggestion here is very similar to the statement "In the mind's eye, a fractal is a way of seeing infinity."[14] This type of infinite projection is what Velázquez attempted some three centuries ago and what all artists who incorporate themselves and their audience into their work continue to attempt. In the case of Ricardo, such a technique represents a possible solution to the colloidal human condition that he himself has helped to create.

Whereas Ricardo implicitly advocates that the solution is to be found in a fragmented, reflected, and iterated art, the third narrator, the Old Man, seems to be the most conscious of the colloidal essence of current discourse, perhaps because he has the advantage of being able to draw on the ideas Carlos and Ricardo have proposed. Indeed, his narration consists in large part of a rereading of their manuscripts. His goal, as he defines it, is to control how people in the future read the past.[15] He justifies his autocratic attitude by calling attention to his "superior knowledge . . . not only of the

14. Gleick as quoted by Sánchez, "*La Regenta* as Fractal," 256. My immediately previous comments represent an obvious metaphorical expression of fractals. According to that geometrical theory, fractals are irregular and fragmented shapes that, viewed in isolation, do not seem to provide any information. But since fractals possess structural irregularities that are repeated at decreasing scale, it may be possible, by comparing multiple examples, to detect a pattern of regularity in their irregularities. In other words, the iteration of fractal irregularities allows the observer to hypothesize something approaching a totalized picture. In addition to Mandelbrot's more technical mathematical exposition in *Fractal Geometry of Nature*, see Hayles, *Chaos Bound*, for examples of how the theoretical concept of fractals can be applied to literature. In the field of modern Spanish fiction, Elizabeth Sánchez has done the pioneering critical work by applying the theory to *La Regenta* (above) and in "Spatial Forms and Fractals: A Reconsideration of Azorín's *Doña Inés*." Gardiner de Arias, "Cosmogonic Myth in *Antagonía*," offers a detailed and perceptive analysis of this passage concerning the reservoir and how it relates to the concept of cosmogonic myth.

15. In "Lost Letters" from *The Book of Laughter and Forgetting*, Milan Kundera states the following: "People are always shouting they want to create a better future. It's not true. The future is an apathetic void of no interest to anyone. The past is full of life, eager to irritate us, provoke and insult us, tempt us to destroy or repaint it. The only reason people want to be masters of the future is to change the past. They are fighting for access to the laboratories where photographs are retouched and biographies and histories written" (22). As noted earlier, Herzberger, *Narrating the Past*, argues that the goal of changing the past by mythologizing it was one of the Franco regime's key projects. Again, we should keep in mind that the Old Man is often referred to as a famous *cacique* or political boss, a reference that inevitably connects him to Franco.

dynamic of creation in general and of the works of the young Carlos and Ricardo in particular, but also of everything concerning the life of each, of the death of each" (336). Faced with the immediacy of his own death, the Old Man's readings will be his legacy, for through them he hopes to "make others see what I see, visions, thoughts and dreams of third parties that I materialize in the form of a virtual projection before their eyes" (316). Rather than an original creator, he is a conduit for others' creations, a speaking subject whose words will be ultimately subjected to a written rendition by someone else.

Yet this man does not consider that his role as conduit contradicts his creative instinct. Indeed, this novel encourages us to draw connections to the other novels of the tetralogy, to view it as a fractal or an iteration of what preceded it. We find, accordingly, an echo in the Old Man in one of the protagonist's statements in *La cólera de Aquiles* (Achilles's fury) as she explains a series of intercepted messages as "respuestas a la respuesta de una respuesta" (replies to the reply of a reply, 42). Her suggestion that every example of writing is merely the graphic expression of a reading applies perfectly to the Old Man and his plagiarism of Carlos's and Ricardo's manuscripts. Not only does he state that by virtue of such duplication ad infinitum we negate the very concept of originality, but he also believes that plagiarism forms part of "the essential devouring nature of the universe" (262). Lest his readers accuse him of excessive cynicism, the Old Man claims that his literary appropriation represents a vital link in the chain of artistic and philosophic creation:

> Los textos que recogen mi pensamiento, por el contrario, cuando dentro de milenios sean hallados junto a un mar muerto, están destinados a revelarse como el eslabón perdido del pensamiento que para entonces prevalezca, relegadas por completo al olvido las creencias hoy imperantes.

> (The texts that my thoughts collect, to the contrary, when millenniums from now they are found next to a dead sea, are destined to be recognized as the lost links to the thought that then prevails, as the dominant beliefs of today are completely relegated to oblivion.) (262)

He is guilty of being, as is every writer, a creative plagiarist. According to him, we form a community of creators whose roots extend in two directions: toward the distant future evoked above but also backward to the very beginning of civilization. For example, when he contemplates a

plastic representation of the famous narrator Aesop, the old political boss
is aware that he is contemplating himself:

> El retrato de un dios que ha perdido sus antiguos poderes, un dios que
> ya no es el ser único, omnipresente y omnipotente que fue, iracundo
> y despótico como un niño; un dios al que ya no le queda más que la
> sabiduría, un viejo. Para los dioses, al igual que para los hombres, la
> creación es la solución de un problema personal.

> (The picture of a god who has lost his old powers, a god who no longer
> is a unique being, omnipresent and omnipotent, who was irascible and
> despotic as a child; a god who now only has wisdom, an old man. For
> gods, the same as for humans, creation is the solution to a personal
> problem.) (303)

The picture is in effect a mirror that projects for him his own image. Just
like Aesop, this former political boss has lost everything but his creative
powers. Yet he has already demonstrated that all creation is an expression
of iteration, a distorted reflection of something inevitably already created.

The combination of fragments, mirrors, and iteration is concentrated in
the last part of the novel when the Old Man hosts a large banquet. Among
the guests are Aesop, Dante, Milton, and Goethe. Tables are set up in the
garden as well as in the house, the group outside forming a mirror image
of the group inside. As he attempts to peer from the outside into the house,
the Old Man must shade his eyes to avoid the reflection on the window of
the garden group. When he does manage to see in, he describes the scene
as follows:

> Los grandes espejos repetían indefinidamente la escena, el empeño de
> los improvisados fotógrafos en obtener fotos que, entre otras cosas,
> recogían su propia imagen en el acto de tomar una foto reflejada en
> espejos y espejos, repetida en fotos y fotos de espejos.

> (The large mirrors indefinitely repeated the scene, the efforts of the
> improvised photographers to obtain photos that, among other things,
> captured their own image in the act of taking a photo reflected in
> mirrors and more mirrors, repeated in photos and photos of mirrors.)
> (326)

The act of photographing is frozen in the eternal present of the photograph,
both of which are in turn reflected ad infinitum; the act and its representation are simultaneously static and dynamic. Whereas all represented acts

and objects are by definition static—including the representation of the act of narrating, which we label *metafiction*—the process of iteration is by definition dynamic since it never ceases. This fractal (the party scene), iterately reflected in reflections, adumbrates the existence of a unifying master text of human existence.

The Old Man expands on the significance of the mirrors in the banquet scene when he explains that Dante was the last artist whose verbal mirror projected a totalizing image. But, according to the narrator, "Then the mirror shattered and humans began to occupy themselves with reproducing the fragmented images of those fragments. Since then what else have painters and novelists been doing?" (309). Limited to representing "fragmented images of those fragments," the only solution to the present colloidal state is, according to the speaker, iteration. Only by means of iteration is there a possibility of realizing the divine wisdom postulated by Aesop and Goethe or of finding the lost paradise imagined by Dante and Milton.

Yet the Old Man does not want to resign himself to the limits he defines for others; he does not want to surrender his ego to the anonymity resulting from infinite repetition, notwithstanding the dynamism implicit in that repetition. Therefore he dedicates himself to taking his own totalizing picture of the group, a shot he describes as

> aquella toma que abarcaba el conjunto de la fiesta en su conjunto, presentes todos los presentes a excepción de mí en calidad de centro, de ojo de aquella cámara cuyo ángulo visual de 360 sólo dejaba fuera al autor de la foto, visible, a lo sumo, en el reflejo de algún que otro espejo.
>
> (that shot that captured the totality of the party in its totality, all those present present with the exception of me as the center, of the eye of that camera whose 360-degree angle only left out the author of the photo, visible, at best, in the reflection of one or another mirror.) (327)

Clearly the photograph he describes belies his vainglorious dream of creating a totalizing representation. No matter how hard he tries, and even with a 360-degree lens for his camera, he cannot transcend the problem of finding a spot from which to present the interconnected whole that is not a part of that whole. He is condemned like everyone else merely to mark another point in time and space on the infinite scale, to offer another fragmented image gleaned from other fragments. As I read this passage then, even the repetitions ("the totality of the party in its totality, all those present present") contribute to the sense of the eternal iteration from which he hopes to save his own ego. Yet finally he has to confess that he has only managed to include an image of himself, for he as the creator is only visible as the reflected figure in a mirror. If he is but a reflection, I as commentator and you as my reader are merely two more mirrors of the potentially infinite iterative process.

Whereas reflections of reflections projected ad infinitum allow us to imagine the interconnected whole, there remains the problem of how to integrate the creator into the creation as something more than a reflection, a mere representation. The Old Man himself underscores the importance of integrating the position of the author within the work when he says that "sólo ve aquel que es capaz de verse a sí mismo mirando lo que ve" (only he sees who is capable of seeing himself looking at what he sees, sees, 308). Perhaps that was the reason for such a large number of metafictional works offering us simulacra of the author within the work during the decades of the 1970s and 1980s. No matter how ingenious such strategies have been, and Luis Goytisolo's should be included among the most ingenious, the question is not of a mere illusion of presence but of one consigned to the background. With his most recent novel to date, Luis Goytisolo has managed to at least change the position of self-representation. Availing himself of autobiography as a model, in *Estatua con palomas* (A statue with pigeons) published in 1993, the "author" commands center stage, while the fictional story is relegated to the background. In a sense the strategy involved in this most recent hybrid work is a simple question of changing the position of the mirrors so as to emphasize the presence of the "creator" in reference to the creation. Yet the new position notwithstanding, both subject and object reflect distorted images of one another, distorted because the subject can never achieve a viewing position that includes itself as a part of the viewed object. Creators, in other words, can only represent themselves in—but never *be* a part of—their creations.

The Old Man's narration posits a theory of knowledge that is really a theory of contemporary art. Since the mirror we used to call mimesis is now broken, artists can no longer aspire to reflect a totalizing image of reality. Rather than art that reflects reality, we now have art iteratively reflecting other art. The implicit message may be that the patterns resulting from this fractal process provide the only means we have of finding our way out of an entropic state. Apparently for that reason the Old Man exhorts near the end of the novel, "¡Cread creadores!" (Create creators! 334).

To summarize, then, the theory that Goytisolo projects in his novel includes the colloidal effect created when two opposing discourses finally amalgamate after some thirty-six years. He then proposes creativity as the cure for this gelatinous and diseased tissue. But the source for creative power can no longer be found in originality. Iteration is offered instead as the solution, a solution reinforced by the alliteration of the three key concepts in the Old Man's narration: reflection, refraction, and repetition. Obviously the creation has to reflect the creator, not mimetically but in the manner of a concave mirror whose refracted images yet other mirrors will repeat. In this way iteration provides the clue for detecting a pattern of regularity from the repeated irregular fragments, thereby transforming a static product into a dynamic process. That is at least one way of reading the theory posited by Goytisolo's *Teoría del conocimiento;* of course, if that were the only way to read it, the theory would lose its dynamism and in effect deconstruct itself.

I think it should be clear from the preceding analysis why I chose Luis Goytisolo's final installment to his tetralogy as an introduction to the decade of the 1980s. *Antagonía* is, without question, one of the more ambitious, complex, and perplexing works to come out of the post-Franco period— though the first segment, *Recuento* (A reaccounting) actually appeared two years before Franco died. *Teoría del conocimiento* not only projects the complexity of the tetralogy as a whole, but, more important for this study, also demonstrates how over the period from 1936 to 1975 (the first date actually could be extended some five centuries to the past) two conflicting discursive practices finally amalgamated to form a single gelatinous tissue whose infection spread from Franco to post-Franco social, political, and artistic reality.

Goytisolo demonstrates in his novel an important dimension of a dichotomized view of reality. *Teoría del conocimiento* implies the need to change the discourse to correct the social system. Now I will examine some alternative discourses as I switch the focus from polarity to patriarchy, which really is a switch of emphasis rather than of direction. As José María Guelbenzu's *El río de la luna* (published in 1981) demonstrates, the same basic discursive practices that separate the world into opposing political and social camps also polarize the sexes.

The Orderly Disorder of *El río de la luna*

Appearing the same year as *Teoría del conocimiento*, *El río de la luna* (Moon river) does not merely address but in effect attempts to redress the issue of Francoist discourse.[16] Luis Goytisolo's novel focuses on how the fusion of a centuries-old bipolar conflict has created the colloidal tissue afflicting Spain today. For its part Guelbenzu's *El río de la luna* suggests that the death of General Franco afforded us the opportunity to end gender phobias. In this sense, Guelbenzu's novelistic project is similar to that of Martín Gaite's in *El cuarto de atrás*. Both of these writers project a semiotic relationship between fascist ideology and sexist attitudes, a relationship that suggests political reform as a viable solution. From this point of view, Martín Gaite and Guelbenzu offer a more optimistic message than Juan Goytisolo, Luis Goytisolo, Mendoza, or Millás about how a change in political philosophy may lead to a change in gender ideology. The disorderly presentation of the story in *El río de la luna* is similar to that of *La verdad sobre el caso Savolta*. The nonsequential order in which we read the events creates a sensation of chaos, yet we discover that governing codes exist underneath the disorder. Mendoza's novel, however, creates a new disorder in the process of resolving an old one, while Guelbenzu's ends with regeneration.

The protagonist of *El río de la luna* is Fidel, whose life parallels the Franco dictatorship: He is born in 1936 and dies in 1975 (shortly before his death Fidel hears grave medical reports concerning Franco). The first narrative level concerns the twenty-four hours or so leading up to the protagonist's death. Within this time frame there are flashbacks, beginning in 1946 when ten-year-old Fidel and his cousin José steal a canoe and almost drown and Fidel is severely punished by his father (chapter 2).

Next in the chronology are the events of 1950 narrated in chapter 1. But intermingled with what is narrated from the past is the present act of narrating. Just before dawn on what turns out to be his final day, Fidel wanders into a hotel bar, deserted except for an obese raconteur, who tells him a bizarre story concerning Fidel's cousin José (the same José of the canoe incident). In the story fourteen-year old José (whose age provides

---

16. José María Guelbenzu's novelistic production began almost three decades ago. His other novels to date are: *El mercurio*, 1968; *Antifaz*, 1970; *El pasajero de ultramar*, 1976; *La noche en casa*, 1977; *El esperado*, 1984; *La mirada*, 1987; and *La Tierra Prometida* (1991).

the clue that it is 1950) is trapped in a tavern inhabited by an all-male cast of grotesque customers and employees, each with a nightmarish tale concerning some woman.

The chronology then skips to 1957 in chapter 4 and concerns Carmen, Fidel's first sexual partner, who jilts him shortly after their affair. The next date in the past sequence is 1960 narrated in chapter 3, when Fidel and two friends force three young women they have picked up to parade nude in front of the car's headlights. The next year, which still takes place in chapter 3 and is the geometrical center of the novel, Fidel and Teresa spend a summer together in the same village in Asturias where the final action occurs.

Chapter 4 is another example where the present act of narrating is juxtaposed with the narrated past. Fidel boasts of his past amorous conquests to a group of men in the hotel bar just a couple of hours before he becomes the audience in the same bar for the obese man who relates José's strange tale, which again is the content of chapter 1. Indeed, presumably one of Fidel's listeners is this overweight raconteur. Fidel's narration in this chapter 4 begins in 1962 and concerns Irene and nights spent in a bar called Jungla, the description of which echoes that of the tavern where José's adventures occur, followed by two years in Paris, from 1964 to 1966, during which Celia is his love interest. In 1967 he returns to Spain because of the illness and subsequent death of his father, where he meets and in 1974 marries Delia with whom he eventually has a son.

The action of the concluding chapter 5 takes place the day following Fidel's and the raconteur's narrations in the hotel bar. The protagonist has a rendezvous with Teresa, they make love, and after they separate someone murders Fidel.[17]

---

17. Unlike Mendoza's novel, *El río de la luna* has attracted a considerable amount of criticism to date. See, for example, Gemma Roberts, "Amor sexual y frustración existencial en dos novelas de Guelbenzu"; David K. Herzberger, "The 'New' Characterization in José María Guelbenzu's *El río de la luna*"; Germán Gullón, "El novelista como fabulador de la realidad: Mayoral, Merino, Guelbenzu"; José María Marco, "El espacio del deseo: La grieta y el mercado"; Robert Saladrigas, "Bajo el signo de la búsqueda"; Rafael Conte, "El precursor"; Horacio Vázquez Rial, "El tormento de los años mozos"; Jorge Rodríguez Padrón, "La narrativa de José María Guelbenzu"; Darío Villanueva, "Como juego y revelación"; Sabas Martín, "*El río de la luna*, de J. M. Guelbenzu, o la doble pasión"; Luis Suñén, "José María Guelbenzu y su camino de perfección"; and Spires, "A Play of Difference: Fiction after Franco."

As this summary makes clear, the order of the *histoire* does not correspond to the order in which we read the events. For example, the major episodes narrated in the first chapter occur after those narrated in the second chapter, and the segments of the first chapter devoted to the raconteur actually refer to the final hours of the *histoire*. The *récit/histoire* relationship can be shown graphically by indicating on a horizontal line the chapters 1–5. Then by assigning a letter, A–J, to each of the major events narrated, along with the year each one occurred, it can be shown how the chronology of the *histoire* (A–J) corresponds to the order in which we read the events (chapters 1–5):

1	2	3	4	5
	A (1946)			
B (1950)				
			C (1957)	
		D (1960)		
		E (1961)		
			F (1962)	
			G (1964–1966)	
			H (1967)	
			I (1974)	
J (1975)			J (1975)	J (1975)

A chaotic sensation results from reading this nonsequential presentation. But since the reader can reconstruct the sequence, Guelbenzu's novel offers a novelistic expression of orderly disorder or of how an underlying system can give meaning to surface chaos. The structure hidden beneath the surface provides textual clues (a date or the age of a character when a particular event occurs) that connect the episodes and reveal the chronological sequence. Without this ordering substructure, the narration would become truly entropic—it would stagnate into a formless equilibrium with no beginning, middle, or end. When a system degenerates into entropy (or chaos), it ceases to yield information; as entropy increases, information decreases.[18] Order, on the other hand, restores form and meaning to a

18. Campbell, *Grammatical Man*, 34, 87.

system. But the concepts *order* and *disorder* depend at least in part on the observer. Sometimes the message includes not only the order but also the disorder (noise) that accompanies it. As Paulson notes: "The theory of self-organization from noise suggests that this ambiguity as well can be converted into information by a change in site of the observer, by a reader who can take into account the ensemble of what has been communicated and the noise that inevitably accompanies that communication."[19] Because the reader has to reconstruct the sequence of events in *El río de la luna,* or convert disorder into order, the aesthetic experience approaches what the protagonist encounters in his search for a meaning-yielding harmony to the events of his life.

A reconstruction of the sequential order of the novel also suggests that normal time/space associations cannot adequately account for human time. Humans experience time as paradoxical—indeed, as contradictory. We are simultaneously temporal and atemporal; as living organisms we are subject to a temporality that precisely limits our existence, but as humans we experience an atemporality in which the past and the future blend into an eternal present. These ideas are not stated in the novel—if they were they would likely be too predictable, too stale—but they form part of the information implicit in a system that both negates and affirms temporal sequence, that confronts us with disorder and challenges us to discover the underlying rules for restoring order. In short, the ability to recognize how noise (disorder) forms an integral part of the overall structure of meaning enriches the message of the novel.

Related to the concept of orderly disorder is disharmonious harmony. Fidel's story is the quest for symmetrical union with his Object of Desire: "No body is free from the need to search for harmony, which provides meaning to life. . .". Yet as he approaches forty, Fidel realizes that the lost opportunities of the past are compounded by his present myopia: "Pero sé algo más, en aquel entonces yo no supe franquear la puerta que conduce a sus dominios y ahora no soy capaz de reconocerla. Dicen que, en algún punto, la atraviesa el río de la luna" (But I know something else, in that moment I did not understand how to open the door leading to its domains and now I am not capable of recognizing it. People say that, at some point,

19. Paulson, *Noise of Culture,* 95.

moon river crosses it).[20] This passage seems to capsulate Fidel's plight. It points to a lost opportunity, his present dilemma, and an ominous future. One person serves as the focal point for these three temporal levels and what each represents in Fidel's quest: "The key is only a name: Teresa" (300). The novel's structure points to Teresa as Fidel's lost opportunity, the reason for his current paralyzing dilemma, and the obsession posing a threat to his immediate future. He believes that she is the true object of his long and frustrated search for harmony, a frustration that, thanks to the nonsequential order of the novel, readers also experience.[21] As the end nears, the readers join Fidel in anticipating from the dissonant combination of "moon river" and "Teresa" the key to a harmonious resolution to the years of frustration.

Since the image "moon river" is also the title of the novel, it is a logical point of departure for considering the concept harmony/disharmony. Although people talk figuratively about rivers on the moon, we know in a literal sense that the moon is totally arid. The image is and is not, therefore, contradictory. On the connotative level, the word *river* often is associated with life and fertility. The moon, so often equated with love and romance, also connotes a life-giving force. Paradoxically, the two often suggest death, with Sánchez Ferlosio's *El Jarama* serving as one obvious intertextual point of reference for the theme of Thanatos implicit in both images. Moon river, then, functions as an oxymoron of contradictory similarities, or harmonious antitheses, concerning life and death. This play of differences, resolved by a suggestion of infinite harmony, points at the object of Fidel's quest, Teresa.

Since Teresa functions as the focal point of Fidel's harmony/disharmony conflict, just as the chapter in which she first appears serves as the novel's structural center, it seems reasonable to consider her as supplement for

20. José María Guelbenzu, *El río de la luna,* 299. Subsequent citations will indicate the page number in parentheses. Of course "Moon River" is the title of a popular song enjoying success at about the time the novel was published.

21. Whether called "acquired knowledge" or "consensus reality," our culture teaches people to reason and read in certain prescribed manners. When I refer to readers, then, I am really referring to conventional logic. By doing so, I am not negating in any sense the possibility that any given individual may reason in a different way. In fact, at times all of us rebel against conventional wisdom, and many works of art seem designed to encourage such rebellions. But before we can rebel, we must first define what we are rebelling against. As I am using the term here, *readers* is synonymous with *conventional* or *institutionalized* logic.

women in general, a function aptly demonstrated by the first chapter. In it José is the protagonist of an all-male cast of characters, with women playing the roles of a powerful, absent presence. Although the men in the tavern range from the violent to the benevolent, each suffers from a malaise that he attributes to a woman.[22]

Fidel's role in this first chapter is contemplative since he is cast in the role of passive recipient of José's story. Such a textual strategy allows the narration to serve as an allegory on gender issues for the benefit of thirty-nine-year-old Fidel. Since he hears the allegorical tale concerning José just hours before he is murdered, one can argue that its lesson comes too late to enable him to avoid his fate. In the episode concerning the canoe, however, ten-year-old Fidel learns by playing an active role, and the gender lesson he draws from it becomes a key to the subsequent events of his life.

The success of the plan to steal the canoe depends on the cooperation of Julia, José's convalescing sister, whom her brother agrees to include in the scheme only because "he was very aware that Julia would not be capable of refusing Fidel" (137). By virtue of her involvement, however, Fidel receives an especially harsh beating from his father, a punishment he endures in manly silence. Based on this experience, the young boy senses for the first time that he can exercise power over the alien "others" known as the female sex but that he has to be prepared to pay a high price for that power. When, therefore, as a young adult he treats women as objects to be conquered and abandoned, a cause-and-effect relationship emerges between childhood experiences and adult attitudes. But because of the *récit/histoire* contrast, the reader must reconstruct that relationship in order to understand the protagonist, just as Fidel must reconstruct the gender relationships between his past and present if he hopes to understand himself.

As a young man, Fidel becomes concerned with proving his manhood. His first sexual experience is in 1957 with a young woman named Carmen, and he resorts to a prototypical male discourse to relate to his barroom audience his feelings afterward: "Era la sensación inenarrablemente placentera de penetrar en un cuerpo ajeno, en ese conducto maravilloso en el que derramé hasta los sesos" (It was the ineffably pleasant sensation of penetrating an alien body, this marvelous act in which I drained myself all the way to my

---

22. See particularly Herzberger's "The 'New' Characterization" and Rodríguez Padrón's "La narrativa" for more on the thematic implications of this male/female conflict.

brains, 225). His sensation of domination was short-lived, however, for soon after his conquest Carmen jilted him. He then explains to his listeners an all too predictable reaction: "Let me tell you that after my experience with Carmen I decided that all women were stupid or whores" (229).

Next in the chronology—but not in the order of presentation—is the corroboration that certain power accrues by virtue of his male gender. It is a verification that he finds both disturbing and satisfying. The moment of irrefutable truth occurs one night in 1960 when Fidel and two companions pick up three young women who are on summer vacation in Asturias with their families. The three couples drive to a deserted spot where Raúl, one of Fidel's companions, orders the women to strip and parade before the headlights of the car. They comply, after Raúl strikes one of them, "appearing and disappearing in the light like mules tied to a treadmill" (160–61). Although Fidel plays a passive role, the narrator notes that "this excited him" (159). He then pairs up with one of the victims, and almost immediately "he sensed in her a certain fear coupled with desire to be with him, to stay here after the scene of the car; but that, deep down, seemed to him unexplainable. He never would have given in after such a humiliation" (160). Her submission is complete when she then allows him to seduce her. By reconstructing the *histoire*, it is possible to read into his past pleasure a certain vengeance against Carmen in particular and women in general. But increasingly he is aware that this type of war between the sexes lies at the root of his current psychological malaise. Reluctantly, Fidel begins to realize that he cannot continue to impose his privileges of gender and still expect to realize his quest for harmony.

When he meets Teresa he must deal for the first time with a woman unwilling to play a submissive role: "He realized that Teresa's strength frightened him, a strength firmly tied to a strange erotic wisdom that, given that she was barely twenty years old, amazed and deeply affected Fidel" (170). His apprehension inspired by her strength is juxtaposed with the memory of the three young women parading like "mules tied to a treadmill." Similar to how their subservience both disgusted and excited him, Teresa's independence both frightens and attracts him.

The key episode in Fidel's relationship with Teresa concerns a car ride through the mountains in which they engage in love play. Fidel, who is driving, becomes so aroused that he realizes he is on the verge of killing them both, and as a result he pulls the car to the side of the road and stops, prompting Teresa to ask, "why . . . why have you stopped, my love; why have you stopped?" (187). The following evening the full impact of the episode strikes him:

> Por primera vez en su relación con Teresa, Fidel tuvo miedo . . . Fidel sabía perfectamente que, cuando sucedió, quizá hasta cierto punto lo estaba aceptando, pero ahora, en frío, le asustaba la locura del hecho. Cuanto más lo pensaba más le asustaba. A la idea de la muerte sucedía otra y ésa sí era el origen de su miedo: había descubierto a un desconocido dentro de él. Lo asociaba continuamente con una frase leída en un libro de Lovecraft y olvidada hasta entonces: "No invoques nunca aquello que no puedas dominar."

> (For the first time in his relationship with Teresa, Fidel was afraid . . . Fidel knew perfectly well that, when it happened, perhaps to a certain degree he was accepting it, but now, removed from it, the insanity of the act frightened him. The more he thought about it the more it frightened him. In addition to the thought of dying was another one that was the true source of his fear: he had discovered a stranger within himself. He associated it with a sentence he read, forgotten until now, from Lovecraft's book: "Never invoke something you cannot dominate.") (188–89)

The stranger he discovers, the true origin of his fear, seems to be blind passion, something over which he has no control. Such an emotion is at odds with the gender codes taught to him by his male and female acquaintances and institutionalized in popular manuals: As the male he is supposed to be all-dominant. Since in the car he was temporarily overcome by passion, and he now feels subservient to Teresa (who is merely asserting her equality), he comes to consider her a threat to the fragile stability of the male-centered system he feels obliged to safeguard. In addition, he realizes that his power is also threatened by another circumstance: "He was alone in a single relationship, more adrift than he had ever been before" (189). Again there is an implicit link with the episode concerning the three young women parading before the headlights. His sense of gender power that evening in 1960 was reinforced by male companionship; his present sense of defenselessness apparently responds to being confronted with a one-on-one relationship. By representing Teresa's eroticism as equal to if not stronger than Fidel's, the text leads us to conclude that, since she refuses to allow his sexuality to displace hers, Fidel considers Teresa a threat to the fragile and false harmony of his male-centered universe.[23]

Finally exasperated by Fidel's irrational jealousy and double standards, Teresa leaves him. But she continues to occupy his thoughts to the point of becoming an obsession. His search for harmony from that point on takes the form of sexual conquests, which he narrates in detail to his barroom audience. But he notes that Teresa's image inevitably imposes itself on the face of each of his partners. He then admits to his male audience that he is unable to understand the connection between Teresa's intimidating strength and the image of harmony she evokes.

When they finally meet again each is married to someone else. They arrange a rendezvous, but someone (maybe Teresa's husband or perhaps a mysterious former lover) seems to be spying on them. As they sit and talk Fidel confesses his attempts to find love and harmony in other women and how her image always ended up superimposing itself. To this revelation she replies: "I *was* each of them, of course, and they were I. But you were only capable of seeing me. How silly!" (318). Although this enigmatic statement elicits polysemic interpretations, in one way or another it seems to be related to Fidel's practice of treating women as sexual objects. That being the case, his sex partners are essentially interchangeable. Perhaps Teresa is suggesting that when he thought he saw her image on the faces of other women, what he was really seeing was the female icon created over the centuries by male discourse and reinforced by official apparatuses of the Franco regime such as the Feminine Section of the Falange and its Social Service. When they were together Fidel could not accept Teresa's deviance from that iconic abstraction, just as he could not accept that same deviance in all the other women he tried to possess. In the flesh, as a physical reality, she (like the others) could not conform to and therefore threatened the idealized and abstract female harmony instilled in him by discursive practices. When they were apart, on the other hand, she "magically" became that very elusive symbol of harmony. Little wonder that, when Fidel says he saw her image on all the other women he seduced, Teresa responds, "I *was* each of them, of course, and they were I."

23. Roberts, "Amor sexual," explains the conflict between Fidel and all the women characters as an expression of his confusion between temporary sexual satisfaction and the existential spiritual union ("interior harmony") for which he is really searching.

As noted at the beginning of this analysis, Fidel's life corresponds to the years of the Franco regime. As an adult, he has been searching for a myth of "woman" that, though not created by the regime, was an integral dimension of its discursive project. A self-proclaimed anti-Francoist, Fidel is, nevertheless, a product of fascist ideology concerning gender roles. Ironically, then, his quest for a romantic ideal is really a defense of a totalitarian ideology.[24] The harmony he seeks is essentially the same harmony the Franco regime champions with its cry for political, linguistic, and religious unity. Inherent in both projects is the need to erase differences, a need that in turn ensures their ultimate failure and demise. Stated in another way, the obsession with equilibrium, one manifestation of which is severely codified gender roles, can be seen as an example of how individuals as well as certain political systems tend to will their own state of entropy.

Fidel's quest ends when he is fatally stabbed in the back after Teresa leaves him to return to her husband. Apparently the murderer is the person who has been spying on them. As the protagonist lies dying he remembers his recent dream of a battle between the knight of light and the knight of darkness. Finally he understands:

> si bien el Caballero de la Sombra luchaba para no morir, el de la Luz sabía—y sus movimientos lo delataban en Fidel—que su victoria no significaba la destrucción del otro, que justamente para vencer necesitaba *no destruir* a su contrario y por esa razón era una extraña grandeza la que le iluminaba.

> (whereas the Knight of the Shadow fought to stay alive, the Knight of the Light knew—and his movements revealed as much to Fidel—that his victory did not signify the destruction of the other, that winning required *not destroying* his adversary and for that reason a strange grandeur illuminated him.) (360)

Again the passage resists a univocal reading, but one possibility is that Fidel finally realizes that his victory (a state of harmony) does not depend on dominating the other. To win means to accept the differences of and the

---

24. Obviously there are echoes of Lacan in this reading. As they relate to this analysis, see particularly his chapters "The Function and Field of Speech and Language in Psychoanalysis," "The Freudian Thing," "The Agency of the Letter in the Unconscious or Reason since Freud," "On a Question Preliminary to Any Possible Treatment of Psychosis ('with Freud')," and "The Direction of the Treatment and the Principles of Its Power," all from *Ecrits*. See also Ragland-Sullivan's *Jacques Lacan*.

inevitable conflicts with others. Whether that is the message Fidel decodes is something we are not told; the narrator only notes that as Fidel dies, "A smile sealed his lips" (362). Perhaps the smile signals that Fidel has finally recognized the harmony of difference. Or if death, as Freud claimed, is the ultimate object of desire as it signifies the end of all disharmony, perhaps we can conclude that it is the only means for Fidel of achieving his quest for unity and harmony.[25] It also allows for the narrative process of *El río de la luna* to come to its harmonious end, which of course is not an end in the conventional sense of the word but rather another deferral of play as Guelbenzu's text awaits and invites the next reading.

Entropy, it is said, is a temporal process that threatens to undermine any system by reducing information to noise.[26] One could argue that by 1975 Francoism was falling victim to entropy; its efforts to control all discourse, to reduce it to a propagandistic function, had reached a point where pronouncements by the government ceased to have any meaning at all, where any officially sanctioned discourse was considered mere noise. By offering the events in a nonsequential order, the *récit* of *El río de la luna* could be interpreted as a novelistic expression of entropy, just as the colloidal metaphor of *Teoría del conocimiento* could be interpreted the same way. But according to Campbell, systems also counteract entropy by means of internalized rules and codes designed to preserve order (99, 113), and order, according to the second law of thermodynamics, makes life possible by enabling new forms to be created out of old ones (41). The clues allowing us to reconstruct the *histoire* of *El río de la luna* may represent an intuitive expression of those internalized rules, of the underlying codes allowing for the possibility of new forms to emerge from an entropic and chaotic system.[27] Whether Guelbenzu had entropy in mind when he wrote *El río de la luna* strikes me as an irrelevant question. What does seem relevant to me is that his novel acts as a powerful register of an episteme. By 1981 totalitarianism, not merely in Spain but globally, was at or near exhaustion. The burning question

---

25. Gullón, "El novelista como fabulador," on the other hand, insists that Fidel never achieves a sense of harmony (68).

26. See Campbell, *Grammatical Man*, Hayles, *Chaos Bound*, and Paulson, *Noise of Culture*.

27. Cohan and Shires, *Telling Stories*, offer a quotation from Sebeok's definition of cultural codes that serves here: "A *code* is 'an agreed transformation, or set of unambiguous rules, whereby messages are converted from one representation to another' " (114).

then (and now) concerned the next stage. Guelbenzu offers us the novelistic solution of orderly disorder, or an underlying body of rules capable of giving meaning to a chaotic system. As this substructure does so, it creates a new form from one that mercifully, for most, was nearing its end. Significantly (perhaps too significantly), as Fidel dies his newborn son seems to herald an emerging new order: "He was awake and excited, vividly moving his hands and bending his legs, as if palpitating to the limit with sensations . . . the moon called to the child. The moon was calling it" (366).[28]

José María Guelbenzu adds another dimension to the discursive renovation of Spanish fiction initiated by Martín-Santos and furthered by Juan Goytisolo, Carmen Martín Gaite, Eduardo Mendoza, Juan José Millás, and Luis Goytisolo. Whereas Martín Gaite focuses primarily on the official apparatuses created with the goal of defining women's role in the society—the already mentioned Feminist Section of the Falangist Party and the Social Service program—Guelbenzu concentrates on the male individual as a product of such a society. Since he incarnates the very gender attitudes championed by the regime, Fidel's death, as did Franco's, seems to signal the possible end of a discursive system—whose roots extended back to pre-Roman times—that the dictatorship took special pains to perpetuate. The next novel we are going to examine, Lourdes Ortiz's *Urraca*, switches the focus from the decaying tree of fascism/sexism with its vertical and predictable root system to the subterranean rhizome of historiography that sends its shoots to the surface in ubiquitous and random patterns.[29]

From Political Authority to Poetic License: *Urraca*

Although the setting is the ninth and tenth centuries rather than the twentieth, Lourdes Ortiz's 1982 *Urraca* (Magpie)[30] follows along the same basic gender path forged by *El cuarto de atrás* and *El río de la luna* and explores a speaker/receptor process somewhat similar to the one found in *Teoría del*

28. There seems to be an echo here to Federico García Lorca's poem, "Romance de la luna, luna."

29. My metaphoric source in this case is Gilles Deleuze and his "Rhizome versus Trees" essay.

30. Ortiz has published six other novels up to this point: *Luz de la memoria*, 1976; *Picadura mortal*, 1979; *En días como éstos*, 1981; *Arcángeles*, 1986; and *La fuente de la vida*, 1995. In 1988 her collection of stories, *Los motivos de Circe*, appeared.

conocimiento. Yet far from being a mere imitator, *Urraca* directs the focus to the dual concepts of *genre* and *gender* as the protagonist attempts to compensate for her loss of political authority by exercising poetic license. The narration revolves around a deposed queen who becomes a speaker/writer and a monk who serves as her listener/reader, the protagonists of a literary power/resistance conflict.

The novel concerns a queen who is more vilified for her acts of adultery than celebrated for her political astuteness.[31] Hers is a story of seductions, alliances, and intrigue as she outmaneuvers her male rivals and ascends to the throne of the emerging Spanish empire. Eventually, however, she is betrayed by both her son and the opportunistic Bishop Gelmírez, who together depose and imprison her. From the monastic cell where her antagonists have isolated her she decides to write the chronicle of her struggle for power.

Urraca addresses, among other issues, the question of historiography or the relationship between history and the historian, between verity and modes of verification—in short, between historical truth and narrating power. Now stripped of her sovereign authority, the protagonist proposes to reassert herself by means of her authorial prerogative: "But Urraca now controls the discourse and she is going to narrate in such a manner that the minstrels may possess the truth and transmit it from village to village and from kingdom to kingdom."[32] In effect she asserts poetic truth here,

31. The historical figure reputedly was born in 1077 to Alfonso VI of Leon and Castile and Constanza of Borgoña. Urraca became queen in 1109 at the death of her father and married Alfonso I of Aragon that same year. In 1123 she was placed under house arrest by her son Alfonso Raimúndez, king of Galicia. She finally died in 1126, reportedly from giving birth to an illegitimate child.

32. Lourdes Ortiz, *Urraca,* 12. Subsequent citations will indicate the page number in parentheses. *Urraca* has received limited critical attention, a most unfortunate oversight. The essays to date discussing the novel include Argelia F. Carracedo, "Síntesis del tiempo en *Urraca* de Lourdes Ortiz"; Nina Molinaro, "Resistance, Gender, and Mediation of History in Pizarnik's *La condesa sangrienta* and Ortiz's *Urraca*"; Elizabeth J. Ordóñez, *Voices of Their Own: Contemporary Spanish Narrative by Women* (see specifically her chapter "Writing 'Her/story': Reinscription of Tradition in Texts by Riera, Gómez Ojea, and Ortiz" and her essay "Rewriting Myth and History: Three Recent Novels by Women"); Angela Encinar, "*Urraca*: Una recreación actual de la historia"; and Biruté Ciplijauskaité, "Historical Novel from a Feminine Perspective: *Urraca*," "Lyric Memory, Oral History and the Shaping of the Self in Spanish Narrative," and *La novela femenina contemporánea (1970–1985): Hacia una tipología de la narración en primera persona,* in which she also discusses works by Fernández Cubas, Martín Gaite, Montero, Riera, and Tusquets. See also my comments on *Urraca* in "A Play of Difference" and "Lourdes Ortiz: Mapping the Course of Postfrancoist Fiction."

which of course always requires to one degree or another a suspension of disbelief. When there is resistance to that narrative convention, attention is directed to the issue of historical truth itself and to who authorizes it and how. By proclaiming that she proposes to narrate "the truth," she effectively sets a clever trap for her male enemies. If they suspend their disbelief, they validate her version of history; if they openly resist her right to author that version, they risk undermining the concept of historical truth itself, which in turn could subvert their own discursive authority. Perhaps sensing the trap awaiting them, her son and the bishop assign a surrogate, the monk Roberto, to monitor Urraca's activities. He, then, becomes a key actor in her subversive melodrama.

Initially Roberto merely provides the writing materials, but, "as if writing were not sufficient," she asks him one day to stay and listen to her story (23). His presence allows her to supplement her written account with oral discourse, her implicit reader with an explicit listener. Now that she has a recipient in front of her, she has to make appropriate allowances for him when she begins to tell how her husband, in the company of the bishop, would fondle her intimately after drinking too much wine:

> No te preocupes, monje, que tu reina no va a seguir por ahí; no iba a contarte mis noches con Raimundo, ni te iba a hablar de su obsesión por las doncellas . . . le gustaban de trece y de catorce años, o incluso más pequeñas: carnes prietas, sin tostar, recientitas, y se encendían sus mejillas cuando quería hacerle compartir al Obispo sus más recientes descubrimientos.

> (Don't worry, Monk, your queen is not going to continue along this line; I was not going to tell you about my nights with Raimundo, nor about his obsession for young girls . . . he liked them between the ages of thirteen and fourteen, and even younger: firm flesh, not weatherworn, really fresh, and his cheeks flushed when he shared with the Bishop his most recent discoveries.) (26)

In addition to her playful strategy of essentially telling him what she promises not to tell him, she conveys an inferred message of moral corruption that concerns the bishop and the church even more than it does Raimundo and his appetite for nubile teenage girls. Not only does the bishop willingly waive for his friend and sovereign the doctrine subjugating corporeality to spirituality but, according to Urraca, this ecclesiastical official clearly demonstrates vicarious pleasure in listening to Raimundo's male discourse of sexual conquests as well. For a modern reader's taste, logically there is a conflict here between Gelmírez's implicit religious values and his explicit celebration of sexual-abuse narrative. Yet Roberto is not bothered at all by what he hears concerning the bishop's moral inconsistency: "As far as Roberto is concerned, Gelmírez is God on earth, his truest image" (23). Roberto's attitude underscores how the church helps institutionalize a discrepancy concerning male versus female sexual as well as textual freedom. As a representative of both the dominant male gender and the church, Roberto serves as a sign pointing directly at two of the forces (which some would argue are really one and the same) that have collaborated, especially in Spanish-speaking societies, to perpetuate this double standard.

Almost immediately Urraca sets out to subvert these oppressive powers by creating a pivotal role for their surrogate in her subversive comedy. First of all, Roberto's pious resistance to what she relates serves to enrich the narrative, providing it with added dimensions of irony. In addition, she makes him an unwitting ally in her attack on institutionalized masculine discursive practices. Although the sexual gratification she gave to others allowed her to achieve temporary political control, she now realizes that only through textual manipulation can she hope to achieve lasting power. Roberto, then, serves as a ready target for her to hone her skills of verbal seduction.

She begins with a strategy of titillation by drawing a suggestive analogy between one of her husband's Moorish warriors and Roberto: "Aben Ammar must have looked like you, Monk; surely he had your same long hands, which I can just feel are destined to caress someone's flesh; he had that slim and firm waist that you castigate with sackcloth and no doubt he bathed with oils" (37). Then, when she begins to describe the scene where Zaida, the Moorish princess, seduced her father, analogy gives way to provocation:

> cuando veo esas manos tuyas diestras en el pincel, sueño yo también con Aben Ammar e imagino los goces de al Mutamid, veo esta celda con los ojos con que Zaida veía sus jardines. Cojines de seda, monje, donde tú podrías recostarte, mientras yo, tumbada a tu lado, iría recorriendo tu cuerpo con mi lengua.

> (when I see your flexible hands on the brush, I also dream about Aben Ammar and I imagine the joys of Mutamid, I see this cell with the eyes that Zaida used to see her gardens. Silk cushions, Monk, where you

could lie down, while I, stretched out at your side, explored your body
with my tongue.) (38)

In spite of its eroticism, this passage seems to serve as an exercise in stylistic
experimentation rather than as a sexual invitation. As Roberto labors with
carnal suppression, she toys with aesthetic expression. Indeed, when she
finally decides to physically seduce him, the results are not entirely satisfying:
"Okay; it finally happened. It was not especially gratifying, but it has
calmed me down" (121). This privileging of linguistic foreplay over physical
consummation suggests that, just as some men seem to feel that discoursing
about sex is as gratifying, if not more so, than the act itself, Urraca begins to
discover the joys of textual stimulation. Over the years the pleasures of sex
have brought her only temporary political power and physical satisfaction;
the newly discovered pleasures of the text promise to bring her much more
enduring discursive authority and psychological fulfillment.

Even though the tools of her trade are now sheets of paper rather than
bedsheets, Urraca finds that a male companion is as essential for her new
vocation as it was for the former. Yet a text partner can become as much of
a burden as a sex partner:

> El hermano Roberto ha estado conmigo toda la tarde y me incita con
> sus preguntas a detenerme en los detalles. Los nombres son para él
> símbolos de una historia de la que nunca fue protagonista, una historia
> que sufrió sin comprender, como la sufrieron todas las gentes de mis
> reinos.
>
> (Brother Roberto has been with me all afternoon and he inspires me
> with his questions to stop and fill in details. For him the names are
> symbols of a story in which he was never protagonist, a story in which
> he suffered without knowing why, as all the subjects of my kingdoms
> suffered.) (76)

Because of Roberto's presence Urraca feels obliged to narrate events that she
otherwise would have skipped, to supply details that, rather than fulfilling
her desire for vengeance, lead her to a recognition of guilt. The initial
pleasure of the text has now turned to displeasure: "I am weary and
I no longer know what I am saying. I have been a prisoner for many
months, too many, and your innocence creates disorder in my narration;
and it is not a good idea to waver because, what then would become
of my chronicle?" (79). His ignorance and innocence now pose major

obstructions to her discursive project. Because of him she must change her chronicle into a diary and thereby sacrifice an authoritative historical mode for a disenfranchised personal style—the latter more typically associated with memoirs and feminine discourse as opposed to the institutionalized masculine discourse of history. Just as when she became queen, male resistance seems to be strategically positioned to usurp her power.

Faced with the prospect of another defeat at the hands of a male opponent, Urraca attempts to write her chronicle when Roberto is not present. But soon she realizes the futility of her efforts. The narrative power she seeks needs a resisting reader to sustain itself.[33] He must therefore play a key role in her creative task: "Tired of writing, worn out by the monologue that will never have a reply, I turn to him to help me arrange my thoughts" (59). As the surrogate for her male enemies intent on excluding her from historical discourse, Roberto supplies the necessary inspiration for her objective: "While I speak for the benefit of the monk I am thinking about my written word, I am dreaming about my chronicle. I heard one day that history should be reconstructed, and I reassemble my origin for the monk" (61). The passage implies that her "I" needs his "other" to reconstitute itself. The monk's presence compensates for the absence of all those male antagonists (including but not limited to her son and the bishop) who wield power against her.

Since her son is the most prominent of the "others" for whom Urraca is writing, she confesses to Roberto: "here, alone with you, in this monastery, when I know that I cannot derive any recompensation nor pardon at all from this confession, I say to myself and I say in writing that I love and loved this son against whom I fought" (84). If "love and loved" seem to contradict the final verb "fought," it is a contradiction that may be inevitable: "From the beginning I saw him as an 'other,' one who emerged not as a prolongation of my body but rather in front of me and only someone who is exterior can be loved and respected" (84). Although their sameness of blood is opposed by their difference of gender, that contrast does not explain the contradiction.

33. In her book *Foucault, Feminism, and Power,* Molinaro expands on Foucault's thesis to posit a relationship between power and resistance that seems also to apply to the novelistic situation of *Urraca:* "The two are viewed not as antagonistic but, rather, as two sides of the same coin; each modifies and sustains the other. Power neither traps nor solidifies resistance. Instead, both suggest mutually responsive and prohibitive strategies" (23).

For if the difference creates rivalry, it also inspires love and respect in her. Indeed, what seems to distinguish this mother from her son is not really biology at all, but her capacity to find in his alterity a motive for adoration. Precisely that ability not merely to accept but also to celebrate difference distinguishes her from all her male opponents, the most recent of whom is the pious recipient of her narrative.

When one day Roberto fails to appear, Urraca realizes beyond a doubt that his absence is a far greater threat to her discursive campaign than his presence:

> de repente, esta crónica me parece vacía. ¿Qué he de contar? Las bata-
> llas, los cambios de humor, los acuerdos . . . Necesito conversar, nece-
> sito contarle al monje aquella jornada para que vuelvan las caras, re-
> suenen de nuevo las palabras pronunciadas . . . para que todo adquiera
> vida.

> (suddenly, this chronicle strikes me as empty. What am I to tell? The
> battles, the changes of mood, the agreements . . . I need to converse,
> I need to tell the monk about that campaign to recapture the faces,
> to make the spoken words reverberate . . . to bring everything back to
> life.) (66)

Obviously Roberto represents an essential element for the success of her narrative project: an identifiable point of male resistance. In her political campaign, amorphous male discursive practices (for which her son and the bishop were mere instruments rather than origins) forced her to acquiesce. That male order publicly rebukes, while privately applauding, a woman who excels in love affairs, while it both publicly and privately condemns a woman such as Urraca who successfully conducts affairs of state. With Roberto present, Urraca has a concrete rather than an abstract antagonist whom she can confront with the irrefutable evidence that it was not her adulterous transgressions that condemned her but rather her political successes.

As she becomes increasingly aware of the interdependency between power and resistance, an action taken by the bishop makes her realize that the very discursive practice designed to exclude her has assured her immortal equality. Gelmírez had a stone sculpture of her carved in the cathedral of Santiago de Compostela as a warning to all men. Little did he suspect its real effect:

> Allí, junto a los temas sagrados, junto a las Tentaciones del Diablo a su Señor, la Adúltera crece y se convierte en símbolo. ¡Ah, Gelmírez! Esa es mi venganza. Igualada para siempre al señor, desafiante al tiempo. Y es el amor lo que me rescata. Yo también en piedra, como el Altísimo, en cuyo nombre decías actuar.

> (There, next to the sacred themes, next to the devil's temptations for the Lord, the *Adulteress* grows and is transformed into a symbol. Oh, Gelmírez! That is my vengeance. Made equal to the lord, eternal. And love rescues me. I also with a stone image, just like the Almighty, in whose name you claim to act.) (129)

The purpose of the stone sculpture was to condemn the adulteress as an impending menace; its effect, ironically, has been to celebrate her as an alluring transcendence. Male discursive practices have transformed her into an icon to stand alongside the holiest of the holy Christian saints. If indeed we live in a symbolic order created by and for males, their attempts to exclude the participation in that order by writers such as Urraca (or Ortiz) ultimately assure her and women artists like her of a position of equality and could even lead to a reversal of the power hierarchy. These writers' feminine power inevitably will grow in direct proportion to the male resistance to it.

Yet Urraca herself falls victim to resistance when, in spite of the textual pleasures she has discovered, she makes one more incursion into the sexual arena and seduces Roberto. Her prosaic synopsis of this sexual anticlimax forms a vivid contrast with the sensual descriptions preceding it. Now she knows for sure that her future pleasures will have to come from discourse rather than intercourse: "All that is transformed into writing. Even Brother Roberto, who sleeps contented, now is part of the text that I have to relate; I no longer experience his flesh except as a dimension of the chronicle. Urraca, you are getting old, you are tired. What would Gelmírez say if he could see you now?" (123). Finally, Urraca thinks, she has discovered the key to absolute control. Promiscuous sex was temporarily gratifying both physically and politically, but ultimately it left her frustrated and powerless. The literary text, on the other hand, promises to bring her lasting fulfillment. Already she has discovered that textualization allows her to compensate for Roberto's deficient virility just as it enables her to transform other fleeting moments of ecstacy into timeless blocks of narrative. With those discoveries she is in a position to realize the culminating subversion of the masculine order represented by Roberto.

Again the act of narrating provides the means of subversion. Recalling a biblical story told to her by her father's doctor concerning David and the spider web, she declares: "For me Roberto is that spider that weaves its protective web over the entrance to the cave and, although there is no Saul from whom I should hide, I know that my only hope is in him" (161). She is relying on three convention-sanctioned tropes: the spider, the web, and the cave. Playing the role conventionally associated with the femme fatale—the spider—is Roberto. His duty is to weave a protective web over rather than to penetrate the vagina and to guard a vagina-centric as opposed to a phallocentric universe. Urraca has turned this particular male symbolic order upside down. Her past political potency never equaled her present poetic power. But her maximum moment of triumph is tempered by the realization that a male presence is also her only hope.

Again contradiction rather than sovereignty reigns. Her immortality resides in the hands of the very person she has managed to textualize. The narrating "I" is inexorably bonded to its narrated "other."[34] Similar to sexual relationships where foreplay is designed to yield to consummation, in textual relationships process at some point must yield to product. The dynamics of one sign responding to another sign eventually must exhaust itself, and the text becomes a mere product, a work.[35] Only the recipient can resurrect a text and restore its dynamic essence, and so Urraca has no alternative but to turn to Roberto: "In this way Roberto, I would like you to complete my chronicle, introducing metaphors, playing with the words" (203). Of course it is possible to interpret this passage as a defeat. Just as she was forced to turn over her kingdom to her male rivals, now she is turning over her text to a male adversary. But even here there is a subtle contradiction, for as she surrenders her discursive power to Roberto she also retains it. That is to say, although she ostensibly grants him poetic license, his creation will inevitably

---

34. By "narrated other," I mean the posited reader implicit in every narrating act. This linguistic dimension has been referred to as the "narratee" (Gerald Prince, "Introduction á l'étude du narrataire"), the "implied reader" (Wolfgang Iser, *The Implied Reader: Patterns of Communication in Prose Fiction from Bunyan to Beckett*), or the "oyente" or "listener" (Félix Martínez Bonati, *La estructura de la obra literaria: Una investigación de filosofía del lenguaje y estética*). Personally I prefer the term *posited reader* as the logical counterpart to Bakhtin's "posited author."

35. For an insightful discussion of the concept of a sign responding to another sign in an infinite process of deferral, see Jonathan Culler, "In Pursuit of Signs." Roland Barthes offers an equally insightful distinction between work and text in his benchmark "From Work to Text."

reveal the traces of hers. His male-centered discourse must respond to, and therefore can never totally erase, the female-centered discourse that inspired it. She has managed to transform a linguistic phenomenon into an aesthetic experience: the dual gender of the word *fe(male)*. Authorship, then, allows her to create a gender equality that her monarchy never allowed her to attain.

The novel ends with Urraca preparing a potion that will unite her and Roberto ultimately in a new order where she hopes to find "una luz que ofusca a todo el que llega y le hace postrarse, y esa luz se propaga a través de los ojos y a través de la inteligencia, de modo que cada uno de los bien aventurados es todo él ojos y oídos y entonces se descorren los velos" (a light that blinds everyone who comes there and makes him or her lie down, and that light multiplies through the eyes and intelligence, in such a manner that each one of the blessed is all eyes and ears and then the shades are drawn, 206).[36] This passage with its "blessed" and its reference to a place where the inhabitants are composed of only eyes and ears has a very definite biblical connotation.[37] Perhaps this Christian imagery in turn points toward a pre-Oedipal union where tolerance and understanding harmonize sexual difference. But whatever the various meanings inherent in the image, the one I find most inviting concerns Ortiz's discursive project. The image echoes her attempt to involve her readers in an aesthetic experience that removes the veils behind which women are expected to hide piously and silently. Her novel allows us to experience the creative force of gender difference and above all the discursive power generated by opposition to this difference. And by virtue of yet another play of difference, Ortiz's "Magpie" does not merely parrot sounds; she speaks with a voice of her own, and the power behind that voice promises to grow in direct proportion to the resistance offered by the "others" who have inspired it and to whom it is directed.

36. Just before she describes her version of heaven, she speaks to Roberto: "Rest now, sleep peacefully. I still have to finish some things, but don't become impatient, because Urraca is going to sleep by your side in just a moment" (206). Although ambiguous, the textual logic indicates that she is preparing a potion to kill only herself, since Roberto has been charged to finish her chronicle. The assumption is, then, that he will join her later rather than immediately in the heaven she describes.

37. Various passages can be cited as sources for this particular biblical discourse. Examples include: "He that hath ears to hear, let him hear" (Matt. 11:15); "Having eyes, see ye not? and having ears, hear ye not?" (Mark 8:18); and "For I tell you, that many prophets and kings have desired to see those things which ye see, and have not seen *them*; and to hear those things which ye hear, and have not heard *them*" (Luke 10:24).

With her novel *Urraca*, Lourdes Ortiz offers yet another version of the idea that power and resistance feed on one another and, similar to rhizomes, spring from a noncentralized root system running horizontally as well as vertically. In the novelistic hands of Luis Goytisolo, we witness an unhealthy amalgamation of the adversarial ideological powers on the Right and the Left. In the case of Martín Gaite, the official efforts to regiment the representation of female roles in popular culture leads to the misreadings of these representations as expressions of freedom and escape. Ortiz offers a protagonist in her novel who gains narrative power by virtue of her resisting male recipient. The narrator's consciousness of power relations and discursive practices marks a vital step in post-totalitarian Spanish fiction. For one thing, fascism and the Franco regime are no longer the point of departure (though the novel does refer to historical totalitarianism). By shifting the focus to medieval Spanish history, *Urraca* dramatically lays bare the foundation on which the present gender edifice has been constructed. The speaker learns through the process of narrating how discourse determines power hierarchies and gender roles and how the key to power is to lay claim to a share of the discourse. The emphasis of *Urraca* on the concept of discursive/gender practices as they relate to power/resistance represents an important step as contemporary Spanish fiction searches for less parochial issues. Goytisolo metaphorically launches this novelistic decade with an interment of Francoist discourse, and Guelbenzu joins him by mercifully ending the life of the regime's sexist progeny. As the ghost of Franco fades with each passing year, the focal points turn increasingly to more universal, epistemic concerns. In the case of the next novel we will analyze, Rosa Montero's *Te trataré como a una reina*, the narrative project concentrates on challenging the authorization of gender roles.

Textual/Sexual Deauthorization in *Te trataré como a una reina*

In addressing the issue of discourse and male/female relationships, Rosa Montero's 1983 novel focuses primarily on popular culture and how it both authorizes and deauthorizes gender roles. The title *Te trataré como a una reina* (I will treat you like a queen), which refers to the line of a bolero, serves as an ironic sign for the myth of Hispanic male homage to women. As is common knowledge, the promise of the title is a purely formulaic expression or *piropo* (flattering comment) that men employ to woo and seduce women. In addition, the image of Urraca still freshly imprinted in our consciousness enhances the ironic impact of the title. Thanks to Ortiz's novel, the word *queen* connotes the total lack of rather than the possession of political power. It is a purely decorative and eminently temporary title, similar to the English concept "queen for a day." All too often, when her day is over (which more likely is really a night in bed), the sovereign becomes a servant to the very man promising her a throne.

The novel presents three primary focalizers: Bella, a café singer accused of attempted murder; Antonio, the victim of her attack; and his sister Antonia. Bella serves as the focalizing point in eleven chapters, Antonio in six, and Antonia in ten. Only chapter 24 is not focalized, and the two secondary characters appearing in it do not provide any source of observation. Interspersed among the regular numbered chapters are four interviews conducted by the magazine reporter Paco Mancebo with the male principals of the story, one of whom is the victim Antonio. An extract from Mancebo's article on the attempted murder serves as a preface to the novel.

The three focalizers share ties that extend all the way back to their childhood. Bella, Antonio, and Antonia grew up in the same village, and Bella and Antonio were lovers as teenagers. Although that relationship ended long ago, almost every night he frequents the Desiré, a sleazy cabaret where she sings boleros and tends bar. Antonio is a bureaucrat who fancies himself as an expert perfume tester. Obsessed with protecting his olfactory gift, he will not tolerate the mixing of perfume scents, and above all he abhors the odor of cigarette smoke. Antonia, his over-forty spinster sister, cooks for him, washes and sews his clothes, and visits the Desiré in the afternoons to talk to her friend Bella.[38]

As the title suggests, love is one of the major themes of the novel. In spite of her cynicism concerning all men, Bella falls in love with the mysterious Poco, supposedly a former legionnaire, who is always either stationed at the bar of the Desiré or hiding in an adjacent room that serves as his living quarters. Poco claims to have a friend in Cuba who will hire Bella, and the two begin to make plans to emigrate there. Another regular at the club is the young prostitute Vanessa, for whom Bella becomes a surrogate

---

38. Two years after *Te trataré como a una reina* was published, Patrick Suskind incorporated the same basic olfactory theme in his best-seller, *Das Parfum*.

mother, a relationship that Poco cites as a pretext for including Vanessa in their projected move to Cuba (really he is secretly in love with the young prostitute). Meanwhile Antonio and Vanessa have become lovers, and surprisingly this apparently confirmed bachelor asks her to marry him. For her part, the spinster Antonia has found a lover in Damián, the shy young janitor of the building in which she lives.

The web of relationships begins to unravel when Inspector García, a friend of Antonio's, watches one night as Antonia and Damián make love in a public park and arrests them when they have finished. Antonio agrees not to press charges if Damián will leave town and never contact Antonia again. At about the same time Poco finally confesses to Vanessa that he loves her, and when she rejects him and refuses to accompany him to Cuba he savagely beats her. Poco then kills himself by stepping in front of a subway train. After his death Bella learns that he is the father of Menéndez, the owner of the Desiré who spends his time secretly reading pornographic novels while Bella assumes the responsibility of running the establishment. She also discovers that Poco was in love with Vanessa and that the Cuba project was a total hoax. When Antonia then tells Bella that Antonio has driven away Damián, the singer goes to Antonio's home and throws him out the fourth-story window. He survives the fall but loses his sense of smell; Bella is arrested and faces a prison sentence; Antonia boards a train with no destination in mind, only to discover that unwittingly (or inevitably) she has picked the train that will return her to the village where she was born and where her mother still lives.[39]

---

39. Concha Alborg, "Metaficción y feminismo en Rosa Montero," argues that the novel has a structure based on the musical composition of a bolero. She notes that the bolero is a dance in which the couples change partners and that the same type of switching characterizes the plot of the novel (72). Unlike Ortiz, Montero has attracted a significant amount of critical attention. In addition to Emilio de Miguel Martínez's study of her early novels, *La primera narrativa de Rosa Montero,* and Alma Amell's book on all her fiction to date, *Rosa Montero's Odyssey,* there are articles on *Te trataré como a una reina* by Alma Amell, "Una crónica de la marginación: La narrativa de Rosa Montero"; Kathleen M. Glenn, "Victimized by Misreading: Rosa Montero's *Te trataré como a una reina*" and "Authority and Marginality in Three Contemporary Spanish Narratives"; José María Navarro, "El lenguaje coloquial en *Te trataré como a una reina,* de Rosa Montero"; Viviana Claudia Giménez, "Subversión en *Te trataré como a una reina* de Rosa Montero"; and Samuel Amell, "El motivo del viaje en tres novelas del posfranquismo." For overviews of her fiction see: Joan Lipman Brown, "Rosa Montero: From Journalist to Novelist"; Elena Gascón Vera, "Rosa Montero ante la escritura femenina"; Luis Suñén, "La realidad y sus sombras: Rosa

As the preceding synopsis should indicate, this involved plot tends more toward soap-opera melodrama than it does to postmodern irony. Indeed, it is easy to point out flaws in *Te trataré como a una reina*, and there is a temptation to dismiss it as a failed novelistic project. Yet even if according to conventional means of evaluating novels it is a failure, it is one of the more discursively interesting failures. Since my focus in this study is on discourse in fiction and how it helps define our episteme, I feel it would be a mistake to exclude Montero's novel. Whether for discursive and epistemic or other reasons, this work has attracted more readers and critics than any of the others we will be examining from this period.[40]

Discourse, the novel suggests, is the principal tool used by the patriarchal order to subjugate women. Whereas Urraca learns how to manipulate a written text to her own ends, in *Te trataré como a una reina* the women characters never manage to "dis-cerne" themselves from the insidious discursive force surrounding them.[41] Bella is a good example. At the beginning she seems to be the one female character too hardened by reality to fall prey to any seductive ploy: "Because Bella was afraid of men. A deep fear that she could not explain. A fear that had grown throughout her life. They were so barbaric, so incomprehensible. So cruel. They were like children, but like children capable of murdering."[42] One day, however, Poco hands her a bolero to sing that he has written, and she assumes he wrote it exclusively for her. Later the reader learns along with Bella that Poco did not write it for her but for Vanessa. When he asks Bella "Do you like it? Come on, woman, tell me the truth" (178), all her defenses crumble:

> Cuando el Poco le llamaba "mujer," Bella se derretía. Entonces se sentía toda ella mujer, la única mujer del mundo, mujer de arriba abajo. "Comprender el más profundo de tus sueños," decía la canción. Era

Montero y Cristina Fernández Cubas"; Roberto C. Manteiga, "The Dilemma of the Modern Woman: A Study of the Female Characters in Rosa Montero's Novels"; and Phyllis Zatlin, "The Novels of Rosa Montero as Experimental Fiction."

40. In addition to *Te trataré como a una reina*, Montero has published six other novels to date: *Crónica del desamor*, 1979; *La función Delta*, 1981; *Amado amo*, 1988; *Temblor*, 1990; and *Bella y oscura*, 1993. She also has published two collections of newspaper articles and interviews, *España para ti para siempre* in 1976 and *Cinco años de País* in 1982.

41. Smith, *Discerning the Subject*, x.

42. Rosa Montero, *Te trataré como a una reina*, 78. Subsequent citations will indicate the page number in parentheses.

exactamente lo que ella pensaba, exactamente lo que ella buscaba. Eran tan iguales, el Poco y ella. Tan parecidos. Idénticos en sus arrugas interiores. Ella le podría hacer feliz. Tenía tanto para darle.

(When Poco called her a "woman," Bella melted. Then she felt like a real woman, the only woman in the world, a woman from head to toe. "Understanding the profoundest of your dreams," the song went. That was exactly what she thought, exactly what she wanted. They were equal, she and Poco. So alike. Identical in their hidden blemishes. She would make him happy. She had so much to give him.) (178–79)

She misinterprets the generic "woman" as his homage to her female essence and the voiced clichés of the song as expressions of the ineffable bonds uniting them. Bella has fallen victim to the prototypical male discourse of popular culture that has become sterile by force of repetition. What she mistakes for expressions of deep emotions are mere rhyming lyrics. Ironically, as a bolero singer she functions as the ventriloquist for meaningless words of romance not only authored by someone else but also directed to someone else. When she finally learns the truth, she realizes that she has been contributing all her life to her own self-deauthorization.

The bolero is only one of many means by which the male gender has appropriated popular culture to spread its discursive message. The movies provide both male and female icons as gender models. Again, even the seasoned Bella is not immune to the pervasive influence of celluloid ideals. For example, when she allows one of the cabaret customers to share her bed one evening, she seems to be coldly calculating: "It was a good idea every once in a while to give some satisfaction to the body" (80). Yet that pragmatic tone is belied by a compulsion to declare that her partner had more to offer than mere male genitalia: "He didn't look like Rock Hudson, but he wasn't altogether bad either" (78). Although almost certainly an unintended irony when the novel was written, that Rock Hudson later revealed he was a homosexual only underscores the lacuna existing between celluloid images and reality.[43] Bella claims that at that moment in the past

43. Largely thanks to the efforts of his Hollywood employers and agents, Hudson's homosexuality was hidden from the public until shortly before he died of AIDS in October 1985. According to his biographer Sara Davidson, *Rock Hudson, His Story,* as late as July 1985, only four people even knew he was suffering from AIDS (18). Of course his public acknowledgment does not preclude the possibility that Montero knew of his sexual orientation by virtue of gossip magazines and the like. Yet very much to her credit there

she merely needed to satisfy her hormonal urges, but in her narrative present she obviously feels obliged to textualize those physiological needs. Her sexual satisfaction, at least in retrospect, must be justified by her partner's possession of at least some of the cosmetic features dictated by Hollywood. For Bella, as perhaps for everyone, even instinct cannot escape the pervasive influence of discourse.

Vanessa is even more a captive of discursive practices. When Poco strikes up a seemingly friendly conversation Vanessa is unable to respond in kind, not because she suspects his motives but because she cannot process his tattoo: "Neither Robert Redford nor Julio Iglesias nor anybody who is really refined and decent tattoos himself" (54), she reasons to herself. Like Bella, she has been conditioned by a world of images. But whereas the older singer may have to rationalize the degree to which her partners conform to the model, the much younger Vanessa can be a little more demanding, and Poco certainly does not even approach the Hollywood standard. Later, when he tells her he can assure her of a singing job at the Tropicana in Cuba, she responds that she does not want to be a bolero singer nor rot in a two-bit cabaret. She wants to be a star and if she goes anywhere it will be to "Jolibud" (136). Even though she almost certainly will never become a star and make it to "Jolibud," Vanessa is all but sure to continue being a product of that factory of celluloid images. By manufacturing (along with the record and television industries) these role models or objects of desire, the movies have also transformed Vanessa and other women into objects; as these modes of discourse authorize icons, they deauthorize being.

Although virtually devoid of Bella's worldly experience and Vanessa's romantic ambitions, Antonia is another product of popular culture's definition of male/female relationships. Bella has to qualify as the heroine of the novel since she alone rebels against the domineering masculine order, but Antonia is both the most interesting and the most pathetic character. Her pathos begins with the similarity between her name and her brother's. Although Antonio is the male and the firstborn, the arrival of Antonia makes the parents question whether their children's respective gender coding has somehow become reversed. Whereas Antonia has a heavy build, Antonio is sickly and frail. The parents, fearing that the boy would not survive and

---

is no textual evidence to indicate that she consciously used his homosexuality and tragic death to underscore the gulf between movie fantasy and real life.

in their obsession with perpetuating the patriarch's name, also baptized the baby girl with it. In short, from birth Antonia was designated to serve the patriarchal order.

She not only accepts her subservient role but she revels in it as well. Indeed, when, as frequently happens, Antonio does not show up at her home to be fed and clothed and does not even bother to call to inform her he is not coming, she feels cheated: "With her brother at home Antonia felt necessary" (15). By failing to appear Antonio does not even allow her to fulfill the role for which she has been bred and which is therefore her only reason for being.

Even her erotic life is defined by the codes imposed on her by patriarchal society. When masturbating she is forced to fantasize that she is being raped, for even imaginary consensual sex would constitute too much of a transgression. And before engaging in even this fantasy, "she turned facing the wall the picture of her brother, Antonio, who ferociously gazed at her from the bedside table" (22).

Finally her fantasy sessions appear to lead to reality, for when she realizes that Damián is spying on her she begins to stage her masturbations for him. Then one day he appears at Antonia's door to collect the utility payments, and after Damián accepts her invitation for a cup of coffee they end up in an awkward and humorous embrace: "ya está, se decía Antonia, ya está, me están besando como besan en las películas, me están besando a mí, me están besando" (now it's happening, Antonia was saying to herself, now it's happening, I am being kissed like they kiss in the movies, I am being kissed, I am being kissed, 119). Even in this key moment of her first kiss, Antonia's feelings and emotions are not her own but rather are those dictated by discursive practices perpetuated by popular culture. The impersonal or passive expression "I am being kissed" underscores the role-playing in which she is involved. Having escaped temporarily from the discursive script written by the church and the patriarchal order, she finds herself cast in a role authored by popular culture. At the same time, these discursive practices have deauthorized her being, along with those of Bella, Vanessa, and, by implication, all other women. In other words, all can be considered mere objects created by a male discursive order.

But whereas Antonio is part of the masculine order that appears to control the discourse, he is also subject to rather than the subject of its practices. In a modern version of Don Juan, Antonio keeps files on the pilots of international flights, and when one is scheduled to be out of town he calls upon the aviator's wife, with the pretext that he is an old friend of her husband's who just happens to be in town. Having gained entry into the home, he relies on his charm to seduce his usually willing victim. But these imitative seductions are not enough; he feels the need to textualize his amorous exploits. One way of doing so is to narrate to his friend Inspector García just how he seduced each woman, with the result that "in a sense it was like possessing them again" (100). But oral narration is not enough either. Apparently only by summarizing his exploits on note cards, by transforming them into a written text, does he feel any real sense of satisfaction. In effect, the physical seductions represent a preliminary step in gathering the material for his writing project. Antonio is caught up in a vicious circle of discourse. He too follows a role written for him and in turn depends on that role to dictate what he writes; he is a deauthorized author. Although the male order appoints him as master of women, he is a slave to that same order.

Underscoring the oxymoron of men as enslaved masters is a framing structure composed of magazine excerpts and journalistic testimony. The novel begins with a passage from an article titled "El extraño caso de la asesina fumadora" (The strange case of the smoking assassin), which appears in the fictitious magazine *El Criminal.* The author of the article, Paco Mancebo (the last name, which means "young stud," is a blatant play on words), writes of the strange and savage attack by a woman on one Don Antonio Ortiz who, according to the information gathered by Mancebo, "looked like a priest or something similar" and was about to marry "a beautiful and honorable young woman" (9), referring, of course, to Vanessa. Citing an eyewitness, the reporter relates how the "the mannish woman [Bella], without any moral principles and capable of all types of fury," entered Antonio's home, threw him to the floor, and, as if that were not enough, "the homicidal beast leveled everything" (10). Then, after pouring numerous bottles of perfume over the man, she blew the smoke of a whole pack of cigarettes into his face. When Antonio managed to free himself from the smoking assassin and tried to run out the door, she grabbed him, and "without further warning, the cold-blooded amazon carried him to the window and threw the hapless fellow to the street from the fourth floor" (11). In addition to conveying the false impression that Bella actually killed Antonio, this is a classic example of yellow journalism, indicating that not only is the author a misogynist but so is his posited reader. In essence, the narrated story serves to deauthorize this "male stud" version of the incident.

The issue of male discursive authority is paramount in the four testimonies interspersed among the chapters. These are interviews, which means that in each case the witness addresses himself directly to Paco Mancebo. The first such testimony is given by Vicente Menéndez, the owner of the Desiré and Poco's son. As noted earlier, he spends most of his time reading pornographic novels and depends on Bella not only to attend to the customers but also to manage the club. But in his testimony to Mancebo, Menéndez declares: "I was always suspicious of her, I can tell you for sure" (93). After confessing that she has worked for him since the day he purchased the club, Menéndez adds:

> Nunca me gustó la acusada, nunca me gustó, que lo grabe bien este cacharro, porque es verdad. Nunca me gustó, y no lo digo hoy porque ella esté con las manos manchadas de sangre. No señor, no. Nunca me gustó. Manteníamos una simple relación profesional. Bella era una mujer . . . grosera. Esa es la palabra. Poco educada. Muy . . . respondona. Una verdulera. Y además un poco fresca, usted ya me entiende.

> (I never liked the accused, never liked her, your machine can record that, because it's true. I never liked her, and I am not saying it just because she has bloodied her hands. No sir, no. I never liked her. We maintained a simple professional relationship. Bella was a woman who was . . . crude. That's the word. Not very well mannered. Very . . . mouthy. Common. And a little uppity besides, you know what I mean.) (94)

His final words, "you know what I mean," are very significant, for they underscore that this is man-to-man talk. Menéndez discredits Bella by listing her nonfeminine aspects, all of which are qualities that men have deemed inappropriate for women: "crude, not very well-mannered, mouthy, common, uppity." Naturally Mancebo will understand what he means, as would any man (and for that matter as would any "proper" woman), for he is relying on firmly institutionalized gender codes. He resorts to these same codes to explain Bella's masculinelike attack on Antonio: "I don't know, but it seems to me that if she did what she did it had to be a question of . . . sex, you must know what I mean. . . . Because of jealousy, she did it out of jealousy, I am sure" (95). As the repetition of the conspiratorial "you must know what I mean" indicates, any man will understand that the explanation for Bella's unfeminine violence has to be jealousy; only love or sexual desire for a man could explain such behavior in a woman. Again, the framed text serves to deauthorize in an unequivocal manner this "framing" testimony.

The second interviewee, Antonio's subservient assistant, Benigno Martí Garriga, presents another dimension of gender coding. Benigno (Benign, another blatantly symbolic name) heaps false praise on his boss, while expressing his resentment that Antonio never allowed him to court Antonia. In effect, Benigno's testimony has almost nothing to do with Bella and the attack. He characterizes himself as an example of a helpless and meek male who wants, and deserves, a woman to take care of him in his dotage. Antonia could have played that role, but now she has disappeared, and as he says, "Now I have nothing, young man, do you understand?" (203). He also depends on his male audience to comprehend what is left unsaid. Antonio, though engaged to Vanessa, insisted on also keeping Antonia to look after his practical needs, which apparently was his motive for running off Damián. This type of commodity hoarding, Benigno intimates, undermines the smooth operation of a male economy. Benigno believes that he has been bankrupted by Antonio's abuse of an economy designed to provide an equitable distribution of the feminine resources to all its masculine clientele.

The final testimony is appropriately by Antonio,[44] but coming as it does almost at the end of the novel, what he says has already been discredited by the framed story itself. His statements represent, therefore, a culmination of the textual process of deauthorizing male discourse, of converting men into the objects of the very discourse they parrot.

Naturally Antonio paints himself as an innocent victim and echoes Mendéndez's reasoning by claiming that Bella acted out of jealousy when she learned that he was going to marry Vanessa. He then adds sententiously, "Women are like that, very possessive, irrational" (238). Thereafter he laments that, because of the plastic surgery to repair his face, he has lost all sense of smell: "It's a mutilation, do you understand? It's a castration. . . . My

---

44. As Glenn, "Victimized by Misreading," points out: "Bella is mentioned only briefly in the novel's concluding chapter. Thus she is in effect 'framed' by two patriarchal texts, Mancebo's and Antonio's . . ." (196). I take the liberty of only slightly modifying this very clever conceit. As far as the structure of the novel, and the legal system, is concerned, certainly she is "framed." But as far as the reader is concerned, this attempt at false incrimination fails miserably. By the time the reader reaches this point, Antonio and Mancebo have lost all credibility, and therefore end up "framing" themselves.

sense of smell was my gift, my art, my reason for being, my life. . . . Without my nose I am nothing, I'm a nobody" (239). Now the "do you understand?" has lost its connotation of gender bonding. When that question was posited by the previous interviewees it was a rhetorical device presupposing that they were drawing on institutionalized male codes to ensure the interviewer's understanding. It was a question of intergender rather than interpersonal communication. Now Antonio is appealing for a very different level of understanding, because by equating the loss of his olfactory nerves with his sex organ Antonio unwittingly provides a humorous challenge to the male myth of virility. Furthermore, the joke is not only on him but also on Paco Mancebo—which of course means on men in general. In effect, Antonio admits that his real sense of manhood—feelings of satisfaction as well as of social power—is centered in his olfactory nerves rather than his testes. Thus we have both a framed text deauthorizing Paco Mancebo's and Antonio's framing textual version of and motive for the attack by Bella and a framing text that deauthorizes the master text equating power and superiority with male genitalia.

Te trataré como a una reina can be seen as another step away from Spanish fiction's obsession with undermining the authority of Francoist discourse well after the regime has ended. Even more than Ortiz, Montero shifts the focus from political to patriarchal hierarchies. Particularly after the failed 1981 coup, not only fascism and Franco but also their most vocal opponents began to recede into the past—perhaps more dispersed than forgotten. With the fading of these political antagonists, the Spanish authors studied here became increasingly aware that discursive systems rather than individuals create power hierarchies. The move away from centric reasoning represents one of the key common denominators for the Spanish fiction written between 1980 and 1984 that has been analyzed up to this point. That decentralizing trend in fiction occurred at a time when international politics shifted from bi- to multipolarities and ethnic as opposed to nationalistic identities, and the scientific/mathematical community turned its attention from absolute and undeviating laws to the search for patterns within randomness.

In the novels examined in this chapter, the focus switched from totalitarianism as an institution to some of the underlying elements such as power hierarchies and gender attitudes from which political absolutism draws its life force. Martín-Santos alerted us as early as 1962 to polarization and patriarchy as two fundamental cornerstones for the modern dictator state, yet it took nearly twenty years after *Tiempo de silencio,* and from five to eight years after the end of the Franco regime, before Luis Goytisolo, José María Guelbenzu, Lourdes Ortiz, and Rosa Montero managed to concentrate their individual novelistic efforts on representing the underpinnings as opposed to the edifice of totalitarianism. In so doing, they pointed to new or different discursive directions for Spanish fiction in the future. In the next chapter I will examine in detail some of these discursive variants that emerged after 1985.

5

The Years 1985–1989

AS DISCUSSED IN Chapter 1, the political upheavals of 1989 within the Soviet Union and the Warsaw Pact member countries overshadowed all other events of the last half of the 1980s. When the breakup occurred, many officials, scholars, and most of the public were caught off guard. Even the disarmament discussions between Reagan and Gorbachev at Reykjavík in October 1986 failed to effect significant changes in the long-standing official Washington position that the United States should dismiss as propaganda all the statements and actions coming out of Moscow. Yet in view of the centrifugal shift in the episteme that has been examined in the fields of science, philosophy, politics, and fiction, one has to express some amazement that by the late 1980s very few Western political observers dared to predict fundamental changes in international alignments. The reluctance to do so is demonstrated in a summer 1989 issue of *International Affairs*. An Oxford professor emeritus of government and public administration wrote a rejoinder to an article in the same issue by a fellow Oxford historian who dared to argue that basic policy shifts were underway in the Soviet Union and that the West should begin considering arms reductions. The emeritus professor all but ridiculed his colleague for being so naive as to believe that meaningful changes within the Eastern bloc were imminent (presumably the rejoinder was written in late 1988 or very early 1989).[1] So it seems that it was not just government officials who preached status quo. Many political scientists also refused to recognize an interconnectedness between international affairs and developments in the scientific, philosophical, and artistic fields.

1. Max Beloff, "1989, A Farewell to Arms?: A Rejoinder," and Michael Howard, "1989: A Farewell to Arms?" respectively.

Meanwhile in the United States, Reagan continued with his domestic policies of shifting more of the tax burden to the individual states in the name of decentralizing the federal government. He also continued his international policy of avoiding any long-term military commitments. The Reagan administration in the case of Nicaragua found itself restrained by an increasing isolationist mood in both Congress and the private sector and as a result limited itself to providing only clandestine aid to the Contras fighting against Ortega and his Sandinista forces. Where the government did exercise force, it struck quickly and declared immediate victory. That formula, first applied to Grenada in October 1983, was repeated in April 1986 with the U.S. air strikes against Libya (Bush applied the same basic formula in the Persian Gulf War against Iraq, though in that case he included ground forces as well). The year 1988 marked the beginning of the Bush administration, with no major deviation from an official domestic policy of less central government control and a foreign policy dedicated to maintaining the status quo by means of periodic and strategically selected demonstrations of military superiority. But when the Soviet bloc disintegrated shortly after the new administration took office, Bush quickly tried to take credit. The elections of 1992 suggested that in this case the strategy had failed. Although most observers believe that economic concerns played the greatest role in the election outcome, that factor might have been neutralized by international successes if the Reagan and Bush administrations had not undermined their credibility by denying, right up to the time of the breakup, that any significant changes were taking place within the Eastern bloc. They had maneuvered themselves into the awkward position of trying to take credit for events after disavowing that those events were even in process. In this sense, the Republicans, ideological advocates of decentralization, were victimized by a decentralizing force that they refused to acknowledge.

Decentralizing forces also appeared within Spain as the decade of the 1990s approached. In addition to the Basques, Catalonians, and Galicians, even the Andalusians and Leónians began to demand autonomy. The Socialists continued to hold political power, but scandals of corruption (most notably in the case of Alfonso Guerra) and an unemployment rate hovering around 20 percent undermined the confidence in and the stability of the government. Yet counteracting these negative factors was a continuing economic boom as foreign investors rushed to beat the 1992 law effectively stemming the flow of non-European capital into the peninsula. Also, the

Madrid sociocultural phenomenon labeled the *movida,* which manifested itself as an uninterrupted party lasting nearly five years and culminating in the years 1985 and 1986, may well have been related to the new economic prosperity and to Spain's admittance into the European Community. Paradoxically, decentralizing sentiments fueled the movement to join that multinational body.

On January 1, 1986, Spain officially entered the European Community.[2] For days preceding that event, Spaniards were saying with bitter irony, "Finally we are Europeans." Of course that remark was partially in response to an historical northern European attitude that Spain is an African rather than a European country. But perhaps the remark also expressed a deep cynicism affecting liberals as well as conservatives. If on the one hand the liberals saw this centrifugal process as an opportunity to create a new, long-overdue value system, they could not ignore the paradox that they were advocating national decentralization at the same time that they were sponsoring membership in a centralized international organization. For their part, the conservatives felt disenfranchised as they witnessed Spain reaching so far outward to be accepted in the European Community that it surrendered a great deal of its national identity and values in addition to much of its economic autonomy. As the end of the millennium approaches, this centrifugal/centripetal polarization may well serve as the next battleground in the historical conflict between "the two Spains." But above all the years 1985 to 1989 were witness to Spain emerging as an authentic post-totalitarian society committed to programs of depolarization, decentralization, and deauthorization.

As the focus shifts to a new or different and, as far as the parameters of this study are concerned, final phase of Spanish fiction, again the literary text expresses the same basic forces influencing Spanish society in particular and Western society in general. As opposed to the novels of the earlier

---

2. Almost from the time the socialists were elected, Spain began jockeying for a leadership position in the international arena. For example, Fernando Morán, González's first minister of Foreign Affairs, argued that since the country enjoyed a special relationship in Latin America, Spain should enhance its standing in Europe by playing a leading role in Central and South America, even if that role conflicted with the United States' interests. Morán, however, overplayed his hand in criticizing American policy in Nicaragua, and González felt obliged to replace him in 1985. See Jean Grugel, "Spain's Socialist Government and Central American Dilemmas."

groups, the emphasis of the fiction I will now analyze falls more directly on the question of gender rather than national identity. Characters see themselves as the products of global discursive practices rather than official Francoist apparatuses. Not only do all texts respond to previous texts but quite often concepts of the self respond to how canonized texts define the self as well, which also raises the issue of canon authorization. Rather than the panopticon functioning as a collective instrument to discipline society, individuals act as agents and objects of a panoptic machine, a machine that now seems to have no relationship to the concept of a commonwealth. To demonstrate how these and other manifestations of the post-totalitarian era find expression in Spanish fiction, I have selected for analysis the following titles: Cristina Fernández Cubas's *El año de Gracia* (The year of Grace), Ignacio Martínez de Pisón's *Alguien te observa en secreto* (Someone is secretly observing you), and Esther Tusquets's *Para no volver* (Never to return), all three of which were published in 1985, Carmen Riera's *Cuestión de amor propio* (A question of self-love), Antonio Muñóz Molina's *El invierno en Lisboa* (Winter in Lisbon), and Javier Marías's *Todas las almas*, the last three of which were published in 1988, 1987, and 1989 respectively.[3]

Disempowerment and Knowledge: *El año de Gracia*

Some will find Cristina Fernández Cubas a surprising choice to head this final chapter. Although her novel *El año de Gracia* (The year of Grace) has not received a great deal of critical attention, I believe that among the works of fiction examined here, it most effectively addresses the issue of knowledge and its relation to human behavior and gender identity.[4] In my attempt to

3. The years 1985–1989 were unusually prolific for Spanish fiction, and the discursive aspects mentioned plus others are also effectively expressed in the following: *La orilla oscura*, by José María Merino, 1985; *Ciertos tonos del negro*, by Beatriz Pottecher, 1985; *El silencio de las sirenas*, by Adelaida García Morales, 1985; *Historia de un idiota contada por él mismo*, by Félix de Azúa, 1986; *Burdeos*, by Soledad Puértolas, 1986; *La voz melodiosa*, by Montserrat Roig, 1987; *La lluvia amarilla*, by Julio Llamazares, 1988; *Uno se vuelve loco*, by Daniel Múgica, 1989; *Morir en sus brazos y otros cuentos*, by Marina Mayoral, 1989; *Juegos de la edad tardía*, by Luis Landero, 1989; and *Obabakoak*, by Bernardo Atxaga, 1989.
4. Cristina Fernández Cubas, born in 1945, is the second oldest of this final group. Esther Tusquets heads the list (born in 1936), and following Fernández Cubas is Carmen Riera (1949), Javier Marías (1951), Antonio Muñoz Molina (1956), and Ignacio Martínez de Pisón (1960). Fernández Cubas has published one other novel to date, *El columpio*, in

help define the current episteme, I have become convinced that the issue of how people learn to think, reason, and act provides one of the keys. In her novel, Fernández Cubas explores the network linking knowledge, education, syllogistic logic, and canonized works to gender attitudes and behavior.

El año de Gracia is similar to Juan sin Tierra in terms of its radical challenge to our Western system of values. Yet there are fundamental differences as to how the respective novels defy cultural practices. Juan Goytisolo's rebellion consists primarily of redefining the subject matter of a novel. He transforms the récit into the histoire by making the novel's own coming-into-being the story of Juan sin Tierra. Cristina Fernández Cubas, on the other hand, writes stories about people and events that, on the surface, seem to be basically conventional and accessible to almost any reader. Yet in spite of its apparent simplicity, her fiction is, if not more subversive, certainly more subtle than Goytisolo's. His efforts are directed primarily to expanding the limits of novelistic form, while hers are to disempower canonical, technological, linguistic, and syllogistic authority. To that end, Fernández Cubas has created in El año de Gracia a story of cultural and intellectual regression in which intuition is privileged over erudition, imagination over representation, accommodation over domination, human communication over rhetorical ostentation, and finally ontology over epistemology.[5]

The anecdote is narrated in the first person by the protagonist, Daniel. He relates that he was a young seminary student specializing in ancient languages when his father died, at which time Daniel decided to abandon

---

1995. She is known primarily for her collections of stories: Mi hermana Elba, 1980; Los altillos de Brumal, 1983; El ángulo del horror, 1990; and Con Agatha en Estambul, 1994.

5. The majority of criticism on Fernández Cubas's fiction has focused on fantastic elements: Kathleen M. Glenn, "Gothic Indecipherability and Doubling in the Fiction of Fernández Cubas" and "Authority and Marginality"; Phyllis Zatlin, "Tales from Fernández Cubas: Adventure in the Fantastic"; Lynne K. Talbot, "Journey into the Fantastic: Cristina Fernández Cubas's Los altillos de Brumal"; Ana Rueda, "Cristina Fernández Cubas: Una narrativa de voces extinguidas"; José Ortega, "La dimensión fantástica en los cuentos de Fernández Cubas"; Suñén, "La realidad y sus sombras"; and Mary Lee Bretz, "Cristina Fernández Cubas and the Recuperation of the Semiotic in Los altillos de Brumal." In my "El concepto del antisilogismo en la novelística del posfranquismo," I explore some of the antisyllogistic implications of El año de Gracia and Alguien te observa en secreto. Focusing more on this novel are the essays of Catherine G. Bellver, "El año de Gracia and the Displacement of the Word"; Julie Gleue, "The Epistemological and Ontological Implications in Cristina Fernández Cubas' El año de Gracia"; and John B. Margenot III, "Parody and Self-Consciousness in Cristina Fernández Cubas' El año de Gracia."

a monastic life for a secular one. To enable him to explore and determine his role in the world he is about to enter, his sister Gracia offers to pay his expenses for a year, to give him a "year of (G)race." He accepts her offer and goes to Paris where, despite a love affair with a beautiful and successful photographer, he decides to sign on as a crew member for a sailing vessel headed for Glasgow. The ship wrecks during a storm, and Daniel is swept ashore on the beach of what appears to be an uninhabited island. A year later, and near the conclusion of the novel, he learns that it is English territory chosen in 1941 for biological experimentation. But it turns out that the island is not uninhabited; in addition to flocks of sheep, a shepherd named Grock lives there. When the scientists learn of Daniel's presence, they send a crew to eliminate him, but, misled by the jackets that Daniel and Grock have exchanged, the agents unwittingly kill the shepherd. Finally some ecologists rescue Daniel and return him to civilization. In an appendix we are told that he meets an Englishwoman named Gruda, they marry and move to Barcelona, and his sister Gracia informs him by letter that she does not want to hear from him again.

The novel is divided into three parts plus the appendix, and part 1 concerns Daniel's departure from the seminary, the brief time he spends with his sister, his days in Paris, and his apprenticeship on the sailing vessel before it wrecks. Although his decision to abandon a monastic life of erudition is precipitated by the death of his father, there is the suggestion of another markedly antirational force influencing him: "The morning, finally, of the 7th of June 1980, I took my leave of the seminary with the same vehemence with which seven years earlier, I left this century."[6] To his sister's offer, he responds, "A year of sabbatical leave?" (24). When the scientists discover his presence on the island, a helicopter appears, and as it hovers over him he is told by megaphone that a boat will be sent "Exactly in seven days" (153). Later, when the ecologists arrive to rescue him from the island, he asks the date, "inspired by something more than simple curiosity. They answered in unison: The seventh of June 1981" (173). The emphasis on the number seven, with its connotation both of games of chance and of theosophy, may signal the first significant conflict between Daniel's heretofore sheltered world of syllogistic logic and Church dogma

---

6. Cristina Fernández Cubas, *El año de Gracia*, 15. Subsequent citations will indicate the page number in parentheses.

and the real world he is about to enter of irrational happenstance and religious unorthodoxy.[7]

In his initial encounter with this new world he must deal with his sister Gracia. After seven years in an exclusively male community, he feels unprepared, even intimidated, by her presence. In fact, he recalls that when Gracia visited him for the first time at the monastery, he asked her not to return:

> En realidad me avergonzaba de ella, del rabioso carmín de sus labios, de la insistencia por aparecer vestida con los modelos más llamativos y excéntricos, de la estela de perfume penetrante que, horas después de su partida, serpenteaba aún por galerías, corredores y claustros.

> (In truth she embarrassed me, with the rabid red of her lips, the insistence on appearing dressed in the most provocative and eccentric styles, the trail of penetrating perfume that, hours after her departure, slithered still through the galleries, hallways and cloisters.) (18)

The narration of this incident serves as a subversion of biblical discourse. "Woman," in the Bible as well as in Daniel's monastic world, represents temptation and sin ("trail of penetrating perfume . . . that slithered"). As Daniel and his monastery colleagues struggle with the scent of Gracia's cosmetics, the text comically echoes Eve leading Adam astray with its catastrophic results for **man**kind. In fact, this passage underscores the pretensions inherent in creating a community from which women are exiled so as not to profane the life of erudition for which men consider themselves so uniquely equipped. (Implicitly juxtaposed to this male domain, of course, is the convent where the novices serve their apprenticeship learning primarily domestic skills.) But Gracia's sensorial presence does not vanish with her physical absence. The thick walls and jail-like cells designed to protect rather than incarcerate the pious monks cannot prevent the infiltration of female reality. Daniel's "firm resolve to live in the world" (19) implies, whether he is conscious of it or not, a commitment to accept the reality of man's other: woman. Since Gracia recognizes that he obviously is not prepared to deal with this fact of life, she grants him a year to make the adjustment.

---

7. The number seven is particularly significant in theosophy. See Virginia Milner Garlitz, "Teosofismo en *Tirano Banderas*," on this unorthodox religious theory and its reliance on numerals vis-à-vis Valle-Inclán's novel.

Paris is his first stop. Soon he discovers a café where students gather, and, to gain stature among them, he ostentatiously reads books in Greek and Latin and one day strategically "forgets" and leaves on a table a copy of Ovid's *Metamorphoses*, in Latin of course. Since, as he smugly states it, "My calling card was left on the table" (27), he soon enjoys the reputation among the students of a true intellectual. In short order he is the center of attention of an admiring group. Included in this group is Yasmine; she and Daniel soon become lovers.

Of Yasmine, Daniel narrates: "I owe to Yasmine almost as much as I do to Gracia, and perhaps for that reason, I played the role with her of a vain and ungrateful disciple" (27). At the root of his vexation in both cases seems to be each woman's departure from what Daniel had been taught in books as well as in his premonastery life was the appropriate female image. Both women are assertive, and Yasmine, for her part, is a successful photographer who has learned the rudiments to communicate in six or seven languages—Daniel, as we remember, has a scholarly command of two dead languages. Even though he rationalizes Yasmine's generosity as the homage due him, he feels increasingly ill at ease in their relationship.[8] Above all, the frequent separations necessitated by her professional trips begin to weigh on him: "I was living her life, Yasmine's life, in a very similar manner to how, months earlier, my sister Gracia appropriated mine. Yasmine and Gracia . . . Who were they really?" (29). Apparently without realizing it he is employing a discourse typical of the neglected and suspicious housewife whose husband is constantly absent. Since reentering the world he has had to deal with two women, and both fail to conform to expected norms. As a result, he concludes that they are involved in some kind of subversive partnership: "Our encounter in the café had not been by chance nor my display of rare abilities as effective as I ingenuously had believed. Yasmine and Gracia knew one another, they were friends or even worse, they were in cahoots" (29). In a sense—but not in the one he suggests—they are in

---

8. Obviously this is a gender role reversal with the man receiving a woman's munificence. As Toril Moi, *Sexual/Textual Politics: Feminist Literary Theory,* explains in her summary of Cixous's feminist theory: "In the Realm of the Proper, the gift is perceived as establishing an inequality—a difference—that is threatening in that it seems to open up an imbalance of **power**. Thus the act of giving becomes a subtle means of aggression, of exposing the other to the threat of one's own superiority. The woman, however, gives without a thought of return" (112). In spite of the sweeping generalization of the last sentence, Moi's summary of Cixous's thesis on gifts can be applied to the novel at hand.

collusion: Both reject the conventional role discursive practice has assigned to them.

Shortly thereafter Daniel and Yasmine go to the port of Saint-Malo, where the sight of sailing vessels triggers in Daniel historical and literary images of high-seas heroes and villains. The characters conjured forth—Morgan, León de Damasco, John Silver, Nemo, Gordon Pynn—are drawn from historical as well as fictitious canonical works for young boys.[9] As if by magic, Daniel imagines that his boyhood cultural orientation has come to life.

His fantasies seem to be even more real when next he sees what has to be a prototypical pirate ship, with the bearded captain in the process of painting the name *Providence* on its bow. This seasoned sailor, Tío Jean, seems so familiar that he immediately inspires Daniel's confidence. As a result, the former seminarian volunteers to help with the sailing preparations. Even though he admits in retrospect that the captain's exaggerated happiness on accepting his offer to help "would have made the most imprudent person in the world take stock" (32), Daniel momentarily is so overpowered at witnessing his literary readings transformed into reality that he signs on as a crew member for a voyage to Glasgow:

> Deseaba vivir, atender las llamadas que me lanzaba el mundo, recuperar a velocidad vertiginosa mis siete años de apacible retiro. Había llegado la hora de abandonar la vida de caricias y algodones, de hermanas y protectoras, y de hacerme a la mar.

> (I wanted to live, to listen to the calls that the world was sending me, to recuperate at a vertiginous speed the seven years of peaceful retirement. The time had come to abandon the life of caresses and softness, of sisters and protectresses, and set sail.) (32)

In his mind the verb *to live* is gender coded. To his way of thinking, this is a call to a life of masculine adventures, which will provide an escape from the feminine world to which he has been subjected. Since he found himself in a subservient position to both Gracia and Yasmine, he feels desperate to find an alternative to "the life of caresses and softness, of sisters and protectresses." The text suggests that rather than witnessing his literary readings being transformed into reality, he is guilty of interpreting the reality he sees by means of the fiction he read: "It was as if my true *Year of Grace*

---

9. See Margenot, "Parody and Self-Consciousness," for an identification of the sources for these references and his analysis of what he considers their parodic function (75–76).

began in that very instant and, with all my childhood dreams as guide, I set out to undergo what seemed to me like the first episode of a great adventure" (33). Clearly this voyage represents an opportunity for him to aspire to the masculine stereotypes his culture has defined.

His first days at sea seem to fulfill the visual images he had formed in his mind from his readings: "Uncle Jean struck me as a fictional character, an old sea wolf who did not have to pronounce a word to convince me that his life had been haphazard and adventurous, a person bursting with humanity and wisdom" (35). Because everything conforms visually to literary models, the young hero does not even need the captain's verbal confirmation of the biography Daniel attributes to him. And although initially he senses that Tío Jean secretly laughs at his lack of seamanship, Daniel is confident that his "argucias" (intelligence) and "ostentación de conocimientos" (ostentatious erudition, 31) will allow him not only to survive but also to operate on an equal level with the captain.

Another literary stereotype appears in the person of the only other crew member, a silent and hostile Egyptian named Naguib. This man expresses open resentment toward Daniel. Turning to his deductive powers of reason, Daniel analyzes the situation: "It was obvious that Uncle Jean had not invited me aboard because of my possible seamanship, but rather because of my simple and pleasant company. It was also evident that as far as Naguib was concerned, since conversation irritated him, I was only a hindrance or an obstacle to his placid life" (39). Drawing on literary models from his boyhood adventure novels to categorize the two men, Daniel is confident that already he has surpassed Naguib in the eyes of the captain thanks to the social and intellectual skills honed in the monastery. Perhaps because of his seven years of isolation as a monk, Daniel has only these literary models to help him interpret the world around him, and unfortunately the sources for those models are excessively gender coded. As a result of the sex bias in both his formal and informal education, he lacks a sense of balance as he tries to make the transition from monastic to secular life, from childhood fantasy to adulthood reality.

The atmosphere on board changes rapidly beginning the day Daniel overhears the captain and the Egyptian in a heated argument over whether they should go to Cardiff, the Egyptian's choice, or Glasgow. Finally Naguib acquiesces but in doing so asserts: "But I will not tolerate any delay" (41). The two men quit talking as soon as they become aware of Daniel's presence.

While repairing a broken door he analyzes what he has heard and seen, and, to hide his concern and perhaps in a vain attempt to reassert his academic superiority, he sings a few verses in Latin.[10] The singing allows him to draw on his training in deductive reasoning to conclude that the two had argued about something they did not want him to hear, that he, Daniel, represents the obstacle to which Naguib referred, that the Egyptian is not merely the subordinate sea hand he appears to be, and finally, "It was obvious that Uncle Jean was faking something in front of me" (43). Suddenly Daniel finds himself in a new fictional plot, one in which his role seems to have changed from hero to potential victim.

With the change of plot Daniel loses his point of textual reference and finds himself forced to decipher a new set of hermeneutic codes. Initially he is certain that the captain is his insurance against the threat represented by the Egyptian, but before long he concludes that the two are partners in a plot to kidnap him, only to decide finally that the captain has some sinister plan aimed at eliminating both Naguib and Daniel. Despite drawing on all his acquired cultural readings and powers of deductive reasoning, he cannot recognize the script or the logic of the plot.[11] Every time he reaches a conclusion, his analysis is contradicted by subsequent events. The tension culminates one night during a storm when the captain and the mate are

10. The words to the first verse are significant:

> In taberna quando sumus
> non curamus quid sit humus
> sed ad ludum properamus . . . (44)

Whereas Latin connotes religion, dedication to scholarly pursuits, and logic, this song refers to our irrational side, our tendency to throw caution to the wind in search of drink, diversions, and good times. The song proves prophetic when Daniel, the supposed prophet, becomes blind drunk at the crucial moment of his voyage on the *Providence*. Also, Daniel sings the song twice more on the island, the first time repeating only the first two lines (80) and the second time merely mentioning the title, "In taberna" (145). This reduction can be considered a sign of the process he is undergoing in which academic knowledge leads to disempowerment rather than empowerment. Interestingly, in Luis Landero's *Juegos de la edad tardía* the protagonist's father undergoes a more radical but yet similar process of sentence reduction. For an illuminating analysis of the role of discourse in this novel, see José García, "*Juegos de la edad tardía*, apoteosis del discurso literario."

11. According to Peter Brooks, *Reading for the Plot: Design and Intention in Narrative*, the novelist depends on plot for the foundational logic of his or her text. It reflects "something in the nature of the logic of narrative discourse, the organizing dynamic of a specific mode of human understanding" (7).

below deck. Daniel hears them arguing, there is a scream, and then the captain appears to announce that there has been a terrible accident. Daniel goes below deck, sees no sign of Naguib, and assumes that the captain has murdered him; then the frightened Daniel, at a time when he obviously needs to be in total control of his mental faculties, irrationally drinks himself into a stupor. He awakens as the ship is breaking apart. He is then swept ashore on the beach as apparently the sole survivor.

The series of incidents on ship make a mockery of Daniel's classical education and childhood cultural orientation. An expert on ancient dead languages, he is forced to create a dictionary with drawings to illustrate the new vocabulary he must learn just to perform basic duties on the ship. Also, his once resourceful use of erudition to gain social prominence fails him miserably, just as his training in logic and deductive reasoning cannot explain what is going on between the captain and the mate. And of course his attempt to follow the script of his childhood adventure readings has led him smack into the middle of a quintessential horror story, but one that he cannot remember from the canon. Once on the island where he discovers that everything works in reverse, he finds himself even more disempowered by his erudite and gender-coded education.

The island is enveloped in a fog so thick that he has to depend on his sense of smell rather than sight to move about, but even this switch of sensory perception works in a contrary fashion. For example, when explaining how he depended on the smell of the sea to find his way back to a makeshift hut on the beach after trying to explore the island, he clarifies, "I did not orient myself by means of smell, but rather by the opposite: its absence" (73). His next discovery is a barbed wire fence surrounding the beach, which leads him to a seemingly logical conclusion: "The barbed wire fence confirmed the proximity of some municipality, the interest of the Administration for the health of its citizens, the precaution taken to prevent that some passerby in this remote area, like me, find himself face to face with a traitorous and deadly sea" (80). Notwithstanding his interpretation of the fence as a reassuring demonstration of the nearby existence of a disciplinary society, whose rules, he assumes, reflect its concern for the well-being of its citizens, he cannot help recognizing that there is another way to read the fence: "Unless it is just the opposite . . ." (80). This new world with its reverse order of things all but forces him to recognize antisyllogistic logic[12] and that the disciplinary motives of a society may not be benevolent: "Because I found myself again contemplating the fence and its barbs now seemed to me to be the bars of an immense box into which I had been imprisoned" (80).

The contradictions continue when he observes that the island has flocks of sheep, but, contrary to the norm, these animals are ferocious and carnivorous. One day Daniel finds a ewe trapped among the rocks, her frightened lamb by her side. But rather than being moved by compassion, he captures the mother, and then makes a bloody sacrifice of her lamb. His barbarity is subsequently matched, or perhaps imitated, by other sheep who resemble lions as they devour a ram that had just been downed in combat by a rival.[13] From the modern world of power based on canonized knowledge, sophistic reasoning, and panoptic discipline, Daniel finds himself suddenly cast into an ancient world where power accrues to those who possess physical strength, are willing to make blood sacrifices, and impose uncompromising justice. It is within this context that he has his first encounter with the other human inhabitant of the island, the shepherd, Grock.[14]

12. Handelman, *Slayers of Moses,* presents an interesting if controversial thesis that begins with the accepted notion that the syllogism forms the basis of Western logic since Aristotle. But, she argues, with the emergence of poststructuralist thought there is an effort to redefine the model and reverse the relationships. According to her, the foundation of this new, antisyllogistic paradigm is rabbinic, and the emphasis is on "an infinity of meaning and plurality of interpretation" (21). From our traditional Aristotelian point of view, the new system would have to be labeled "irrational." According to Handelman's thesis, that is an arbitrary label inherited from the Greeks, and she would argue (along with many others) that syllogistic logic is no more rational than antisyllogistic logic; they are merely two different approaches to reality, one traditional and the other what many now label "postmodern."

13. The battle in which the ram was defeated echoes the Book of Daniel and the prophet's dream. In the biblical story, Daniel the Prophet is unable to interpret the meaning of the combat between the rams. In Fernández Cubas's version, the protagonist does not dwell on interpretations; he merely returns to the shackled ewe and kills her, much as he callously sacrificed her lamb. His cruelty and lack of meditation seem to serve as another subversion of biblical discourse and the consensus interpretation of its message as one of benevolence and reason.

14. With questionable textual evidence to back his thesis, Margenot, "Parody and Self-Consciousness," suggests that the referent for this character comes from Charles Adrien Wettach (84), a circus performer whose ring name was Grock and who wrote an autobiography, *Grock, King of Clowns* (note 14). In an interview with Julie Gleue, Fernández Cubas asserts that she had never heard of Wettach nor his autobiography. The

When he meets Grock for the first time, it is like coming face-to-face with a caveman. Yet Daniel narrates: "I could not help but be amazed and to understand that who really turned out to be inappropriate and grotesque in that inhospitable environment was I, and everything that previously seemed to me monstrous assumed the most natural and tranquilizing appearance" (105–6). In science fiction and the movies, trips back in time are fairly commonplace; *El año de Gracia,* however, offers us a trip backward in the cognitive course of action. Daniel undergoes a type of aphasia. He must, in effect, unlearn the signs and codes that Western society has created and by which it trains, disciplines, and rewards its citizens. Since the time he became a crew member of the *Providence,* he has been forced to abandon the classical paradigms and learn a more primitive and denotative linguistic system. Stated in Lacanian terms, Daniel can be said to have left the realm of the symbolic order of codified language and patriarchal law and returned to the prelinguistic imaginary stage of harmony.

Language itself is the foundation of any social order, and Grock's is based primarily on simple denotation: "it was extremely similar to some primitive languages and, in addition, to that of many of our children when, having acquired a certain vocabulary, they begin to express their needs" (107). In his efforts to understand the shepherd, Daniel must "often resort to his imagination, at times to pure innovation" (109). Rather than the codified and systematized language systems to which he was accustomed—underscored by his specialty in classical languages during his seminary days—Daniel now is confronted with speech, or *parole,* in its primordial and intuitive essence. The canon and the syllogistic paradigm, which began to fail him on board the ship, increasingly reveal their inadequacies. Furthermore, he has discovered that this new order based on imagination, invention, and oral discourse leads to an unsuspected sense of unity.

Ironically, however, as Daniel gradually learns how to live in harmony with this new world, an increasing disharmony develops between him and Grock; they become male rivals for power, perhaps fulfilling the prophecy inherent in the combat between the two rams. By virtue of his strength

---

novelist says that in an attempt to create a name with an English sound to it, she merely added K to the end of the Catalan word for yellow, *groc.* Although Margenot's article offers some valuable insights into the novel, this example concerning the name underscores some of the dangers inherent in source hunting.

and experience, the shepherd clearly holds the upper hand until one day when Daniel discovers a Bible that Grock has among his possessions. When the former seminarian begins to read the Scriptures aloud, he notes that "all signs of authority and anger had disappeared from Grock's expression" (132). Again, this episode tends to subvert biblical discourse since Daniel does not read the Scriptures aloud with the spiritual intent to instruct, convert, or save his companion but rather to dominate him. This episode also conveys gender implications. In the opinion of some people, the Bible has served men in general over the centuries in their campaign to dominate women. The reemergence of the equation of power and knowledge from his previous order becomes a key moment in Daniel's "year of (G)race."

A short time later Grock is mistakenly murdered by the government agents, and the sheep immediately accept Daniel as their new master, thereby affirming that he is the uncontested sovereign of the island. Yet he is not satisfied with ruling a natural order, and so he makes a fateful decision. There is a mysterious forest that Grock refused to enter but where Daniel now proposes to go "to find the tree of knowledge, eat its fruit and acquire wisdom" (170). Yet he had entered that forest earlier only to find that the trees are actually dead, and so he should realize, since the acquisition of knowledge is his goal, that the fruit he seeks has to be rotten. By refusing to recognize something so obvious, by suppressing deductive reasoning even as he seeks the source of that reasoning, Daniel further betrays the unity and harmony he has found. He is a myopic prophet incapable of foreseeing a future order with no central base of knowledge and authority. His year of (G)race indeed has been in vain. He has thrown away the opportunity provided by his sister to be "otherwise."

The appendix relates that one day in Saint-Malo after his rescue he enters a bar named Providence, the same name as the ship that wrecked, and discovers that the owner is Naguib, the Egyptian crew member he was certain the captain murdered the night of the storm. There is also a photograph of the captain hanging on the wall. For his part, the Egyptian shows no indication of recognizing Daniel. Although he is back in a society that supposedly is grounded on epistemology and syllogistic concepts of cause and effect, it does not take him long to discover a loose thread, which, if he were to pull, could very well unravel the whole fabric of this social order. Daniel shows no inclination, however, to test the integrity of the webbing.

Soon after meeting Gruda, who as the winner of a supermarket contest is on a free vacation to Paris, the two marry and move to Barcelona. Then Daniel narrates how, during the night when he is awakened by Gruda's wheezing and snoring, he imagines himself once again shipwrecked on "the peaceful and tranquil Isle of Grock" (184). Only the memories of the sense of harmony he enjoyed there enable him to return to a state of blissful sleep. With this confession, Daniel ends the narration of his year of (G)race.

There is a paradox inherent in offering a written account of an experience that in essence challenges the authority of writing. That paradox also emerges within the novel. As noted, on the ship Daniel begins by recording the new maritime terms he has learned from the captain and drawing sketches to explain their meaning. Then when he begins to suspect a plot against him, he writes even more feverishly, but by then the captain has ceased explaining things to him; since Daniel is afraid to write down his suspicions, he writes words with no message, a discourse that conveys no information. He begins, therefore, to write letters, at least one of which is addressed to the woman left abandoned back in Saint-Malo: "I believe that I sincerely fell in love with Yasmine, and I communicated as much to her in one of the numerous letters with which I attempted to occupy my mind and escape from cruel reality" (48). If indeed, as Jacques Derrida argues in *The Postcard*, not all letters reach their destinations, this one almost certainly will not. The Frenchman was referring to communication theory and how the received message is never the same as the one intended, how at least part of the message sent is lost in transmission. Daniel, however, is much more solipsistic than philosophic when discussing letters. He does not even intend to send his missive to Yasmine. Daniel's letter is directed to himself, perhaps to soothe his conscience—when he abandoned Yasmine he left a note saying he was returning to Paris and would call her—or perhaps to avoid any real commitment implicit in his confession of love. At any rate the act of writing serves as an avoidance of a reality that refuses to conform to the fictional world of his childhood books.

When confronted with the strangeness of the island, his impulse to write intensifies, though now he begins to express some inner doubts: "I decided to write and, upon doing so, I closed my ears to a second voice that demanded a practical and ephemeral death by fire for the unblemished book" (81–82). This other voice suggests that a part of Daniel now reacts against a cultural tradition based on the written word, perhaps because he realizes that these words have disempowered and betrayed him. In addition, he cannot ignore that since the first days on board the ship, he has not been writing to convey information, but to indulge himself. In defiance of the sacred stature our civilization has placed on published works, and therefore of the inquisitional connotations of the word *fire* in reference to any book, a part of Daniel now dares to voice the sacrilege that perhaps it is time to put an end to our blind faith in the sanctity of the written word.

Still convinced that writing does serve a purpose, Daniel ignores that other voice and, inspired by the discovery that fate left him ink and pens among the ship wreckage, he begins to write a different type of narrative, to which he affixes the title, "*El año de Gracia . . .*" (84), followed by these initial words: "Aunque los mejores años de mi vida transcurrieron de espaldas al mundo . . ." (Although the best years of my life unfolded outside of the world . . . , 85). These are the very words with which the novel we hold in our hands begins. The text does not tell us what effect this incident has on Daniel, but it leads me to conclude that the justification for writing lies in its very fictionality; all writing is merely a response to other writing, and therefore behind every author there is another author. Daniel dramatizes this concept. As he writes his novel, we are well aware that he has been written into the role he performs. Thus the message implicit in this focus on writing is that, by subverting the facade of textual authority, writing can best serve the community we call Western civilization by not pretending to represent anything other than itself.

But no matter what kind of writing one engages in, it always explicitly or implicitly involves a "hypothetical reader" (99). As he continues with his narrative account, Daniel provides a revealing outline of who this reader is, or what *he* is like:

> Mi hipotético lector, nacido sin rostro, habría ido adquiriendo, poco a poco, facciones y características concretas. Tendría más o menos mi edad, veinticuatro, veintisiete, tal vez treinta años; sufría con mis infortunios y se alegraba ante mis hallazgos. El hecho de suponerlo inteligente e instruido me daba arrestos suficientes para intentar la mayor concisión en mis descripciones, para no sucumbir a la pereza de lo ya sabido y limitarme a anotar . . . a la manera de una agenda de negocios o una sucesión de mensajes telegráficos. Fue una gran idea. Porque aquel complaciente y amigable lector me proporcionó, desde su lejana existencia, la compañía y el apoyo necesarios para esperar,

lo más equilibrado posible dentro de las circunstancias, la inminente llegada de mi liberación.

(My hypothetical reader, born without a face, probably had slowly acquired concrete looks and characteristics. He probably was more or less my age, twenty-four, twenty-seven, perhaps thirty; he suffered my misfortunes and rejoiced with my discoveries. The act of imagining him intelligent and educated gave me the courage to strive for the maximum conciseness in my descriptions, and avoid succumbing to the lazy practice of stating the obvious, and limit myself to schematic notes . . . just like in an appointment notebook or a succession of telegraphic messages. That was a great idea. Because that agreeable good old boy from his distant existence provided me with the company and support necessary for waiting for, as clearheaded as possible given the circumstances, the imminent arrival of my rescuers.) (139–40)

The lonely shipwreck survivor can barely contain himself on discovering this kindred spirit whose sex, age, intelligence, and education mirror Daniel's own. Now he has someone with whom he can bond until the day of his liberation from the island and reintegration into the fraternal order. Yet it does not tax the imagination excessively to conclude that his "agreeable good old boy" does not really represent an "other," but rather Daniel's own male alter ego. Possession of Grock's Bible has suddenly placed Daniel in a position of power. The power of writing, in turn, points him in the direction of his salvation: "Now my reader, from his remote existence, was going to save me from Grock's barbarity" (142).

But again Daniel's prophecy proves false, and after witnessing how the scientists murder Grock, our contemporary seer expresses his disenchantment with the very community he has been so intent on rejoining: "The time had come to embark on the authentic, unpredictable adventure, about which, the face of that distant, unreal and obnoxious reader having disappeared, I was not going to mind leaving a record" (170). His quest centers on the pathetic hope of discovering the tree of knowledge in the dead and rotting forest and then to declare a new religion with himself as both leader and sole follower. Although finally he recognizes the need to free himself from the community personified by whom he now characterizes as a "distant, unreal, and obnoxious reader," obviously his lack of determination and imagination, combined with fate, will prevent him from achieving that freedom. Accordingly, on June 7, 1981, he is "rescued" and restored to the civilized world of supermarket lotteries, Gruda, interrupted sleep, and dreams of escape back to "the peaceful and tranquil Isle of Grock."

Knowledge, as represented in *El año de Gracia,* features classical studies, but it also includes science and technology, two of the prominent targets in *Tiempo de silencio.* Notwithstanding this fundamental similarity, it is important to note a basic difference between these two novels. *Tiempo de silencio* projects its messages primarily by means of stylistic strategies, while *El año de Gracia* depends much more on intertextuality. If in part that difference may be explained by the censorship with which Martín-Santos had to contend, I suspect it is more likely a case of reader expectations. Martín-Santos could not rely on reader familiarity with concepts such as horizontally dispersed power hierarchies or logic derived from contiguity as opposed to continuity, and so he depended on stylistics to enable his readers to experience more than intellectualize these concepts. Fernández Cubas, thanks to the pioneering efforts of Martín-Santos and others, can count on a different horizon of reader expectations. Intertextuality, therefore, reflects her confidence in her readers' competence, in their familiarity not only with the Bible and *Robinson Crusoe* but also with the contemporary discourse on imaginary versus symbolic orders, on rabbinic versus syllogistic interpretations, on absence versus presence, on *parole* versus *langue.* By appropriating that critical discourse, she manages to extend the boundaries of postmodern aesthetics and in fact thematize some of the concepts only hinted at in Martín-Santos's groundbreaking stylistics.

El año de Gracia represents, therefore, a significant challenge to prevailing practices and attitudes that trace their roots to the beginning of Western civilization. The novel subverts the tradition of biblical discourse by underscoring its sanction of violence, power structures, and gender hierarchies. The story also undermines our bases for defining learning and erudition and the power that accrues with knowledge. For example, when Daniel lands on the island and thinks it is deserted, his reason will not accept that situation: "But in the second half of the 20th century, in Europe, there was no room left for uncharted lands, mysterious islands and anachronistic Robinsonian adventures" (72–73). The reference to *Robinson Crusoe* is significant, for many consider that work as one of the discursive benchmarks for our scientific-technical age. But whereas Robinson with the aid of his man Friday demonstrates the technical ingenuity of man (I use the masculine form purposely), Daniel proves to be totally inept and cannot even build a raft.[15]

15. As Margenot, "Parody and Self-Consciousness," points out, *Robinson Crusoe* also is often cited as one of the key discursive expressions of imperialism in the name of

In short, this intertextual reference also plays an integral role in Fernández Cubas's novelistic project to challenge our Western heritage of privileging logic, science, and technology, all of which have played key roles in sustaining a patriarchal legacy. That challenge also underscores a basic difference between *El año de Gracia* and the novels analyzed earlier. Fernández Cubas addresses discursive practices whose authority is much more amorphous and ubiquitous, indeed much more pernicious, than that of Franco or his legacy. For her the issue of dominion involves the means by which gender roles and attitudes are formed and perpetuated, and accordingly her fiction seems designed to disempower the acquired knowledge and logic sustaining those roles. The next work of fiction we are going to examine, Martínez de Pisón's *Alguien te observa en secreto*, demonstrates how gender roles relate to a panoptic legacy devoid of any supposed civic function.

The Discursive Eye in *Alguien te observa en secreto*

Back in 1986 Martínez de Pisón was recognized as one of the more significant new writers to emerge in post-Franco Spain.[16] Since that time Eduardo Mendoza, Antonio Muñoz Molina, Juan José Millás, and Rosa Montero are prominent names that seem to have passed him in terms of both sales and critical reception of their works. As in the case of Fernández Cubas, Martínez de Pisón's lack of recognition may be partially attributable to his cultivation of short fiction, a genre still striving for recognition in Spain.[17] There is

---

Christianity. One of Robinson's possessions is a Bible, which he uses to proselytize Friday. In the case of *El año de Gracia*, Grock has the Bible and, as noted, Daniel uses it solely as a source of power and domination. This subversion of biblical discourse has, therefore, imperialistic as well as gender implications.

16. "Los nuevos narradores" (*El País* [Madrid], May 29, 1986, pp. 2–13). That same year Javier Goñi presented an interview with him: "Entrevista con Ignacio Martínez de Pisón." To date Martínez de Pisón has published two novels, *La ternura del dragón* in 1985 and *La ciudad secreta* in 1992, plus two other collections of stories, *Antofagasta* in 1987 and *El fin de los buenos tiempos* in 1994. Kathleen M. Glenn has published an article on one of the stories, " 'Alusión al tiempo' and Hitchcock's *Rear Window*: Voyeurism and Self-Reflexivity," and I have written on the final one, "A Play of Difference."

17. Fernando Valls, in "El renacimiento del cuento en España (1975–1993)," claims that the genre is in the midst of a renaissance in Spain. Santos Sanz Villanueva, "Prólogo," is considerably less enthusiastic, though he also admits that there is motive for optimism. Ana Rueda more or less echoes Villanueva's guarded optimism in her article, "El cuento español: Balance crítico de una década (1980–1990)."

reason to hope that as the frontiers between the novel and the short story become more blurred, writers such as Fernández Cubas and Martínez de Pisón will have less trouble attracting critical attention.

The most obvious link between the fiction of Ignacio Martínez de Pisón and that of Cristina Fernández Cubas is a novelistic world that takes its readers beyond consensus reality and syllogistic logic. But it is also possible to draw lines leading from Martínez de Pisón to Mendoza on one end and Muñoz Molina on the other and the role of enigma in fiction, to Martín-Santos and the issues of power and discipline, to Millás, Montero, and on to Muñoz Molina in reference to the influence of cinematographic discourse on human behavior, to Martín Gaite, Guelbenzu, Ortiz, Montero, Tusquets, Riera, and Fernández Cubas and the destructive effect on both sexes of inflexible gender roles, and above all to Millás and the force of the panopticon.[18]

As Millás and the other writers we have examined represent it, a panoptic system serves a civic function; it operates as an extension of the state. For better or for worse, it is a discursive practice dedicated to imposing order and discipline on the citizens of a commonwealth. Martínez de Pisón offers a new twist to the concept of a panopticon by reducing it to an individually inspired rather than a communally motivated force. In three of the stories of *Alguien te observa en secreto* (Someone is secretly observing you), the discursive eye aspires to impose an idiosyncratic discipline that underscores an epistemic shift away from the state as the center of authority.[19]

The first story of the collection, "El filo de unos ojos" (The cutting edge of someone's eyes), demonstrates how the gaze of the other inspires the protagonist to imitate a behavior that he initially finds reprehensible. The anecdote concerns a young man who makes a business trip to Barcelona

18. In an earlier article, "A Play of Difference," I trace similarities between the aesthetics Juan Benet defines in his essays and the fiction Ignacio Martínez de Pisón writes. In an intriguing statement, as an homage to Juan Benet, Eduardo Mendoza stated that every current Spanish writer (including himself) is influenced by Benet, even those who have not read him.

19. "Otra vez la noche" (Nighttime again) is the one story that does not fit into the focus I have established for this study. It concerns a female student who nurses back to health a wounded bat she finds in the street. Her room becomes the home for a whole flock of bats, who then begin to kill one another, apparently vying in this way for her affection. In the end she finds the bats more loyal and comforting than either of the two men in her life. The story is interesting, but unlike the others, it does not feature an observing eye.

and during his visit stays with a cousin. The protagonist works for a literary magazine, and his assignment is to persuade various authors living in the Catalonian capital to publish their works in the journal. His very first contact leaves him bitter and disillusioned when the writer demands a flattering review of his latest novel in exchange for agreeing to submit one of his unpublished essays to the magazine. Upon returning to his cousin's house, the protagonist encounters a furious man who is just leaving. His cousin explains that the man was a salesman who had been trying to sell him a history of Christianity. A few days later the protagonist is in an adjoining room when a home remodeler arrives to offer recommendations and estimates concerning the kitchen. After a long period the protagonist hears the carpenter and his cousin begin to argue loudly, until finally the man leaves shouting insults. His cousin then laughs uproariously as he describes the remodeler's frustration upon hearing that he had changed his mind and would not make any decorative changes. The protagonist is left speechless by these displays of sadism.

Similar episodes follow in which the protagonist observes as his cousin initially expresses enthusiasm over buying something a salesman is offering —for example a method for learning English or a set of encyclopedias— only to then change his mind. The cousin even goes so far as to ridicule the deformed back of one of the salesmen. In each case his radical switch causes the unfortunate vendor to leave either devastated or extremely angry. During all this time the protagonist becomes increasingly apathetic and makes only one other halfhearted attempt to contact his list of writers for the articles. Finally, one day a salesman of kitchen appliances arrives, but the cousin says he is about to take a bath and cannot talk to the man. The protagonist then begins enthusiastically to inquire about the most expensive items in the man's catalog only suddenly to declare definitively that he has changed his mind and is not interested in buying anything. The hapless man leaves in a state of total dejection. Finally for the first time since his arrival the protagonist feels good about himself and awaits the expected approval from his cousin. But when the latter emerges from the bathroom, and the protagonist looks into his eyes, he sees reprobation rather than approbation: "I felt the habitual glow of discontent, of a perhaps faked dissatisfaction. He never praised me, and was never satisfied with what I did."[20]

---

20. Ignacio Martínez de Pisón, *Alguien te observa en secreto*, 40. Subsequent citations will indicate the page number in parentheses.

This story of exerting power for the sake of power is very disquieting, perhaps because the advantage gained serves no apparent purpose. Other than eliciting despondency or anger from the victims, there is no point to the game; the cousin, and then the protagonist who imitates him, has nothing to gain socially, economically, politically, or romantically. Power itself is the only motive. And as he peers into his cousin's gaze at the end, the protagonist realizes that he is destined never to win approval from his observer. The ending leads to the conclusion, nevertheless, that this same gaze will inspire him to continue his cruel acts of imitation in the vain hope of gaining approbation.

The second story, "Alusión al tiempo" (A temporal allusion), concerns a voyeur and two possible acts of violence. The narrator is an elderly man who writes in a diary the events he observes in the apartment directly across the street. The old man is confined to a wheelchair, an anecdotal situation that echoes Hitchcock's *Rear Window,* though the denouement is markedly different.[21] The object of his gaze is an attractive young woman, often in various stages of undress, living in the apartment across from him. But he is not the only one who observes her. From an apartment above him he sees tobacco ashes float by whenever the young woman is in view. The narrator is intent on hiding his presence not only from the object of his gaze but also from his neighboring observer. In this way he enjoys a panoptic position or illusion of power over both the observed object and his fellow observing subject.

A dramatic twist occurs when the narrator writes in his diary of the mysterious murder some time back of a young woman who lived in the very same apartment as the one now occupied by the woman under his surveillance. He then remembers that tobacco ashes were found on the body of the victim and writes a notation: "My imagination has gotten carried away and has tried to create a novelistic plot around that apartment, my upstairs neighbor, and Turkish tobacco" (57). This is a classic example of an implicit negative that actually affirms. Not only does it have a metafictional effect, but by supposedly dismissing the connections he has drawn as a mere fictional strategy, he has in fact drawn the reader's attention to the novelistic plot being created. Since he has underscored that this is a work of fiction, he has also alerted his reader to look for cause-and-effect combinations typical

---

21. Glenn explores this intertextuality in "'Alusión al tiempo' and Hitchcock's *Rear Window.*"

of the genre and therefore to anticipate a series of empirical clues to solve the developing enigma.

The dramatic tension increases as a male photographer with a huge and vicious dog moves in with the young woman. After a while the man leaves but the dog remains. Then one day the dog, apparently agitated by the narrator who has begun to whistle to him, jumps from the balcony to his death in the street below. In his diary the narrator notes that he believes the dog had in its teeth a bloody piece of the young woman's clothing.

In *La verdad sobre el caso Savolta*, Mendoza undermines the epistemological base of the detective genre; in "Alusión al tiempo," Martínez de Pisón parodies it.[22] The observer not only fails to prevent the apparent acts of physical violence but also contributes to rather than solves the enigmas of the story. To provide additional context for Martínez de Pisón's narrative, the protagonist's viewing position in *Rear Window* compensates for his confinement to a wheelchair; observation translates into knowledge and knowledge into the power to effect change. In "Alusión al tiempo" the wheelchair functions as a metaphor pointing at voyeurism; the protagonist's viewing position only dramatizes his moral as well as physical invalidism. As incarnated in this old man, the panopticon functions as an obsolete and unproductive yet perpetually operating machine.

Not only is the title story the best of the collection, but it incorporates many of the discursive practices we have analyzed in the previous texts as well. I propose to use it, therefore, as the display text for the collection. As I do so, it will become apparent that Martínez de Pisón's story is not a mere imitation, for in addition to its shockingly violent conclusion, the observer in "Alguien te observa en secreto" becomes the object of an observing eye originating within his own imagination.

The anecdote begins with the arrival of the protagonist Manuel at his friend Bárbara's country home after a six- or seven-year absence. He is an entomologist, and as every time in the past, he intends to regale her with a butterfly collection. From the moment he arrives Manuel is confronted

22. This story would certainly seem to support Spanos's efforts to link the contemporary detective genre model with its antisolution to postmodernism: "The Detective and the Boundary." Martínez de Pisón's story also should be seen within the context of recent Spanish detective literature as outlined by Bravo, "Literatura de la distensión"; Vázquez de Parga, *La novela policíaca en España;* and Colmeiro, *La novela policíaca española.*

with a series of enigmas. Although the same house, the garden looks as if it has been devastated by a plague. The dog is pregnant and after giving birth smothers its three pups before also dying. Bárbara has only artificial plants and flowers in the house. In one moment she comes on to him sexually, and in the next she treats him with absolute disdain, even humiliating him with the hated nickname Besugo (Sea Bass). Every day at the same hour Bárbara receives a phone call, and he hears her talking to someone in French. Bárbara gives him a list of rules, one of which is that he is never to spy on her, and then she tells him enigmatically that he has to do everything she tells him as well as some things she does not articulate. If he obeys her, she promises to show him how to appreciate the supreme beauty of inanimate objects.

In the meantime, Manuel has the sensation that someone is always observing them. One afternoon he betrays Bárbara and spies on her, and the next day he discovers that there is a growth of hair on the bathroom fixtures and the furniture. Then he descends the stairs and finds Bárbara in a yoga trance. Imitating the way he mounts specimens in his butterfly collections, he removes a giant lance from the family crest and impales her against a floor tapestry. Afterward when he lies down, he feels the teeth and lips of the sofa close in on him.

The story outlined above is focalized through the eyes of the protagonist, and initially the reader shares Manuel's sensation of an aura of strangeness surrounding Bárbara. As the protagonist attempts to cope with her un-orthodox behavior, he increasingly resorts to fantasy, which in turn leads to an atmosphere of strangeness surrounding him. Finally his make-believe world culminates in an act of violence that, while unreal for him, is too horribly real for her and the reader.

The very first sentence conveys the protagonist's sensation of wonder as he enters Bárbara's home: "There she was, unexpectedly naked" (105). By beginning the story with this statement devoid of any background context, a bond is created between the protagonist and the reader; we cannot help but share his surprise at this woman sitting there in the nude. As he silently approaches her, however, the scene becomes a little less unusual: "After a few seconds of indecision he became aware of the unusual nature of that yoga position of a Bárbara who was distant and yet so close" (105). Since she is in a yoga trance, the surprise in the initial scene at seeing her nude now is more attenuated. But Manuel seems less reassured and focuses on the paradox that she is both distant and near, conveying his confusion that a separation obtains between the psychological and the physical. And since she is seated on a Gobelin tapestry with the mythological scene of "the three apathetic goddesses who are waiting for Paris's decision" (106), Manuel must sense that Bárbara does not conform to the classical representation of a woman as subservient to the judgment of a man. She is different, and he is perplexed, and perhaps threatened, by her difference.

Again he experiences confusion as he contemplates through the window the desolation of what was once a neoclassical garden and the pride and joy of Bárbara's father. Logic tells him that Bárbara, in addition to having fired her father's gardener, had all the trees cut down. In fact, it occurs to him that some people would think that the place looked like it had been ravaged by a plague of locusts, but he knows differently: "His doctorate from the USA was worth something" (107). Ironically the knowledge certified by his American graduate education tells him only what did not happen to the garden, while it is essentially useless in helping him understand why Bárbara did what she apparently did to it. Readers no doubt share Manuel's confusion, but when he compensates by referring to his academic credentials (underscored by the initials *USA*), reader reactions can be expected to range from scorn to pity, from laughter to social indignation, and from these to frustration. What, one wonders, is behind Bárbara's compulsion to eliminate living organisms from the premises (Manuel has noted that all the plants and flowers in the house are plastic). But by ignoring that logical question, the protagonist not only fails to address the most significant enigma but in effect creates one concerning himself; however abnormal Bárbara's behavior may be, Manuel's supposed orthodoxy is not without its own aberrant elements.

Manuel's insecurity becomes even more transparent when Bárbara, having emerged from her trance and now wearing panties, comes up behind him and kisses him on the neck but then says as a greeting: "You still have a sweaty face, and the same bulging eyes of a sea bass" (108). Disturbed by her use of his former nickname, "Besugo," he first compensates by familiarizing her conduct: "Bárbara was the same aggressive girl, the same dark-eyed Lauren Bacall" (108). After encasing her in familiar roles, he proclaims for himself a brand-new persona: "But he shouldn't back off, she had to recognize how much he had changed, how self-assured he was, because now nobody got bored being with him" (109). Again, the textual strategy serves to mock his self-assessment as he reaches into his suitcase for her present,

but before he can retrieve it she asks: "Another butterfly collection?" (109).
Sure enough, he has brought her one box of butterflies and another of their
corresponding larvae.

As she examines the collection, Manuel sees "those momentary and feline
characteristics of an unquestionable Lauren Bacall. They looked at one
another intently and, Lauren Bacall again, she lowered her dark eyes that
gave her away" (110). At this point she seems to collaborate in the Bacall
illusion, a collaboration that becomes even more direct as she suddenly
kisses him passionately:

> Fue primero el aliento cálido, aquellos labios húmedos, aquel beso
> violento, después el olor inmediato de su piel. Cuando Bárbara le cogió
> la mano y la llevó a su pubis, internándola bajo la tensa gomita del
> slip, advirtió el calor pujante, incontenible, de aquellos dos muslos
> que atraparon furiosos su mano. Manuel, casi instintivamente, retiró
> la mano al contacto con aquel sexo tan vivo.

> (First it was her warm breath, those wet lips, that violent kiss, afterwards
> the odor of her skin so near. When Bárbara took his hand and placed it
> on her pubis, slipping it under the tense elastic of her undergarments,
> he felt the vivid warmth, uncontrollable, of those two thighs that
> furiously grasped his hand. Manuel, almost instinctively, withdrew his
> hand from contact with that sex organ that was so alive.) (110)

At this point clearly Manuel's behavior rather than Bárbara's qualifies
as aberrant. Although she may be guilty of violating certain gender codes,
she acts in a quintessentially human manner. For his part, the recoil from
the physical contact with her qualifies as an abnormal, indeed antihuman,
reaction. The reference to Lauren Bacall offers one possible explanation for
his response. Lauren Bacall is, of course, only an icon, a celluloid illusion of
reality. Bárbara, by way of contrast, is for him an all too physical presence.
It is precisely this overwhelming physical reality of her body that prompts
him to recoil from contact with her. Increasingly it seems that rather than
an abnormal being, Bárbara is merely different, and a great deal of her
difference is a question of social codes. Significantly, Manuel cannot erase
the memory of rumors he had heard that when she was living in Paris she
had had a lover who was dark-skinned and that she had posed nude for
a magazine under the caption, *"l'amour l'aprés-midi"* (114). Because he is
unable to accept her difference, increasingly Manuel appears to us as truly
alien, a misfit who opts for abstraction over presence, illusion over reality.

After being rejected, Bárbara imposes a set of rules, one of which is that he is never to spy on her, and she assigns him to his own bedroom. When she takes him to his room, he cannot escape the feeling of being punished as if he were a small boy. At every turn Bárbara betrays the image he had created for her: "Sus miradas se cruzaron por un instante y Manuel pensó que en aquellos ojos negros de falsa Lauren Bacall siempre habría esa hostilidad latente de tigre en la jaula" (Their gazes crossed for an instant and Manuel thought that in those dark eyes of a pretend Lauren Bacall there would always be that latent hostility of a caged tigress, 113). Not only does she betray the image forged in Hollywood and within which he has caged her, but with increasing intensity he also senses danger if this rebellious feline ever manages to break loose.

That night as he falls asleep to the sound of a rainstorm, he finds temporary solace in a dream: "Ahora, en cambio, aludía a un mar inmenso en temporal y ella a merced de las olas y yo rescatándola de los núcleos mortales de la tempestad. Le reconfortó reiterar la visión de aquellas pupilas de Bárbara que eran la gratitud del náufrago" (Now, on the other hand, it alluded to an immense turbulent sea and she at the mercy of the waves and I rescuing her from the mortal center of the storm. It comforted him to repeat the vision of those eye pupils of Bárbara that expressed the gratitude of a shipwrecked person, 117). But this anachronistic dream of the male hero rescuing the helpless damsel in distress whose eyes express her gratitude— as opposed to the hostility he saw that afternoon in Bárbara's gaze—is immediately disrupted by another dream image:

> . . . el vuelo de tus faldas de Marilyn Bacall o el tácito desafío de tu risa o esos senos que cobran vida *l'aprés-midi* Bárbara desnuda por supuesto . . . esa piel blanca como Lauren Hayworth sus hombros desnudos luminosos sobre un fondo negro de guantes que caen con lentitud y que de pronto asedian a esa Bárbara que no es Bárbara. . . .
>
> (. . . the upward sweep of Marilyn Bacall's skirt or the tacit challenge or her laughter or those breasts that come to life "after midday" Bárbara in the nude of course . . . that white skin like Lauren Hayworth's bare and shining shoulders with a black background of gloves that slowly fall and that suddenly seize that Bárbara who isn't really Bárbara. . . .)
> (117)

This dream underscores Manuel's basic insecurities. The words in French are obvious references to the rumors he had heard about Bárbara in Paris, which, contrary to his claim that he never believed them, continue to obsess him. Perhaps even more significant is the confusion of names: Marilyn Bacall and Lauren Hayworth. Up to this time he has tried to compensate for Bárbara's unconventional behavior by identifying her with Lauren Bacall. Of course the Lauren Bacall to whom he referred was not the real woman, but her cinematographic image, the icon created in Hollywood. But in his dream this supposedly fixed image becomes fragmented and pluralized. Just as the Lauren Bacall projected on the screen is a mere simulacrum, and as such easily confused with other simulacra such as Marilyn Monroe and Rita Hayworth, so Manuel has attempted to reduce Bárbara to an abstraction. But she is a reality that continues to impose itself in all its dynamic essence; she refuses to be confined by static representations of women, whether classical (Aphrodite, Athena, and Hera) or modern (Bacall, Hayworth, and Monroe). Not surprisingly, therefore, Manuel refers to her as "that Bárbara who is not Bárbara."

Shortly thereafter Bárbara initiates a reconciliation by first asking him to name his favorite movie scene (his mind jumps to *To Have and Have Not* with Lauren Bacall and Humphrey Bogart), but before he can answer she begins to plan a formal meal for that night. When dinnertime arrives, he watches as she descends the staircase ridiculously dressed in her father's tuxedo, "confident of her beauty, with a ceremonious hesitancy learned from Hollywood movies. She was Lauren Bacall two times over, her coiffure featuring a lateral part just like in *How to Marry a Millionaire*" (120). This parody of a movie-star entrance indicates that Bárbara enjoys playing with the make-believe world of films. Later she claims to have invented an after-dinner drink (cognac with egg yokes), only to confess that it is something she really saw in a movie: "'*Cabaret*' Manuel said with a certain roughness, nothing disgusted him more than a drunk woman" (121). His brusque intervention underscores the difference between him and Bárbara. Whereas she creates a game based on the make-believe world of movies, for Manuel the movies are not a game of fantasy but a grim representation of what he thinks reality is or should be—at least concerning gender roles and the image of a proper woman.

Again there is a gender reversal as she becomes the sexual aggressor, and when he resists her advances she slaps, curses, and spits on him. After he finally manages to subdue her, he becomes convinced that she wanted to kill him. In spite of their conflict, she announces the next day that they will begin sleeping together. When she then kisses him, "Manuel responded without closing his eyes, with a Bogart half smile" (126). After dinner he moves his things into her bedroom, while she, wearing only a "very masculine" bathrobe, leads him to her bed and undresses him. As she plays the role of the blindly passionate seducer, he assumes that of the partner reluctantly resigned to the seduction: "That increasing odor of close-by skin and perspiration disgusted him. With admiration, however, he verified the feline properties of that body, that false Lauren Bacall" (127). In addition to the masculine role she plays, he cannot reconcile her physical reality with the abstract image he has created for her. As her aggression continues and her physical imminence engulfs him, she becomes an "Impossible Lauren Bacall" (128). The following night there is a similar scene with Bárbara astride him: "A vague apprehension prevented him from looking her in the face, from confronting those eyes of an impossible Lauren Bacall. You are killing her, Bárbara, you are killing Lauren Bacall . . ." (132). As these examples demonstrate, Manuel increasingly interprets Bárbara's sexual aggression as a threat; not only does he feel personally threatened, but almost as significantly he feels the threat to one of the icons so essential to his existence as well.

A key moment occurs when he defies her orders and spies on her as she practices yoga in the nude with the Gobelin tapestry as a background: "adoró a aquella Bárbara inmóvil de expresión serena. La sentía por fin toda suya, así, en aquella postura caprichosa y, sobre todo, indefensa. La sentía indefensa sobre ese fondo magnífico" (he adored that stationary Bárbara with the serene look. Finally he felt that she was his, like that, in that capricious position and, above all, defenseless. He sensed her defenseless against that magnificent background, 134). Absorbed in her trance, she offers him the illusion that he is in control of her; like the female figures in the tapestry, she now fits the image of statuelike repose and apathy that he has been trying to impose on her. "Manuel would have liked to love her like that all his life, with that serene face and those closed eyes that allowed him to observe her removed from time" (135).

In her trance she is indeed an object seemingly existing outside of time, but for Manuel this proves to be one of those moments that "concern looking at the female body as the object of desire while conceiving its potential as desiring subject."[23]

23. Brooks, *Body Work*, 84.

The dreaded transformation occurs almost immediately as Bárbara awakens and asserts her position in temporal reality:

> Cuando la vio abrir los ojos y recuperar su figura habitual, esa fórmula agresiva de su juventud, no supo calcular si habían pasado diez minutos o diez horas. Se sintió súbitamente ridículo, inferior; mucho tiempo antes, cuando eran adolescentes, ella le había descubierto espiándola mientras se duchaba y le había insultado y gritado con odio.

> (When he saw her open her eyes and recover her habitual form, that aggressive formula of her youth, he could not calculate if ten minutes or ten hours had passed. He suddenly felt ridiculous, inferior; a long time ago, when they were adolescents, she had caught him spying on her while she was taking a shower and she had insulted him and shouted at him in hatred.) (135)

With her return to reality, his sensation of power and serenity yields to insecurity and guilt. At this point the reader can anticipate the denouement. It seems inevitable that for Manuel to achieve his own mental stability, he will need to find a means for stabilizing Bárbara.

The next morning while shaving he thinks about the Hitchcock film *Rebecca,* as Laurence Olivier and Joan Fontaine stand at the edge of a cliff and the audience expects him to throw her over the side. "[N]ada malo le ocurrirá a Joan Fontaine, *celle-ci est ma situation avec lui, celle-ci est ma situation avec lui*" (but nothing bad happened to Joan Fontaine, that is my situation with her, that is my situation with her, 139), he thinks to himself as he peers into the mirror. Then, he looks in wonder as hair begins to grow on the sink and other bathroom fixtures. After descending the stairs and finding Bárbara again practicing yoga, he removes the lance attached to the family crest of arms, and "he steadied its point against Bárbara's inverted stomach and with a superhuman effort plunged it completely through, nailing her to the middle of the magnificent Gobelin tapestry before which she was practicing her yoga, naked and beautiful, defenseless like a dead butterfly" (141). Finally he has reduced her to a nonthreatening inanimate object of beauty.

Even though apparently in his twisted mind Bárbara had metamorphosed into a butterfly and he had merely added her as another specimen to his collection, Manuel continues to feel that he is imprisoned in a panopticon. From the moment he entered the house and stood gazing at Bárbara seated in the nude, Manuel "was uneasy, he had that vague sensation in his heart telling him that they were not alone, that someone was observing everything" (106). After their formal dinner and just before her second unsuccessful attempt to seduce him,

> sonrió indulgente y notó otra vez aquella sensación en el pecho: a él le gustaba pensar que era un sexto sentido que detectaba peligros latentes, presencias que acechan, pero, qué bobada, sabía que siempre lo notaba cuando se encontraba a disgusto en algún sitio.

> (he smiled indulgently and again noted that sensation in his heart: he liked to think that it was a sixth sense that detected latent dangers, things that were lying in ambush, but, how silly, he knew that he always felt it when he was somewhere where he was in a bad mood.) (121)

Later, when she does manage to seduce him and in his mind he accuses her of killing Lauren Bacall, more doubts arise: "Why was his sixth sense again detecting a latent danger, an unknown presence? Who was secretly observing him?" (132). To a degree this secret observer can be dismissed as a figment of Manuel's own imagination, an expression of his insecurities and increasing insanity. But in another sense the observer can be considered a trope for the discursive forces influencing Manuel, forces that cause him to confuse the division between illusion (Lauren Bacall and other movie star-lets) and reality (Bárbara). Since he feels he is the object of observation, he must play his role as it has been written—"with a Bogart half smile" (126). But as the make-believe and real worlds merge in his mind, the responsibility to human life disappears; if nothing bad really happens to Joan Fontaine, nothing bad can really happen to Bárbara. Everything is part of a script, and he must remember that in his backlit cell he is always on stage before the critical eye of a secret and omnipresent jailer/director (most assuredly male) ready to pass judgment on how well he conforms to and plays his role.

But even in death Bárbara looms as an absent presence intent on rewriting the script. After impaling her, Manuel falls on the couch, and then "sintió una presencia tibia, unos dientes inmensos que nacían del sofá y le atrapaban por la nuca y por las corvas, unos labios que se cerraban sobre él y le sumían en una oscuridad húmeda y total" (he felt a warm presence, immense teeth that were growing out of the sofa and closing in on his neck and knees, lips that closed around him and submerged him into a damp and total darkness, 142). This image seems to echo an earlier love scene:

> Exploró también su sexo, que ofrecía una boca esperando la suya, ingresó entre sus piernas para atraer sus zumos amargos, sus líquidos

urgentes . . . se refugió aún más en aquella boca accesible, aquellos labios deformes esperándole y adaptándose obedientes a sus propios labios. Intuyó más dura la mirada de Bárbara cuando cesaron sus murmullos de placer. . . .

(He also explored her vagina, which offered a mouth awaiting his own, he dug between her legs to attract her bitter juices, her urgent liquids . . . he took even more refuge in that accessible mouth, those deformed lips awaiting him and obediently adapting themselves to his own lips. He intuited that Bárbara's gaze hardened when her murmurs of pleasure ceased. . . .) (132)

Even though she pays with her life, the ending leads us to believe that he does also. Just as surely as he murdered her because of her sexuality, that same sexuality avenges itself on him. Both can be considered victims of the violent, male-driven legacy of a panoptic system that no longer seems to function as an extension of the state.

As in *Visión del ahogado* and several of the other novels examined earlier, women in *Alguien te observa en secreto* continue to serve as objects of the male gaze. For Manuel, however, the machine has become internalized, and he becomes the object of a gaze created within his own psyche. Perhaps because the panoptic system has lost its link to a civic disciplining function, its effects are more violently destructive than what we have witnessed up to this point. By representing in these three stories how a decentralizing force can translate into a destructive separation between the individual and the state, Martínez de Pisón expresses an important dimension of the post-totalitarian episteme. To appreciate the connection between the fictional representation of the equation of decentralization and violence and its expression in political reality, we need merely look to the former Yugoslavia, and perhaps to Spain itself and ETA.

In the next novel to be analyzed, the emphasis shifts back to institutional practices more directly tied to the state. In Esther Tusquets's *Para no volver*, the issue is how psychoanalytic discourse functions as a game designed to impose gender conformity.

The Games Men Play: *Para no volver*

Perhaps by virtue of the author's age and sociocultural history, *Para no volver* (Never to return) serves as both a temporal and an artistic bridge between the first and second half of the 1980s.[24] It addresses some of the same issues raised by Carmen Martín Gaite, José María Guelbenzu, Lourdes Ortiz, Cristina Fernández Cubas, and Rosa Montero concerning institutionalized discursive practices and gender roles. Tusquets presents gender issues by means of a modified bildungsroman. The protagonist and focalizer, Elena, undergoes an adult learning experience, which begins with the distinction between gender as a theme and discourse as a means for positioning certain groups in a subservient role. That lesson is first provided by her best friend, Eduardo, who, to her claim that a woman can do anything that a man can do, "answers with absolute seriousness that what no woman will ever be able to do is make a figure eight by pissing on a wall."[25] Humor aside, this is a serious message concerning the absurdity of confusing biological functions and differences with social roles and status. Eduardo helps the protagonist see that distinction, which in turn helps her focus on the underlying causes rather than the surface manifestations of gender attitudes. Her task, then, is to discover how to manipulate the rules of the game that a postfascist society has invented to impose its own brand of patriarchal discipline.

The anecdote of *Para no volver* concerns Elena, who like the author at the time she published the novel, is faced with the disquieting reality of her fiftieth birthday. In addition to that crisis, the protagonist's husband is in New York with a much younger woman, where one of the films he directed is previewing in New York. Recently she also has had to face the painful conclusion that her two adult sons have forsaken her and the values

24. Tusquets is the author of four works of fiction in addition to *Para no volver: El mismo mar de todos los veranos*, 1978; *El amor es un juego solitario*, 1979; *Varada tras el último naufragio*, 1980; and *Siete miradas en un mismo paisaje*, 1981. Molinaro's *Foucault, Feminism, and Power* represents the benchmark of criticism on Tusquets's fiction. See also Barbara F. Ichiishi, *The Apple of Earthly Love: Female Development in Esther Tusquets' Fiction*, and the analyses of Luis F. Costa, "*Para no volver*: Women in Franco's Spain"; Gonzalo Navajas, "Civilization and Fictions of Love in *Para no volver*"; Elizabeth Ordóñez, "*Para no volver*: Through the Mirror and over the Threshold of Desire"; Catherine G. Bellver, "Intertextuality in *Para no volver*" and "Assimilation and Confrontation in Esther Tusquets' *Para no volver*"; Mercedes M. Rodríguez, "Narrative Strategies in the Novels of Esther Tusquets" and "*Para no volver*: Humor vs. Phallocentrism"; Maarten Steemeijer, "El relevo del mito: Sobre *Para no volver* de Esther Tusquets"; Geraldine C. Nichols, "Minding Her Ps and Qs: The Fiction of Esther Tusquets"; Spires, "The Dialogic Structure of *Para no volver*"; and Elizabeth Espadas, "An Annotated Bibliography of Works by and about Esther Tusquets."
25. Esther Tusquets, *Para no volver*, 75. Subsequent citations will indicate the page number in parentheses.

she tried to instill in them. A long-standing friendship with Eduardo (who at one point in the past was her paramour) and a recent love affair with an Argentine named Arturo provide Elena with at best partial solace. But when her fiftieth birthday arrives she can no longer cope, and decides to begin therapy sessions with an Argentine psychoanalyst.[26] By means of a third-person narration the novel conveys her flow of consciousness as she discovers in those sessions that the root of her problem has much more to do with a birthright than with a birthday.

Since the novel presents Elena's nonlinear flow of consciousness, at times the narrated utterances make little sense—they approach what information theory labels *noise*. As the reading process continues, however, and as readers become more accustomed to a style characterized by seemingly endless digressions and subordinate clauses, what initially seemed to be noise becomes information;[27] the chaotic style itself conveys a message concerning conformity versus subversion, syllogistic logic versus free association, and linear sequences versus an interconnected web.

This process of noise becoming information is also aided and abetted by a narrator who tells only what the character knows.[28] The combination of a chaotic style and a narrator limited to telling only what the character says and thinks serves to make the reader an active participant in the process of discovering the rules of the particular discursive practice represented in *Para no volver.*

The sessions with the analyst clearly are related to that practice. Elena begins her therapy looking for a cure but quickly discovers that psycho-

26. Tusquets undoubtedly plays with the stereotype of Argentina as a country obsessed with psychoanalysis. Elena corroborates that intertextual reference when she observes: "tal vez se trate en definitiva de una pésima costumbre, un hábito nefando de los argentinos, que ellos sí se habían psicoanalizado en masa, habían estado años y años tumbados en el diván, para pasar luego a ocupar detrás de él una mecedora o para andar por la vida interpretando pavadas" (perhaps it is a fundamental question of an annoying custom, an infamous Argentine habit, which they themselves have analyzed ad infinitum, that they had spent years and years stretched out on a couch only then to occupy a rocking chair behind it or go through life interpreting stupid acts by others, 138). Nichols, "Minding Her Ps and Qs," finds chauvinistic implications in this type of stereotyping.

27. Molinaro, *Foucault, Feminism, and Power,* offers a brief but insightful analysis of how the use of subordinate clauses in this novel (and in all of Tusquets's fiction) defers closure and subverts institutionalized writing logic (98–99).

28. See Cleanth Brooks and Robert Penn Warren, *Understanding Fiction,* 588–94, and Gérard Genette, *Narrative Discourse: An Essay in Method,* 161–211.

analysis is "a particularly vigorous exercise of power."[29] As she reflects on her two months of sessions, it appears that Elena's motives have changed from seeking a cure to subverting this particular practice of authority: "perhaps she had gotten something during the process of those two months of psychoanalysis, and it was, among other things, the almost permanent habit of turning every issue upside down . . ." (10). This nonconformist mode of reasoning represents a point of resistance inherent in any system: Every assertion implies its own counterassertion. Elena seems to corroborate that discursive law shortly thereafter in the narrative when she recalls an incident in which she felt like murdering a saleswoman who could not understand her order for fitting six prints of unequal dimensions into six frames of exactly the same size. The clerk was totally confounded by this unorthodox, and from her point of view illogical, request until, in a sudden flash of insight, she exclaimed, "But then the borders will not be equal!" (15). The response is humorous but also revealing. The saleswoman is a product of a logic that finds it difficult to accommodate variations from norms. Obviously Elena likes to break from norms, and it is the analyst's charge to cure her, to discipline her unruly behavior by assigning her a fixed position not only in the clinic but also in society.[30]

Because my focus in this book is on discursive practices, I cannot ignore a connecting link between the emphasis in Tusquets's novel on psychoanalysis and the new Spanish sociopolitical order, which of course anticipates an emerging world order. In the new post-Franco democratic society, psychoanalysis is one of the primary ideological apparatuses for imposing discipline and conformity on the upper middle class. And as opposed to the former totalitarian system with its overt repression, the new practice is to turn the disciplining process into a game. Consistent with all games, each player—doctor and patient in this case—has a prescribed area to occupy and a position to assume. But since in the beginning, "Elena was still ignorant of the most elementary rules of the game" (18), she tries to

29. Bersani, "Subject of Power," 7. Subsequent citations will indicate the page number in parentheses.
30. According to Althusser, *Lenin and Philosophy*, beginning with childhood we are interpellated and thereby positioned by discourse within ideologies, which interpellation in turn determines the way we think and behave. What the capitalist system is for Althusser, psychoanalysis is for the posited author of *Para no volver*. Both interpellate and then subjugate the individual within determined ideologies.

sit facing her analyst. He makes it clear, however, "that he definitely wanted her lying on the couch with him seated beyond her head" (10). Although at the beginning she does not know the rules, immediately she realizes "how dangerous that game could be—that the analyst-patient relationship was necessarily asymmetrical" (22). Elena realizes that the asymmetry of this clinical situation is a double-voiced image and reflects the role she has been assigned in society. She clearly understands, then, that the proposed "cure" begins with accepting the all too familiar assigned position. In fact, everywhere she turns she finds herself the participant in a game of essentially the same arbitrary and often ridiculous rules. In this case, as she lies subserviently on her back, she can only see the toe of the analyst's shoe, a situation whose absurdity prompts her to observe to herself, "and it is a little ridiculous, to tell the truth, to go around telling who knows what to a shoe" (47).[31] But of course this is not just any shoe but that of the male referee always already present—at least from Elena's point of view—to ensure that the rules, however absurdly arbitrary, are not violated.

In this novelistic world of psychoanalysis, dialogue is a transgression; for the psychoanalytic process to function effectively, the analysand must engage in a monologue to which the analyst merely listens. Although the doctor may prompt her and ultimately finds it his responsibility to interpret what she says, during these sessions the psychoanalyst's function is to discipline, to ensure that she plays the prescribed institutionalized gender role. Soon she recognizes that the rules in the clinic trace their roots to ancient times: "there Elena learned that the Great Enchanters of the Tribe have made vows of silence, just like the hermits of other centuries" (39). Although packaged in a new scientific wrapper, this time-honored discursive practice is dedicated to reaffirming for the male gender the power of silence. But Elena is determined to resist that system by ridiculing her analyst's authority and engaging him in imaginary dialogues.

In challenging the analyst, Elena is taking on a powerful institution. As Leo Bersani explains, "psychoanalysis has produced a discourse of knowledge in almost absurd excess of the theoretical 'needs' of its own operations as an institutionalized practice" (7). The analyst personifies this excess. He

---

31. See Molinaro, *Foucault, Feminism, and Power,* for a fascinating analysis of the dustcover, which is based on a photo of Freud's couch and includes the toe of the shoe of the analyst, who is sitting just off camera at the head of the couch.

prominently displays his academic credentials on the walls of his office, thereby providing visual evidence of his acquired knowledge. Bastioned in his archival sanctuary, "he appeared to be confident of possessing all truth" (19). In addition to his certified professional status, he has effected an ecclesiastical demeanor appropriate for someone "who possibly spoke with God every night" (20). Elena's sarcasm linking acquired knowledge with divine insight provides a key in her search for a means of empowering herself. The sessions are helping her to recognize that such a link is in reality a social construct justifying men's right to subjugate women. That being the case, logically the same construct could be appropriated to free women. The force that oppresses her also provides her with the strategies to oppose and ultimately to control it.

As Elena gains knowledge, she sharpens her attacks. For example, she baptizes her Argentine analyst with sarcastic nicknames or titles, the likes of which include "el Señor Mago" (Mr. Magic, 13), "el Gran Invisible" (the Great Invisible Man, 100), "el Gran Brujo de la Tribu" (the Great Witch Doctor of the Tribe, 198), and one of the "Grandes Hechiceros de la Tribu" (Great Enchanters of the Tribe, 39), plus other epithets that mock his stoicism. The names or titles undermine his facade of divine erudition by equating his profession with that of primitive and medieval wizards. Whereas his precursors conjured forth imaginary demons or relied on sleight of hand to gain credibility and power, the epithets suggest that the psychiatrist relies on the mystique of erudition, certified by his diplomas, to accomplish the same end.

The analyst also lays claim to another title, as he reassures Elena after an early session "with paternal pats on the back" (12). Since his attitudes make clear that in his own mind patriarchy and pedantry are mutually dependent, she baptizes him "Papá Freud" (18). Driven to analysis by an inferiority complex, Elena discovers that the world of psychoanalysis is indeed structured on the same hierarchical premises as the community that has rejected her and that she in turn has rejected. She feels trapped for she knows she needs the therapy, even though she forces herself to ask the painful question, "what was there about psychoanalysis that made her, almost inevitably, act like a stupid little spoiled brat?" (24). Obviously she is the product of discursive practices that dictate attitudes and behavior that she abhors. In order to build an arsenal of defenses against these practices, she needs someone to help her identify them. For that reason she cannot afford to reject this clinical world where, she is becoming more convinced, the secrets of power are hidden. Her only immediate recourse, therefore, is to imagine scenes in which she ridicules the underlying discursive rules and codes; she must undermine their authority and that of their professors in her own mind before she can do so publicly.

As the sessions continue, Elena increasingly recognizes the double voicedness inherent in psychoanalytic discourse. It functions as an extension of the basic game society teaches to women, which they in turn play with consummate skill: "a dirty game, so feminine, of adoring a man as if he were a god and of protecting him as if he were a child" (101). The analogy is obvious. The analyst has substituted himself for her husband, Julio, in the role of god, and she of course has the same role as always, that of worshipper. She notes with bitter irony that it is inexcusable that she did not know her part immediately, since "it has been assigned to women from the beginning of history" (188). Also inscribed since the beginning of civilization are the female rituals for enticing the male deities.

The role of seductress is not only an integral part of our social and cultural history but it also has been refined in modern times thanks to Hollywood. Indeed, this is the one role that has the potential for dethroning even the godlike presence of her Argentine psychiatrist: "it would have been really magnificent to be able to go up to the Stranger, with the long and serpentine body of Bacall, with a tight-fitting suit jacket, a raised eyebrow, and profess her devotion and love in a brief and unforgettable sentence" (14). The subjunctive mood of the initial verb says everything. Elena can only fantasize. Divine status is a birthright for nearly all men and may even increase with age for those who acquire education and wealth. Yet only a few select women are born with the seductive powers of a Lauren Bacall, powers that—as opposed to the process for many men—decrease rapidly beyond a certain age. But even an actress's charms, at least in part, are based on celluloid illusions. In fact, the glamorous trappings of movie stars are especially useful for hiding some very nonalluring moments for Elena: "of course it was crazy but she has even bought some sunglasses, extra large and dark like Garbo's, to serve as a mask and hide from other passersby the spectacle of her crying" (45). One suspects that the reality behind Elena's mask is not all that different from what was behind Greta Garbo's made-in-Hollywood facade—which may well explain that actress's early retirement from the movies and her subsequent life of seclusion. The film world, so it would seem, reinforces the role of woman as pure image. But what happens, when at age fifty, the image begins to fade and the role of seductress becomes impracticable, perhaps even pathetic? Elena knows only too well that she cannot depend on her imitation of Bacall and Garbo to break down the Magician's sacred wall of silence. Perhaps for that reason she sweeps aside those romantic daydreams and replaces them with yet another image drawn from that great modern conveyer of discourse, children's films.

Her new model is her childhood matinee idol, Lassie: "badly treated by its master . . . a ridiculous dog that alternately and simultaneously detests and loves a cruel master whom it never understands and upon whom it fatefully depends" (29). Only this subservient status of a dog to its master seems to provide the reader with an answer to a question posited by Eduardo that even Elena cannot answer. When the former asks her why she does not leave the Argentine doctor and find a Catalonian woman analyst her own age, the narrator explains: "because she has fallen into an absurd trap from which she cannot escape, but she opts to remain silent, because it would take a long time to explain it and besides she herself doesn't quite understand it" (82). The domestication of the dog from a wild beast to a household pet took centuries of discipline and breeding. Elena seems to sense, without fully understanding, that as a woman she has undergone a similar process of socialization. Breaking away from the obedience that discourse has ingrained in her is, therefore, difficult. Yet ironically psychoanalysis, which some would argue was conceived to ensure gender conformity, has provided her with the basic tools to rebel effectively by dramatizing the arbitrary essence of sex roles, and more significant, of some of the discursive strategies employed to perpetuate them.

Elena's first cautious attempt to seize control of the discourse comes in the form of a seemingly innocent question directed to the psychiatrist. She merely asks him whether, when he fled the dictatorship in Argentina, it was before or after Franco's death. When she manages to get him to indicate that it was after, the narrator explains that she has won this hand by resorting to a "a complex, ingenuous, and dangerous game that Elena has invented, a private game that is uniquely and exclusively hers, a game that she keeps secret within the other large game that Papa Freud invented and that the Magician reproduces to the best of his ability" (50). This is an excellent example of how the double voicing of the novel turns over to the reader the task of creating meaning. Neither Elena nor the narrator explains exactly what this game is or why it is dangerous. In effect, her game becomes the readers' game as they try to decode its rules, as they try to transform its noise into information.

As players, readers may first conjecture that the danger resides in the possibility that, despite her strategy, the analyst will elect to ignore her. In all likelihood that reaction would only intensify her feeling of nonbeing. But by eliciting a response from the Magician, by manipulating the discourse, she has learned (as have the readers) something significant about him when he confesses that he did not merely exchange one totalitarian state for another, but he fled Argentine dictatorship for Spanish democracy. Yet even this victory is tempered by her realization that she cannot transcend her discursive context, that however private and unique her game may be, it is informed by Freud's strategies. She and the Magician are equal in that both are subject to Freudian interpretations of human behavior—he as an avowed disciple, she as a resisting parishioner; psychoanalytic discursive practices limit his as well as her freedom and originality. It would seem, then, that Elena needs the confirmation that she is capable also of manipulating the strategies within the Freudian paradigm. She needs to prove to herself that she, a woman, is capable of controlling rather than merely being controlled by this discourse. In effect it is a dangerous game she plays, for to lose would be to recognize that she, and by extension her gender, truly has been disqualified from the competition.

However small her initial victory may seem, it provides the launching pad for her determination to rebel openly, "to determine for once the course of the game, for once not to be the besieged, the one who is ordered, the one who is sought, to feel that she is not forced, obliged, to do anything" (200). She first asserts herself by seducing rather than being seduced by her friend Arturo. Arturo's Argentine nationality leads us to assume that he merely represents the practice session prior to the championship. But Arturo is also significant because the first time they were together she tried to use him as a confessor, only to conclude:

sí había debido de estar escuchándola, aunque fuera a medias (es posible, se le había ocurrido a Elena, que ese interlocutor válido del que hablan los tipos como Arturo, ese interlocutor que andan buscando a lo largo y lo ancho del mundo, sea un interlocutor que, no sólo no comprende ni responde, sino que ni tan siquiera escucha).

(yes he must have been listening to her, even if only partially [it had occurred to Elena that it is possible that the authentic interlocutor about whom guys like Arturo spoke, that interlocutor that they go around the

globe searching high and low for, not only does not understand nor
respond, but that he does not even listen].) (138)

Again, the responsibility for interpretation, for transforming into information what may sound like noise, is passed on to the readers. One possible
reading, therefore, is that if one knows the discourse well enough, there
really is no need to listen, for there can be no new information forthcoming.
That, apparently, is the Magician's great secret, his source of power. Armed
with this new insight as she enters her final session with him, she feels she
now has accumulated a formidable arsenal of knowledge to use against him.

She asserts herself in their final session by refusing to lie down, though she
does so with certain trepidation: "Then, after a pause and in another tone of
voice or her couch voice, although she remains seated, because she cannot
bring herself to lie down now on the couch, although she would prefer, she
has to admit, to be stretched out on it" (202). By sitting rather than lying
down, Elena has changed the game. She has abandoned the position of the
one who confesses and assumed that of confessor; she has placed herself
on an equal level with Mago. But she realizes at the same time that it was
much more comfortable in the old position, if for no other reason than she
had so many years to become accustomed to it. Now even more than before
she finds herself "straddling two worlds, always out of position and without
knowing exactly which position was hers" (52). But at least she has reduced
the options, because however ill at ease she may be, she cannot bring herself
to lie down on the couch. From now on her position in the game is going
to be different.

Shortly thereafter her husband, Julio, returns from the United States, not
in triumph as he had anticipated but devastated by a negative review of his
film published in an Oklahoma newspaper. His young companion does not
return with him, and Elena realizes that now "he could only tell her about it,
not anyone else . . . because only she possessed the sufficient codes, not only
to understand what he meant, but also to know immediately how to react,
what is the right sentence, silence, caress" (214). Finally she is in control of
the contest, for she knows the rules. If she chooses to do so, she will not
even have to listen. Just as in the sessions in which she did all the talking and
the analyst controlled the discourse by means of his silence, now she can
do the same with Julio. Her meditations, then, can be seen as an instinctive
attempt to change the game, to turn the tables on her male interlocutors, to

free her own discourse by usurping their position of authority, their strategy of silence.

When the story draws to a close the protagonist and her husband are back together, but we know things have changed:

> Elena dispone pues su instrumental, sus armas, y sonríe, y no le dice que ha estado pensando que mañana, cuando el Mago le abra la puerta de la consulta, le cogerá la mano que él le tienda y no se la soltará, no dejará que inicien el tortuoso camino hacia el prostíbulo-santuario, sino que antes, en el mismo umbral, le comunicará la gran noticia: "Sabés una cosa, Mago, me voy a psicoanalizar."

> (Elena lays out her surgical instruments, her weapons, and smiles, and she does not tell him that she has been thinking that tomorrow, when the Magician opens the door of his clinic for her, she will grab the hand that he extends to her and she will not let loose, she will not allow him to begin the tortuous path to the bordello-temple, but before that, right there in the doorway, she will tell him the great news: "You know what, Magician, I'm going to psychoanalyze myself.") (217)

Once again the reader is called upon to decode the messages, though naturally the text establishes parameters as to what will be judged acceptable or unacceptable conclusions. Following the textual pointers, then, "surgical instruments" and "weapons" suggest the forces now at her command after serving her discursive apprenticeship. Furthermore, her smile indicates confidence and power, even a hint of vengeance. All this leads to the reflexive construction "me voy a psicoanalizar" (I'm going to psychoanalyze myself), which is not devoid of ambiguity. But given the context indicated, it can be seen first of all as a declaration of freedom from her frequent reference to the clinic as a "bordello-temple"—a place connoting both sexual exploitation and spiritual comfort. But now she is ready to face the inherent risks and, as the reflexive construction suggests to me, analyze herself. If the "me voy" (I'm going to) is not intended as a true reflexive, the implication would be that she is leaving ("me voy" "I'm out of here") to find another analyst.[32]

---

32. Nichols, "Minding Her P's and Q's," labels as a misreading the suggestion that the construction is a true reflexive, adding that self-psychoanalysis is an oxymoron since psychoanalysis must involve two people. The critic cites a statement uttered by Tusquets to support her reading. Although Nichols may be right in reference to the author's intention in writing "me voy a psicoanalizar," what Tusquets wrote grammatically militates against that intention. The English verb "to psychoanalyze" is transitive, and since technically the

Either way her words signal the termination of further pseudodialogues of the type she has been having with the Magician, Arturo, and Julio (interlocutors who do not even listen to what she says). If indeed she is going to become her own analyst, from now on she truly will be engaged in monologues or at least until such time that real dialogues, with real listeners, are possible. Until then, as far as she is concerned, the rest may well be silence.

If the protagonist finds her voice in voicelessness, the opposite is true of the narrator. Elena's path to silence refracts into the narrator's avenue of expression. By giving voice to Elena's thoughts, the narrator dominates the text. The protagonist has to learn what the narrator already knows. An analogy thus can also be drawn between the narrator/reader and the Magician/Elena relationship.

As noted, though Elena does almost all the talking, the Magician controls the discourse. He uses silence as a defensive strategy to deny her access to his territorial claim. But by tricking him into finally revealing the codes, Elena is able to wrest at least some of that control from him. In the narrator/reader refracted version of that relationship, the narrator exercises another type of silence by conveying only Elena's thoughts and utterances. Although her voice dominates the text, she withholds any clarifying comments and leaves it primarily up to the reader to decode the messages. And again parallel to Elena's situation where she must operate within the prevailing discursive parameters, the reader's interpretations must fit within the parameters set by the text. An additional refraction emerges from this dialogic process. Elena's conversation is with a concrete character who is a present absence—in addition to being a fictional character, Elena merely imagines almost all the exchanges between herself and the Magician, and so he is not even there fictionally to hear her discourses. The narrator, on the other hand, addresses an absent presence—though her reader is only implicit in the act of narrating, a linguistic construct, real readers give corporeal presence to that construct in the act of reading. All fiction is double voiced, but *Para no volver* projects a conscious effort to exploit that elastic quality as a means of making the reader an active participant in the game of discourse.

Spanish verb here is an anglicism, sentence logic dictates that the Spanish construction also should be reflexive. If Tusquets did not mean it to be reflexive, she is guilty of writing a defective construction.

In what I will offer as a final example of the elasticity of the reading experience created by this novel, as the ending is reached readers are all but ricocheted back to the beginning and the epigraph, borrowed from Rubén Darío's "Canción de otoño en primavera" (Autumn song in spring): "Juventud, divino tesoro, / ya te vas para no volver . . ." (Youth, divine treasure, / now you are leaving never to return . . .). This passage can be read as nostalgia, an anguished lament over lost youth (the conventional reading of Darío's poem) and therefore appropriate for the just-turned-fifty Elena, for Esther, and for all those readers who have experienced or are anticipating the same rite of passage. On the other hand, one can read these verses as a celebration of change in discursive practices, social values, and gender roles, and therefore an ironic reference to the past. My own reading of these verses and of the novel as a whole combines these two tones. Just as the aging process for an individual can be motive for both nostalgic longing (even anguish) and a celebration of change, so the evolution of discursive practices and social values can elicit similar emotions. Not everything in the old system was bad, nor will everything in the new one be good. The process of both aging and social change is complex, contradictory, and, for better or worse, inevitable. The novel invites readers to share with Elena the mixed experiences of crisis and exhilaration, anger and amusement, bitterness and nostalgia in the face of an ending that is also a beginning.

In many senses *Para no volver,* like its protagonist Elena, finds itself straddling two worlds—Francoist Spain on the one side and the new democracy on the other. One of Elena's laments addresses this dichotomy: "Perhaps one of the causes of her depression and sadness is centered there, in the small degree to which the world has changed for the better, in the small degree to which those of her generation have managed to change the world" (46). She echoes Ricardo of *Teoría del conocimiento,* another anti-Franco liberal whose actions had no apparent effect on the political change that occurred. It seems significant that the novelists behind these two characters both have turned their focus to discursive practices as a means of reconciling the two worlds and their role in each. For her part, Esther Tusquets has elected games as the trope to lead us into the issue of discourse. In fact, *Para no volver* is itself a game. Readers either accept the author's rules and participate in her pastime of transforming her version of noise into information, or they can close the book (and with it their minds, to one degree or another). But if they elect to play the game of fiction as she has designed it, like Elena they are offered the opportunity to discover that what they tend to dismiss as noise may actually convey very important information and to find their own strategies for assuming control of the contest we call *discourse*. In the final analysis, Tusquets offers readers the challenge in *Para no volver* of being more tolerant of alterity, and thereby enriching their very existence. In the next novel to be analyzed, *Cuestión de amor propio*, published in 1987 by Carmen Riera, a similar theme emerges but is conveyed by very different textual strategies.

Oppositional Reading and *Cuestión de amor propio*

Carmen Riera places the emphasis in her *Cuestión de amor propio* (A question of self-love) on the issue of a listener/reader for a female speaker and in that sense echoes Esther Tusquets. *Para no volver* suggests that the only solution may be for a woman to become her own listener, to subject herself to self-psychoanalysis; *Cuestión de amor propio*, on the other hand, implies another type of solution.[33] According to the reading I am about to offer, this novel proposes that the communication problem for women may be solved by creating a reading subject who actively cooperates with the writing subject to wrest control of the discourse from the masculine order.

Riera's short but finely crafted novel has an epistolary format and consists entirely of a letter of apology and explanation written by Angela to her sexually liberated Scandinavian friend, Ingrid. Angela is a middle-aged Catalonian writer, divorced some seven years ago, who finds herself torn between the old and the new Spanish moral codes. She is inspired by an ultimatum from Ingrid that she received the day before and promises at the beginning of her response to provide a detailed account of the events over the last year that prevented her from answering the Scandinavian's

---

33. The Catalan edition of this novel appeared in 1987, and the Spanish version, translated by Riera, appeared one year later. This is Riera's third novel to date. Her first, *Una primavera para Domenico Guarini*, appeared in 1981 (the Catalan edition is the same year), and her second, *Joc de miralls*, appeared in 1989 (the Spanish edition, *Por persona interpuesta*, appeared the same year). Her most recent novel to date is *Dins el darrer blau*, 1994. Her collections of stories *Te deix, amor, la mar com a penyora*, 1977, and *Jo pos per testimoni les gavines*, 1977, were jointly published in Spanish under the title *Palabra de mujer*. Another book of stories, *Epitelis tendríssims*, appeared in 1981, while *Contra l'amor en companvia i altres relats* and its Spanish edition were published in 1991.

letters. She also warns that after her explanation, she will be asking some favors.[34]

Approximately the first twelve pages of the fictional response deal with the difficulty of communication and the need to find a reader capable of bridging the gap between language and reality, between what is said and what is really meant. Recently Angela mistakenly thought that her writing projects "had finally found the only recipient who interested me, a 'you' that from that moment on would justify my existence,"[35] but that reader seduced and betrayed her. Her act of writing a letter to Ingrid can also be labeled a *seduction,* in Ross Chambers's sense of luring the reader's "interests and desires in favor of those of the narrative."[36] By convincing Ingrid that their interests and desires are really identical, she hopes to entice her friend into playing the role not only of a reading or interpretive subject but also of an avenging comrade.

When Angela finally turns the focus to the events of the past year, Miguel, a prominent writer whom she met at a literature conference in Valencia, holds center stage. She confesses that during a discussion period the second day of the meeting she challenged his reading of Ana in *La Regenta* just to attract his attention. Her strategy worked, and Angela narrates how for the rest of the convention they were inseparable companions (though they were lovers for only one night, approximately one month later at her home in Barcelona). After the conference Miguel sent flowers and notes and called her regularly until he finally managed to come to Barcelona to see her. That night together was followed by a single orchid he sent her, with the laconic note "Muchas gracias" (46). When he failed to contact her after that, she made many unsuccessful attempts to call him.

---

34. For useful overviews of Riera's fiction, see Roberta L. Johnson, "Voice and Inter-subjectivity in Carmé Riera's Narratives," and Glenn, "Authority and Marginality," along with the interview in Nichols's *Escribir, espacio propio.* Akiko Tsuchiya, "The Paradox of Narrative Seduction in Carmen Riera's *Cuestión de amor propio,*" and Sandra Schumm, "'Borrowed' Language in Carmen Riera's *Cuestión de amor propio,*" have contributed provocative analyses of this novel, and Emilie L. Bergmann, "Letters and Diaries as Narrative Strategies in Contemporary Catalan Women's Writing," discusses *Cuestión de amor propio* more briefly in her essay.

35. Carmen Riera, *Cuestión de amor propio,* 24. Subsequent citations will indicate the page number in parentheses.

36. Chambers, *Room for Maneuver,* 13. Subsequent citations will indicate the page number in parentheses.

After she had finally reached the point of accepting the definitive end of the relationship and had written off the whole affair as but another bitter lesson of life, he sent her a copy of his new novel. Angela explains to Ingrid that it concerns a love affair between a dynamic and successful young writer and an aging woman, who in her possessiveness threatens to strangle the young man's talent and vitality. Most of the dialogue in the novel, she says, is an almost exact transcription of conversations she had with Miguel, including their debate over *La Regenta*. There is also a scene in the novel concerning the protagonists' single night of lovemaking, which in the fictional account is a total disaster because of the woman's frigidity and sexual complexes. Angela then reveals the favors she mentioned at the beginning.

First she asks Ingrid to read the novel to confirm that it is a roman à clef, with her, Angela, cast as the older female protagonist (in reality, Miguel is five years older than Angela). Next, and more important, she reveals that Miguel is going to Norway to write some travelogues about the region and its culture, which will be published throughout the Spanish-speaking world. Since Angela has told him all about Ingrid (including that she is a very good friend of the most influential member of the Nobel Prize committee), he is certain to look her up. Knowing that Miguel will not bother to do his own research if he finds someone who will provide him with information, Angela asks Ingrid to volunteer to do just that, but with data, traditions, and lore that are totally erroneous and will discredit him as a writer when the articles appear in print. Ingrid's role, then, is not merely to serve as the empathetic but passive narratee of the communication act but as an active participant who will help both affirm and avenge the speaker as well. Angela wants and needs to form a partnership of agency with Ingrid so that between them they can effect a change in the rules of discourse.

The partnership begins immediately, for although supposedly as reader Ingrid has no voice, in fact she speaks through Angela, as the initial words of the novel demonstrate: "You are right. I accept your enraged ultimatum. You will never want to hear from me again if I do not answer immediately and explain to you, in full detail, my motives for not contacting you for so long a period" (11). As this example shows, the narrative we read carries Ingrid's words clearly imprinted on it. Unlike what occurs between Elena and her male interlocutors in *Para no volver,* this is an authentic dialogue, even though one of the participants is physically absent.

Dialogues, however, are complex discursive practices. In a strategy cleverly designed to demonstrate to Ingrid that even when she thinks she is in control she may in fact be controlled by others, that the person speaking is not always the speaking subject, Angela actually quotes several passages from Ingrid's previous letters. In doing so, she demonstrates the power of the reader in narrative. Although the words were written by Ingrid, as the recipient Angela is in a position to subject them to her own purposes. Ingrid's quoted words, therefore, automatically become double voiced; standing behind Ingrid's quotes is Angela who is quoting them, and therefore the reader should read not only what Ingrid's words say, but also what Angela is saying through them. The first such example of this type of double voicing concerns the difference between Nordic and Mediterranean light. Angela quotes Ingrid in a letter written just as winter was beginning in Scandinavia:

> yo, como todos los años, me desesperaré por los verdes del sur, las flores del sur y vuestra luz. La luz que no viene del norte—como tú, remedando la crítica de Maragall a *La Intrusa*, me aseguras, burlona, siempre que me quejo de lo mismo—sino del Mediodía, donde perfila los contornos y los ofrece con toda nitidez.

> (like every year, I became desperate for the green south, the southern flowers and your light. The light that does not come from the north— like you, imitating Maragall's criticism of *The Intruder*, jokingly assure me every time I complain of it—but from the southern zone, where it sharpens the outlines of objects and offers them clearly.) (14)

By means of this quotation, Angela is demonstrating to her friend (and of course to the reader) that she, Ingrid, is guilty of writing clichés, of engaging in the northern European custom of romanticizing the Mediterranean south. Thus Angela as a reader turned writer can discredit Ingrid who is now cast as a writer turned reader. This role shifting is similar to what happens with first- and second-person pronouns in discourse: " 'I' and 'you' are reversible: the one whom 'I' defines by 'you' thinks of himself as 'I' and can be inverted into 'I,' and 'I' becomes 'you.' "[37] By shifting her role from the

---

37. Benveniste, *Problems in General Linguistics*, 199. Deleuze and Guattari in *What Is Philosophy?* present a similar paradox in reference to interpersonal relationships: "In fact, if the other person is identified with a special object, it is now only the other subject as it appears to me; and if we identify it with another subject, it is me [*sic*] who is the other person as I appear to that subject" (16).

reading "you" of the day before to that of the writing "I" of the present, Angela has positioned herself to offer her own "reading" of the bright light of southern Europe:

> nos muestra con crudeza lascas, aristas, protuberancias, y sin disimulos, con la máxima precisión, nos hace caer en la cuenta de que los objetos tienen perfiles ásperos, los vegetales tallos escabrosos y todo, o casi todo, muestra la agresividad del cuchillo, la incisiva dureza del buril, cuando no la terrible, por más bella, del diamante. Y a causa precisamente de esa poderosa luz, el mundo que divisamos parece erizado, como si estuviera en perpetua erección.

> (it reveals to us crudely, without facades, and with the maximum precision the rocks, arris, protuberances, and it makes us realize that objects have rough edges, plants have stems with scales, and everything, or almost everything, reveals the aggression of a knife, the harsh incision of the scalpel, or even more appalling, because of its beauty, of the diamond. And precisely because of that powerful light, the world that we see seems to be standing upright, as if it were in a state of perpetual erection.) (15)

Obviously Angela's reading is anything but objective, yet her excessively pessimistic images underscore Ingrid's excessively romanticized ones. Angela even humorously mocks her friend's tendency to stereotype this region as the home of hot-blooded Latin lovers when she suggests that the bright sunlight of the south gives the illusion that this is a world in a state of perpetual erection. By virtue of her liberated ideas concerning sex, Ingrid apparently considers herself a freethinker. Angela demonstrates to Ingrid that, to the contrary, her Scandinavian ideas about the Mediterranean are clearly a product of discursive stereotypes inscribed in her. By alternating roles in this way, Angela underscores how writers need readers, and vice versa, to balance one another. Only by means of a partnership can they maneuver themselves into a power position.

With an eye to strengthening the partnership she has begun to forge, and as a demonstration of how discursive practices work in both directions, Angela quotes another of Ingrid's letters, this one written in response to one of Angela's novels: " 'Your novels,' you were saying to me, 'would be a lot better if you were capable of resolving your sexual life for yourself, rather than through the orgasms of your characters . . .' " (20). In this case Angela responds defensively. She argues that for her, and for the majority of the women of her generation, tenderness is more important than sex. She goes on to admit that her life's fantasy is "that someone would call me little one, tiny one while he embraced me . . ." (22). With this confession, Angela reveals that she also is subject to a discursive practice that has imprisoned her. On the one hand her need for tenderness is, at least presumably from the point of view of Ingrid, something society has inscribed in her psyche. Angela seems to concede that possibility when she adds, "although my feminist principles would be seriously scathed and my scruples excessively compromised if I had to admit that I not only accepted, but desired to be diminished, objectified, almost degraded" (22). But in confessing her desire to be dominated and noting how it contradicts her commitment to gender issues, she raises the question as to whether these feminist principles are not also attitudes inscribed in her by society, albeit a different segment; perhaps *they* represent the alien force that obstructs her natural needs for tenderness. I believe that her strategy, however, is not designed to question the validity of feminist convictions but rather to make Ingrid aware of the pervasive influence of discourse, of how we can never be sure whether we are the real source of what we feel and believe.

The strategy up to this point, according to the way I read the textual clues, has been designed to seduce Ingrid into participating in this project, to convince her that she too is a product of discourse and therefore has a vested interest in the partnership. Angela's next step is to confess her helplessness and put her fate into Ingrid's hands.

The confession starts in earnest when, in referring to her fateful meeting with Miguel in Valencia, she writes: "noté el momento en que el arquero divino disparaba sus flechas doradas y mi mitad perdida, tras la catástrofe que nos condenó a una larguísima escisión, se soldaba por fin con mi ser" (I was aware the moment the divine archer shot his golden arrows, and after the catastrophe that condemned us to a lengthy separation, my lost half was finally fused with the rest of my being, 23). This series of clichés represents a radical stylistic change in the narrative. In part we can consider it self-parody as Angela mocks her schoolgirl reaction to Miguel. But by means of a parenthetical intrusion of her present being, "I know that it is a cliché to affirm it, but that is the way it was" (23) indicates not only self-parody but a realization by the "narrating self" that her "experiencing self" could not help reacting as she did.[38] Now she can analyze how her emotional response

---

38. As defined by Franz Stanzel, *Narrative Situations in the Novel: "Tom Jones," "Moby-Dick," "The Ambassadors," "Ulysses,"* 59–70.

to Miguel was programmed by cultural indoctrination; she now recognizes that she was a product of *novela rosa* definitions of gender roles. Yet in spite of this ability to analyze her past being, Angela in the present does not feel that she is free from other discursive forces. As she engages in self-analysis, she positions her former self to help her effect a solution.

That same positioning strategy underlies her reference to canonized works whose message is essentially the same as their popularized clones, the *novela rosa* or the Spanish version of Harlequin Romances. During their idyllic time together in Valencia, Miguel resorted to quoting love poems, explaining that "These borrowed verses would serve better than my impoverished words to express to you everything that you make me feel" (34). This admission that, despite his supposed magical command of language, these appropriated verses express his feelings better than his own defective word combinations indicates that Miguel is really a manipulator rather than a creator of the discourse he uses—a creator in the sense of using his own turns of phrase rather than other people's. Obviously the implications of that admission were lost on Angela in Valencia, but they are not lost on her as she now writes about this incident:

> Ausias March le prescribió la receta adecuada y la luna de setiembre rielando en el mar echó el resto. Aunque no era un canto ronco, ni gemía el viento en la lona, ni estábamos en la popa de ningún bajel, su voz debería haber sonado pirata en mi oído, y aún más corsarias sus palabras.
>
> (Ausias March prescribed the appropriate recipe for him and the September moon sparkling on the sea provided the rest. Although it wasn't a sonorous ode, nor was the wind howling over the sail, nor were we standing on the bow of some ship, his voice must have had a pirate tone to my ear, and his words an even more buccaneering ring to them.) (34)

Parody serves as a subversive strategy as Angela mocks first Ausias March and his fifteenth-century love poetry and then that pillar of nineteenth-century romanticism, Espronceda, and his "Canción del pirata" (Pirate's song). In doing so, she is discrediting not merely Miguel and his reliance on borrowed verses in lieu of artistic originality but also the very foundations from which he appropriates his material. By canonizing these poets, the academy has played a key role in preaching gender roles to its female parishioners; it has perpetuated a discourse of which Angela is a parishioner and therefore an easy target for one trained by the same academy as a proselytizer. But now thanks to the act of writing her letter, Angela realizes how to subvert this literary discourse by enlisting the power of her reader.

Her newly developed analytic skills also lead her to recognize that pedantic is even more insidious than artistic discourse, because it hides behind the pomp and circumstance of the academy and the mystique of individual scholarly disciplines. Yet somewhat paradoxically, those most easily seduced by the mystique are precisely the members of the particular discipline. Angela clearly fell into the latter group when she heard Miguel speak for the first time at the conference in Valencia:

> toda esa propensión a maravillarme ante la habilidad de un encantador de palabras . . . Miguel tomó la palabra. El mago de mi adolescencia, el prestidigitador capaz de sacar de la chistera una bandada de palomas, anudar y desanudar pañuelos en un abrir y cerrar de ojos y, en la apoteosis final, cortarle el cuello a su ayudante para volvérselo a unir al torso en un santiamén, apenas sin otra ayuda que unas palabras . . . correspondiendo feliz a los aplausos del público.

> (A word enchanter . . . Miguel seized the podium. The magician of my childhood, the sleight-of-hand expert capable of pulling from his top hat a flock of doves, of tying and untying scarves in the blink of an eye and, in the final deification of his act, cut off his assistant's head only to reunite it in a flash to her body, with little more than words as his props . . . and happily acknowledging the audience's applause.) (27)

As she presents the scene in retrospect Angela creates her own style to subvert Miguel's, which was the very style that in the past seduced her. She underscores her victimization by equating her ingenuousness at the time with that of an innocent child hypnotized by a magical sleight of hand. But as the tricks progress from the engaging (doves drawn out of a hat and knots tied and untied in colorful bandannas) to the grotesque (a be- and reheading), enchantment yields to abhorrence. The innocence of childhood is sacrificed to the morbidity of adulthood as this linguistic mutilation draws applause rather than outrage from the audience (practice dictates that the be- and reheaded assistant is virtually always a young and attractive woman).

Angela's tropes suggest that the modern Don Juans are those writers and academics who seduce with clever linguistic manipulations rather than daring invasions of sanctuaries; the new breed of magicians are those intellectuals whose verbal adroitness rather than motor dexterity creates the illusions. The real trick is to be in a position of control, and in her narrative present Angela is making Ingrid aware that Miguel is but one member of the controlling literati fraternity. Angela's letter is designed to enlist Ingrid's support in forming a competing discursive sorority and to convince her that between them they have the creative tools at hand to subvert and supplant Miguel and his fraternal order.

Along with recognizing how she was a product of discourse and how her attitudes toward men and romance were inscribed in her by pop culture *(novela rosa)* as well as academe (March, Espronceda, and other canonized writers), Angela also becomes increasingly aware that Miguel and other men are equally discursive products. In Miguel's case, the key moment occurs when she reads him into the characters of his own novels. On scrutinizing the literary text, she discovers that the cosmopolitan views on art expressed in his fiction are plagiarized from *Michelin Guides,* that his characters' informed comments on baroque music are usually erroneous, and that his triumphant masculine protagonists display a fundamentally brutal attitude toward the opposite sex. In effect, Angela has textualized Miguel. He is now subject to how she, his reader, interprets him. Once his role as writing subject ends, he is transformed into a written object at the mercy of his reader. After this discovery, Angela realizes that for Miguel everything was a text: "our relationship, based eminently on literary words, had ended like that, suddenly, because he had nothing more to say to me . . . Perhaps neither he nor I were anything other than a stack of words" (49). Miguel's fatal error, and by association men's fatal error, is to fail to realize that discourse depends on two components, not one. Angela has just demonstrated that only by enlisting the partnership of the reader can anyone hope to control the discourse. Since Miguel never made provisions for a female reader/partner in his texts/life, he has given Angela room to maneuver into a position of assuming control, of extracting her vengeance. But of course she also must forge a partnership with her reader if she hopes to take advantage of this opportunity. Unless Ingrid cooperates, Angela will also be trapped in the text she writes. Now she at least realizes that she is at the mercy of her reading subject.

For her the first fateful moment comes when Miguel finally calls her, only to reveal that he had to defend her work from the attack of an influential critic. Later she learns from a friend that it was the opposite, that Miguel had questioned her talent and the critic had defended her. She then concludes that Miguel used her as a mirror in which he could see his own image reflected. But when he began to sense that his seductive charms as well as his writing talents were on the wane, "he sensed that my mirror had broken into a thousand pieces and that he would never be able to reconstruct in it his seducer image" (65).[39]

An even greater crisis emerges when he sends her a copy of his novel and she recognizes herself as the female protagonist. Once again she finds herself reduced to the product of someone else's discourse: " . . . I still desperately search for myself in the pages of his novel" (71). In spite of the freedom she had begun to create for herself, Miguel temporarily has outmaneuvered her again, forcing her to read herself as pure text. But thanks to her own textual strategies, she now has, or at least assumes she has, an ally to help her: "I fervently need you, Ingrid, to give me your opinion and tell me if I really am the protagonist of the book, or if I am mistaken when I recognize myself in the mirror created by its pages" (71).

The novel ends with this appeal plus the one to provide Miguel with false information. As a result of such a nonclosure, readers never know whether Ingrid provides Angela with the reading she hopes for nor whether Ingrid tricks Miguel. In both cases, nevertheless, fictional logic or verisimilitude provides every reason to assume that Ingrid will do whatever she can to help her friend.

If, however, a thread of uncertainty remains concerning whether Ingrid will be willing to deceive Miguel—and if willing, successful—there should be no doubt about her answer to Angela's ontological question concerning her presence in the novel. As a writer and critic herself, Ingrid surely will answer that Angela's "I" can never be the protagonist of the book, that in spite of all Miguel's maneuvers to reduce her to language, the sign can never be the object to which it refers. Only people like Miguel, who allow themselves to be absorbed by discourse, who try to transform their narratees into mirrors, are susceptible to being transformed into mere verbal constructs. Furthermore, Ingrid's implied presence is conclusive proof that Angela and the protagonist of Miguel's novel are not the same at all. By incorporating Ingrid into her text, by making her a partner in this writing project, Angela definitively has separated her self from the literary personage Miguel created.

---

39. See Schumm, " 'Borrowed' Language," for a perceptive and much more detailed analysis of the use of mirror images in the novel.

Angela's Angela has molded herself to Ingrid, to an "other" who can affirm being, while Miguel's Angela is molded to his own mirror image, which ultimately leads to nonbeing. Even the referent to which he refers in his novel is another Angela, an Angela who had not yet learned the strength of a partnership. The new Angela and her ally Ingrid, on the other hand, are about to reduce him not only to discourse but to a discourse fashioned by the two women to discredit him in the eyes of his future readers as well.

As demonstrated, this epistolary format is double voiced so as to constitute a dialogue and debate on the nature of discourse and the possibility of forging new alliances to control it. As a dialogue/debate, it is not merely between two friends but between conflicting generational and cultural attitudes—respectively advocated and contradicted by both Ingrid and Angela—and between the posited author of the novel and her posited reader, and ultimately between Carmen Riera and her readers. Ross Chambers argues that oppositional reading consists of seducing the reading subject away from the subject position of narratee into that of interpretive subject. As my analysis has demonstrated, in *Cuestión de amor propio* the strategy is to discourage Ingrid from ever assuming the position of a passive narratee—a dimension of literary discourse itself. From the beginning she is maneuvered into the position of active reading subject. By quoting her words back to her, Angela creates a dialogic role for Ingrid, one in which she is both reading and speaking subject. This process seems to correspond to Chambers's concept of seducing the reader, since from the beginning she is not allowed to identify herself as a conventional narratee.[40]

More than any other work we have examined in this study, *Cuestión de amor propio* proposes a plan of action or a strategy for wresting control of the discourse. Yet significantly it does not lead us to the point where we can verify that the strategy is successful. Of course we can speculate in a number of ways as to why the novel ends without a clear resolution, but I am inclined to think that the ending represents the posited author's strategy for forming a partnership of agency with her reader. This is not a question for just

---

40. Chambers, *Room for Maneuver*, specifically 17. My reading of Ingrid's role in the novel differs from that of Tsuchiya, "Paradox of Narrative Seduction," who argues that Angela tricks Ingrid as well as Miguel. In a sense, "to trick" and "to seduce" can be considered synonyms, but since I am following Chambers's use of the latter, I suspect that the difference between Tsuchiya's reading and my own involves more than semantics.

Angela and Ingrid and not even for the abstractions labeled *posited author* and *reader*. I have to believe that the real author hopes for real readers to join her in challenging and changing desire itself or what Ross Chambers defines as "ideas, attitudes, values, and feelings" (1), or more specifically in the case of this novel, the discursive practices that define and reify gender casting. If that reading sounds excessively forced, it might be well to remember that behind the posited author of the novel is Carmen Riera who is, in addition to a novelist, a professor and critic. Significantly, I have to believe, the project outlined in *Cuestión de amor propio* focuses on issues in academia, such as sexual stereotypes in canonized works, the academy's practice of authorizing the use of discourse and of valuing linguistic dexterity or jargon over creativity, and the concentration of discursive power in a fraternal order. Of course in all these issues, academia serves as a microcosm for society at large. As she explores these issues in a novelistic context, perhaps Carmen Riera is counting on at least some of us, if for no other reason than a question of self-respect, to see the reality in her fictional model and to form a new collective discursive agency against such abuses of human dignity.

Elena of Tusquets's *Para no volver* suggests that she is going to become her own analyst, while Angela's project of oppositional discourse in *Cuestión de amor propio* is much more radical. In effect, she proposes to act as agent for a whole new kind of reader. With the next novel we will examine, *El invierno en Lisboa*, there is a much more restrictive opportunity for agency. Antonio Múñoz Molina's characters find themselves already cast into screenplays, with their freedom to improvise limited by the roles already assigned to them.

The Improvised Script of *El invierno en Lisboa*

Among the previous works analyzed here, the 1987 *El invierno en Lisboa* (Winter in Lisbon) forms the most direct proairetic links with *La verdad sobre el caso Savolta*, *Visión del ahogado*, and "Alusión al tiempo."[41] Eduardo

41. *El invierno en Lisboa,* published in 1987, winner of both El Premio de la Crítica and El Premio Nacional de Literatura in 1988, is Muñoz Molina's second novel. His other novels to date are: *Beatus Ille,* 1985; *Beltenebros,* 1989; *El jinete polaco,* 1991; *Los misterios de Madrid,* 1992; and *El dueño del secreto,* 1994. He also has published a book of stories, *Las otras vidas,* 1988. In 1995 Muñoz Molina was elected to the Spanish Royal Academy.

Mendoza resurrects some of the elements of the conventional whodunit story into Spanish fiction, and Juan José Millás and Ignacio Martínez de Pisón each follows with his own version of that same format, but, as demonstrated earlier, even in the case of Mendoza's novel the model is subverted rather than imitated.[42] Antonio Muñoz Molina also emphasizes story and enigma in a manner that is conventional only on the surface, and his model is drawn expressly from the world of cinema or the film noir. In fact, the dust jacket states that Muñoz Molina's novel is an homage not only to the movies but also to jazz.

The tribute to jazz appears most obviously on an anecdotal level with the protagonist, Biralbo, cast as a pianist who plays in clubs around the world, most prominent of which in the story is the Lady Bird of San Sebastián. The structure of the novel is, like jazz music, a familiar melody subjected to improvisation, resulting in a harmonious blending of different voices and temporal levels.[43] In effect, jazz qualifies as perhaps the clearest example of a fusion between classical and popular art forms, and in this sense the narrator points to this musical hybrid as a metaphor for the novel as a whole: "I don't understand much about music, and I was never particularly interested in it, but listening to Biralbo in the Lady Bird I had become aware with some relief that music does not have to be unintelligible and it can tell a story."[44] By means of this self-referential statement—and self-referential does not necessarily imply that it is self-conscious on the speaker's part—the narrator positions *El invierno en Lisboa* squarely between the polarities of high and low culture. I propose to examine the novel from this cultural midposition.

As a summary of the action demonstrates, the story narrated in Muñoz Molina's novel is indeed accessible.[45] The action begins in 1985 when the

42. As already noted, one of the trademarks of novelistic postmodernism is a subversion of the detective-novel format. If, as McHale, *Postmodernist Fiction*, argues, the detective novel is the example par excellence of the epistemological mode, it makes an inviting target for those who wish to undermine the very tenets of epistemology.

43. In "El jazz y la ficción," Antonio Muñoz Molina makes a clear distinction between jazz as a discursive theme and as a structural principle. Of course the concept of artistic improvisation—the elaboration of a familiar model into a new expression—can also be equated with Luis Goytisolo's implied theme of iteration as the key to creation.

44. Antonio Muñoz Molina, *El invierno en Lisboa*, 10. Subsequent citations will indicate the page number in parentheses.

45. In view of his fairly recent arrival on the literary scene, Muñoz Molina's work has attracted a reasonable amount of critical comment. See the essays by Rafael Conte, "Antonio Muñoz Molina o la conquista del estilo"; Andrés Soria Olmedo, "Fervor y sabiduría: La obra narrativa de Antonio Muñoz Molina"; José Ortega, "La dimensión temporal en dos novelas

anonymous first-person narrator encounters Santiago Biralbo, a pianist and old drinking buddy, playing under the name Giacomo Dolphin in a Madrid jazz bar. After the musician finishes at the club, the two renew their friendship over a bottle of gin in Biralbo's hotel room where he begins the story, interrupted and resumed over a span of several days, about his life the past five years. It is a love story concerning a beautiful and mysterious woman, Lucrecia, whom the narrator also met briefly in San Sebastián.

The events from the past begin in 1980 at the Lady Bird. Biralbo is the pianist of a jazz group headed by Billy Swann, and the speaker is an infrequent customer of the club. One night a new and captivating face appears among the customers, Lucrecia, and shortly thereafter she and Biralbo become lovers. Sometime later her husband joins her, an American named Malcolm who reputedly deals in stolen artworks and who buys some paintings from the narrator (cheating him in the process). Suddenly Malcolm and Lucrecia depart for Berlin, and she leaves a note for Biralbo with her Berlin address and a promise to write him.

For a while the letters arrive every two or three weeks, but then they stop. The jazz group breaks up, and Biralbo quits his job at the Lady Bird and begins teaching music at a school for girls. One day in 1981 Billy Swann, who has been on a tour through Europe and America, reappears to say that he saw Lucrecia in Berlin in January, and he delivers a letter to Biralbo from her (the last one the pianist is to receive). The letter is written on the back of a map of Lisbon, with the name Burma written at a spot marked with an X.

When Lucrecia finally returns to San Sebastián from Berlin in November 1983, she explains that during this time she and Malcolm were in Germany with another couple, a black man named Toussaints Morton and a blonde woman, Daphne, whom Toussaints said was his secretary. One night Lucrecia witnessed Toussaints and Malcolm murder a man called El Portugués for a map that, Lucrecia confesses, she stole and fled with while the others were sleeping. She says only that the map had something to do with a Cézanne painting. Since then she has been hiding from Malcolm, Toussaints, and Daphne.

---

de Antonio Muñoz Molina"; Juan Antonio Masoliver Ródenas, "Antonio Muñoz Molina: Un paisaje del tiempo"; William Sherzer, "Tiempo e historia en la narrativa de Antonio Muñoz Molina"; Randolph Pope, "Postmodernismo en España: El caso de Antonio Muñoz Molina"; and Gonzalo Navajas, "El *Ubermensch* caído en Antonio Muñoz Molina: La paradoja de la verdad reconstruida."

Biralbo relates that earlier, in July of the same year, Toussaints and Daphne appeared and questioned him about Lucrecia. Now Lucrecia says that they and Malcolm are back in San Sebastián searching for her. In short order Toussaints and Daphne try to ambush Biralbo at night, but he manages to elude them. Biralbo then borrows a car from the owner of the Lady Bird, Floro Bloom, to take Lucrecia to Lisbon. Before they arrive there, however, she convinces him to return to San Sebastián. Later he discovers that she took from him the last letter she wrote, the one written on the back of a map of Lisbon with an X on the spot marked "Burma." Biralbo shortly thereafter goes on a two-year tour with Billy Swann to Copenhagen, New York, and Canada (where he adopts the pseudonym Giacomo Dolphin). On December 12, 1984, he is listed on a program under that name for a concert in Lisbon.

Biralbo says that he arrived at the capital at the beginning of December, coming from Paris where he had received news that Billy Swann was in a Lisbon hospital and gravely ill. Once in the Portuguese city he wandered into the neighborhood he vaguely remembered marked on Lucrecia's map, and entered what he thought was a bar but that turned out to be a bordello called Burma. The waiter informed him that a year earlier, before a police raid, it had been a coffee warehouse that was really a front for an illegal weapons operation. Burma, the waiter explains, was the code name of a secret organization dedicated to the reconquest of Angola.

At this moment the waiter vanished and Malcolm appeared, followed by Toussaints and Daphne. They were still looking for Lucrecia, from whom Biralbo had not heard since he left her two years earlier. As they questioned him at gunpoint, he learned that the owner of the warehouse and founder of Burma, known as El Portugués, had been a wealthy landowner in Angola before he was forced to leave after that country's independence. He had sold his art collection to buy arms, but when the project collapsed and the police were alerted, he had abandoned the warehouse, leaving behind a small but very valuable Cézanne painting. Since Lucrecia had had the map for which they murdered El Portugués, the three were convinced that she had absconded with the painting before the building was taken over by its current owner. Borrowing a script right out of the movies, Biralbo at this point knocked the gun out of Malcolm's hand and managed to escape. He then took a train to the hospital on the outskirts of Lisbon where Billy Swann had been admitted and on the way he saw Lucrecia on a train headed in the opposite direction. He learned from Billy that she had paid in advance his enormous hospital and doctor bills and that she lived in a place called Quinta dos Lobos. On the train back, Biralbo had a confrontation with Malcolm, and during a struggle the American fell onto the tracks and was killed. Biralbo looked up the address of Quinta dos Lobos and found Lucrecia there. She confessed she did find the painting but sold it, using the money to pay Billy Swann's medical bills. After a night together (December 11), they decided to separate, because in addition to Toussaints and Daphne, the police were now after them. Biralbo played at the concert the next day under his pseudonym, Giacomo Dolphin.

During the nights when Biralbo tells this story in his hotel room, he and the narrator can see Toussaints on the sidewalk below watching the building. The narrator has to make a trip to another city for a few days, and when he returns he is told at the club that Giacomo Dolphin (or Biralbo) no longer works there. He goes to the hotel where he hears two police officers questioning the receptionist, and when they leave she tells him that Dolphin has not been there for days, but that a black man and a blonde lady had just left the musician's room before the police came. The narrator goes to it, sees that it has been ransacked, and as he drinks from a bottle of whisky left behind, Lucrecia enters. After he tells her what he knows, she rushes out of the room in search of Biralbo.

One of the metaphorical keys to the novel is provided when Lucrecia returns to San Sebastián from Berlin. In a love scene that takes place in the Lady Bird after hours, Biralbo plays "All the Things You Are" for Lucrecia, and upon finishing confesses that he has always played for her. That is his destiny, she responds, and then adds: "Yo he sido un pretexto" (I have been a pretext, 81). In effect, the whole novel is constructed around not one but a whole series of "pre-texts," one of which is the beautiful and mysterious heroine. But there are others, from *Casablanca* and the whole genre known in Spain as *cine negro* (dark cinema) to *La vida es sueño* (Life is a dream). In short, the love story itself is familiar, a pastiche of popular and classical art.[46] But the story, just like Lucrecia, is a "pre-text" created from a series of pretexts whose purpose is to provide a model on which to improvise. Improvisation, *El invierno en Lisboa* suggests, is the best and perhaps only

---

46. According to Jameson, *Postmodernism*, the pastiche is one of the distinguishing characteristics of postmodern art.

defense against the scripted roles (cultural, social, and economic) that, in Althusser's terminology, "interpellate individuals as subjects" (162). Since we cannot afford to be ignorant of the scenarios, or indifferent to them, our only recourse is to learn how to improvise from them. And the key to that, at least in the case of this novel, is in the telling.

In effect there are two tellers of the tale: the anonymous narrator and Biralbo himself. As already indicated, the story is far from original and in effect reflects a very self-conscious re-creation of several cinematographic, and at least one classical, sources. Biralbo's telling of it, however, represents an improvisation on this very familiar love theme. For example, during their first night together after her return from Berlin, and after they have made love, Lucrecia lights a cigarette before beginning what promises to be a very painful review and explanation of the three years since she left Biralbo. The narrator recounts the moment: "Lucrecia waited silently for a question that Biralbo never asked. Her mouth was dry and her lungs hurt, but she continued smoking furiously, completely oblivious to pleasure" (105). By telling how she felt, the narrator breaks the rules of verisimilitude (the assumption is that he is merely reporting what Biralbo told him). Biralbo, of course, has access to his own psychological and physiological sensations at that time, but he is not supposed to know that her mouth was dry, her lungs hurt, and that she felt no pleasure in the cigarettes. Yet what would be objectionable in a realist, or even a neorealist, work somehow fits here. It seems that Biralbo was projecting his own anguish onto Lucrecia rather than inventing what she was experiencing. In effect, she is not really another person for him but a part of his very being; it is not a case of using her as a mirror for his own image but of his empathetic fusion with her. The description of Lucrecia in this dramatic moment is, I would therefore argue, "realistic."

But the narration of the story is complicated by the presence of the first-person witness narrator. Since he represents the speaking voice of the novel, Biralbo's story is filtered through this speaker who is really a listener and recorder. Even when he assumes the role of directly narrating a portion of the story, for example when he describes Lucrecia the first time he saw her at the Lady Bird in San Sebastián, the narrator defies convention by expressing his lack of narrative authority: "I don't know if I am remembering her as I saw her that night or if what I see while I describe her is one of the photos that I found among Biralbo's papers" (24). Aware that his memory is influenced by things he has seen and heard since the moment in the distant past that he has tried to describe, he does not trust what is generally considered empirically verifiable data. Nor will invention or eyewitness accounts serve for the reality he hopes to convey. As a result, to describe adequately the lovers' first meeting after her absence of three years, the narrator must make it his own experience:

> No imagino estas cosas, no busco sus pormenores en las palabras que me ha dicho Biralbo. Los veo como desde muy lejos, con una precisión que no debe nada ni a la voluntad ni a la memoria. . . . Lo veo todo desde el porvenir, desde las noches de recelo y alcohol en el hotel de Biralbo. . . .
>
> (I am not imagining these things, I am not searching for the details in the words that Biralbo uttered. I see them from a great distance, with a clarity that owes nothing to will or memory. . . . I see everything from the future, from the frightening and alcoholic nights in Biralbo's hotel. . . .) (67–68)

Reality, he implies, transcends not only empiricism but also individual and private incidents. It is shared human emotions that exceed even consensus reality, for it is not quantifiable or merely observable behavior. As I read the implicit message, the novel would have us believe that a narrator does not record facts nor does he or she invent incidents. To narrate, to tell a story, is to draw on consensus reality and acquired knowledge and then to transform them into feelings and sensations. Biralbo and Lucrecia's love affair belongs to timeless human essence; it extends beyond them as individuals and the moment of their embrace; it is part of the person who tells their story and of the persons who listen to it. It truly represents an eternal present.

Biralbo himself seems to capture this concept of atemporality as he explains that for musicians the past does not exist. Music ceases to exist in the very instant in which the musician stops playing it. "It is pure presence" (13), he explains. In spite of Biralbo's metaphor, the lesson to be learned from jazz comes to the speaker only as he listens simultaneously to his friend's narration and to his music on a record. From this combination he comes to understand the art of giving new life to what is as old as human existence:

> Sigo escuchando la canción: como una historia que me han contado muchas veces agradezco cada pormenor, cada desgarradura y cada

trampa que me tiende la música, distingo las voces simultáneas de
la trompeta y del piano, casi las guío, porque a cada instante sé lo
que en seguida va a sonar, como si yo mismo fuera inventando la
canción y la historia a medida que la escucho, lenta y oblicua, como una
conversación espiada desde otro lado de una puerta, como la memoria
de aquel último invierno que pasé en San Sebastián.

(I continue to listen to the song: like a story that has been told to me
several times I appreciate every detail, every fissure and every pitfall that
the music leads me into, I distinguish the simultaneous voices of the
trumpet and the piano, I almost direct them, because at each moment
I know what sound is going to follow immediately, as if I myself were
inventing the song and the story as I listen, slowly and obliquely, like a
conversation overheard from the other side of a door, like the memory
of that last winter that I spent in San Sebastián.) (83)

At first glance his sensation of invention is belied by his confession that
he already knows the story and can anticipate all the twists. Information
theorists say that if we already know or can anticipate the message, it ceases
to provide us with information and tends to become noise.[47] Yet what he
hears is music and not noise, because he is reexperiencing something akin to
the delights of an oral literary tradition in which the mastery of telling lends
vitality to familiar stories; the invention concerns the art of improvisation,
the method rather than the content, the how rather than the what. Again,
the speaker's words tend to turn inward and point at the novel itself. It
relies on a timeless love theme and a familiar story of intrigue upon which
to improvise a new aesthetic experience. In fact, improvisation may be the
only recourse against the tyranny of scripts always already written for us.

The movies represent the clearest expression of how our actions tend
to respond to written scenarios. On the one side are those who fail to
recognize that art, popular or classical, provides existential rather than
merely monetary enrichment. Indeed this group, composed of El Portugués,
Malcolm, Toussaints, and Daphne, treats art strictly as a commodity. By
doing so, these characters allow themselves to be converted into products,
commodities of materialistic discursive practices. On the other side are Billy
Swann, Floro Bloom (the owner of Lady Bird), and of course Biralbo and
Lucrecia. Whereas these people also are threatened by the tyranny of art
forms, they accept the challenge of harnessing the creative and liberating

47. Campbell, *Grammatical Man,* and Paulson, *Noise of Culture.*

potential of those forms. The latter four realize that art is a means of transcending and escaping the enslavement of a materialistic world order. Significantly, when Lucrecia explains that she had to sell the Cézanne painting to pay Billy's medical expenses, she adds: "I had it and I sold it. I will never be resigned to not seeing it any more" (159).

But whereas classical art traditionally has been cast as the enricher of human existence, popular art has been assigned a more problematic role. As one of the more influential modern purveyors of discursive practices, it often enslaves more than it enriches, sometimes serving as an all too handy substitute for creative imagination. For example, when Floro Bloom cannot muster the linguistic dexterity to describe Lucrecia, he resorts to a celluloid model: "A ghost woman. Very impatient. She constantly lights cigarettes and leaves them half smoked. *Phantom Lady.* Have you seen that movie?" (82). Of course in addition to serving as a handy crutch for Floro Bloom, it is possible that Lucrecia is indeed a product of this movie, that she has modeled herself, consciously or unconsciously, after *Phantom Lady.*

The problem of one's life following a movie script affects the narrator as well. After listening to the beginning of Biralbo's story, he returns to his room and puts on a record by Billy Swann titled *Burma.* The music seems to conjure forth a memory that he cannot quite recall because, he explains, it "did not come from my life, I am sure, but from a movie that perhaps I saw as a child and whose title I will never know" (21–22). His problem, like that of all humans, is being the product of sources he will never be able to identify fully, sources that extend from his infancy and beyond. But the problem of being controlled by exterior forces is aggravated when Malcolm buys some paintings from him, and he feels he has fallen victim to something more than this American con artist: "I had the dual and troubling sensation of having been robbed and of acting in a movie for which they gave me only a partly written role" (25). This is one of the few times that the narrator is actively involved in the story, and clearly he feels ill prepared to play his part. But just as he is really a listener more than a narrator, even when cast into the action he prefers the role of spectator rather than actor. It is from his position in the audience that he sees Toussaints for the first time at the Lady Bird: "He spoke as if he were mocking a French accent. He spoke exactly like the blacks in the movies and he said ameguicano and me paguece and he smiled at Floro Bloom and me as if we were buddies from before the time we could remember" (52). Everything is indeed older than their memories, for they are witnessing the forces of fraud and evil assemble themselves. In times of Shakespeare, Lope, and Calderón the actors could be said to be assuming their positions on the stage; in modern times their images more typically are projected on a screen and more often than not on a television set in someone's living room. But really only the costumes and speech patterns have changed. The drama still concerns a conflict between the forces of good and evil, and all the world truly is a stage or screen for it.

But whereas the narrator is primarily a spectator, or a bit player at most, Biralbo has the leading role in this film-script version of life. From the beginning he feels he is reading lines written for him. Even though he does not know Lucrecia is about to accompany Malcolm to Berlin, he senses in their last meeting that she will leave him when she comments on the rain: "I answered her that it always rains like that in the movies when people are going to say good-bye" (38). Then, after her departure, he confesses that he found solace in pretending that he was in a world of make-believe: "I aspired to be like those heroes in the movies whose biography begins at the same time as the action and who do not have a past, only imperious attributes" (40). Lucrecia's return after three years only adds to the sensation of celluloid unreality, as demonstrated one night when they go to the Lady Bird after hours and Biralbo sits down to the piano and plays. When he finishes, Lucrecia says, "mocking herself and Biralbo and what she was about to say and loving it more than anything: 'Play it again. Play it again for me.' 'Sam,' he said, calculating the laughter and the complicity. 'Samtiago Biralbo'" (80). Although *Casablanca* provides the referent for this scene, the two actors are sufficiently conscious of the source to be able to parody it and mock themselves and one another, while still conveying their admiration for the source along with their mutual affection. Actually, they are improvising, finding a means of converting what could be an enslaving structure into a liberating mode of expression. They have found the same transcending value in popular art that traditionally has been attributed only to works labeled *high culture*.

Yet works from high culture also play an important role, and a theme from one of them is masterfully blended into *El invierno en Lisboa*. During their single night together in Lisbon as they try to define some order in their turbulent lives, Lucrecia finally suggests that perhaps all their acts were merely vile, to which Biralbo argues: "we weren't vile . . . we were merely searching for impossible things. The mediocrity and happiness of others disgusted us. . . . There will never be anything better than what we had then." To which she replies: "It's probably so because it is impossible" (167). By virtue of the myths created by the cinema and other popular art, we have familiar models of impossible dreams and love affairs and examples of codes of ethics that dare to depart from the norm. Also thanks to Calderón there is an antecedent for this type of popular art, for "el hacer bien ni aun en sueños se pierde" (good deeds are not wasted even in dreams). Although their existence may be a fiction scripted by the culture in which they were raised and now live, Lucrecia and Biralbo are sufficiently conscious of these influences to be able to select models of human dignity and love. They are true masters of improvisation.

Their opponents, on the other hand, either are completely ignorant of the cultural codes working on them (Malcolm) or dismiss any ethical values implicit in these codes (Toussaints and Daphne). In Lisbon, Malcolm himself defines the gulf that separates the two lovers from him when, as he and his partners question Biralbo at gunpoint about Lucrecia and the Cézanne painting, he suddenly refers to the past:

> Hablabais mucho, lo hacíais para poder miraros a los ojos, conocíais todos los libros y habíais visto todas las películas y sabíais los nombres de todos los actores y de todos los músicos, ¿te acuerdas? Yo os escuchaba y me parecía siempre que estabais hablando en un idioma que no podía entender. Por eso me dejó. Por las películas y los libros y las canciones.
>
> (You two were always talking, you did it so that you could look each other in the eye, you knew all the books and you had seen all the movies and you knew the names of all the actors and musicians, remember? I used to listen to the two of you and it seemed to me that you were talking in a language that I couldn't understand. That's why she left me. Because of the movies and the books and the songs.) (132–33)

Malcolm feels that he has been cuckolded by a discursive system. By not learning its codes, he realizes now, he left himself defenseless. His resentment, as a result, is not so much against Biralbo as against a system that Biralbo and Lucrecia learned to avail themselves of so masterfully: "nobody nor nothing mattered to the two of you, reality was too impoverished for you two, isn't that right?" (141). Malcolm, of course, has guessed their secret. Art, whether in the form of jazz, the movies, or a Cézanne painting, allows them to transcend everyday reality. Furthermore, since the two of them can share that experience, the hapless Malcolm cannot hope to compete with Biralbo for Lucrecia. The novel points to the conclusion that he is a tragic figure not because he dies a violent death beneath the wheels of a train but because he excludes himself from cultural discourse and therefore from the forces that help give meaning to human existence.

While Malcolm is hopelessly ignorant of contemporary cultural codes, that is not the case with Toussaints and Daphne. For example, during the same interrogation in Lisbon, Biralbo at one point says, "Shoot, Malcolm. You would be doing me a favor." When Toussaints asks where he has heard those lines before, his companion responds: " 'In *Casablanca*,' Daphne said, indifferently and accurately. 'Bogart said it to Ingrid Bergman'" (141). Daphne and Toussaints know the codes, but for them it is more like a game of "trivial pursuit"; obviously they do not experience any transcendent value from these art forms. Just as much as Malcolm, they have condemned themselves to an impoverished existence. Having denied themselves the existential wealth that art can provide, they dedicate themselves to stealing works of art for material wealth. In yet another ironic twist, by attempting to reduce art to a commercial product, Malcolm, Toussaints, and Daphne reveal themselves to be the real products; they are commodities of a discursive practice known as the modern consumer society.[48]

The novelistic structure itself of *El invierno en Lisboa* defies the concepts of commodity and product. Rather than leading to closure, the ending points to eternal iteration. After Lucrecia leaves the hotel in search of Biralbo, the narrator watches her from the window of the musician's room as she merges into the crowd of Madrid's Gran Vía or "Broadway": "ya convertida en una lejana mancha blanca entre la multitud, perdida en ella, invisible, súbitamente borrada tras los paraguas abiertos y los automóviles, como si nunca hubiera existido" (now transformed into a distant white spot in the multitude, lost in it, invisible, suddenly erased behind the open umbrellas and the cars, as if she had never existed, 187). With this fading that is typical of jazz as well as vintage film noir, the readers sense that they have been offered a segment of an eternal theatrical event. The drama is

---

48. While conceding that Malcolm is marginalized from the others, Navajas, "El *Ubermensch* caído," does not seem to distinguish between Biralbo and Lucrecia on one end and Toussaints and Daphne on the other in reference to the influence of pop culture on the respective couples.

real, whereas the characters may well be phantasms. There is every reason to assume that not only will this story of an impossible love continue but it will be repeated in both popular and so-called high art forms for ages to come as well. *El invierno en Lisboa* has now joined a long list of other "pre-texts" to facilitate the next improvisation on the themes of love and intrigue.

Without question, Muñoz Molina has emerged as one of the leading new Spanish novelists. While one suspects that the reading accessibility of his novels goes a long way in explaining their success, it seems almost certain that, at least on a subconscious level, readers are also captivated by his response to the influence in our lives of discourse in its multiple forms. It has become something of a cliché to say that everything is intertextual and that there can be nothing new or original in literature or anything else. What Muñoz Molina has accomplished with *El invierno en Lisboa* is to rise above the cliché of "everything new is old" by making it the very focus of his writing project.

Many theorists argue that humans cannot escape the influence of discourse, or the fact that every text emerges from a previous text. As a result, people are limited to repeating lines spoken by others and familiar to all. Not surprisingly, many are convinced that communication itself is a threatened practice. Modern communication theory has helped pinpoint the threat by arguing that to effect communication, a message must involve an element of surprise, something not evident or anticipated. I would like to argue that *El invierno en Lisboa*, at least by implication, challenges that thesis.

When the narrator happens onto Biralbo at the jazz bar in Madrid and they sit down to talk for the first time in years, he verbally paints the following scene:

> Nos quedamos solos Biralbo y yo, mirándonos con desconfianza y pudor sobre el humo de los cafés y de los cigarrillos, sabiendo cada uno lo que el otro pensaba, descartando palabras que nos devolverían al único punto de partida, al recuerdo de tantas noches repetidas y absurdas que se resumían en una sola noche o en dos.

> (Biralbo and I were left alone, looking at one another with suspicion and fear over the smoke of coffee and cigarettes, each one knowing what the other was thinking, discarding words that would bring us back to the only point of departure, to the memory of so many repetitious and absurd nights that were compressed into one or maybe two nights.) (30)

Although there is no exchange of ideas or concepts, nor even words up to this point, these two old friends are definitely communicating. As the preceding analysis of the novel has demonstrated, there are several similar examples in *El invierno en Lisboa* of this type of omniscient empathy where one person not only knows what the other is thinking and feeling but actually thinks and feels as his or her "other." Paulson and others argue that at least since the printing press, only in the sciences and technology has any new information been generated.[49] Perhaps the fading importance of the humanities can be traced in part to critics' efforts to prove that communication in the arts involves the creation of information rather than the transmission of feelings and emotions. Muñoz Molina may be suggesting that what is needed in literature are linguistic constructs that deemphasize the importance of information based on new plots or surprising twists. The unexpected turn of events was not a part of oral literature, and he seems to be striving for a minstrel effect by relying on familiar intertextual models in *El invierno en Lisboa*. Indeed, the surprise factor is not a question of a new plot but of an empathy whereby a first-person narrator can convincingly say of his meeting with a friend that each knew what the other was thinking.[50]

Muñoz Molina follows the strategy initiated in this period by Martín Gaite and Millás—and further developed by Montero, Tusquets, and Martínez de Pisón—of focusing on the discursive practices perpetuated by popular art forms, especially the movies. The next and last author whose work I am going to examine, Javier Marías, does not concern himself with that particular discursive practice but focuses instead on how perturbations in a cultural system can become an important source of information.[51]

49. Paulson, *Noise of Culture.*

50. Again in "El jazz y la ficción" the author makes a revealing analogy between music and literature: "And literature, just like jazz, attains its highest presence and its only true justification when it establishes a sense of simultaneity: the one who is playing and the one who is listening experience the same emotions, and music would not exist if there were no one listening to it" (25–26). The shared experience defined here is similar to what I label a nonverbal communication between the characters in the novel.

51. Paulson, *Noise of Culture,* explains the phenomenon of perturbations as follows: "Before there can be communication, there must have been precommunicative utterances, perturbing signals to which there was not yet a stable or recognizable response" (147). Later Paulson states: "What is studied in literature appears, if placed in opposition to what is communicative and functional, as a *perturbation* of contemporary culture, as something at least partially unexpected that comes from the outside" (152).

Perturbation/Information: *Todas las almas*

Javier Marías's novel *Todas las almas* (All souls) concerns a young Spaniard who spends two years at Oxford University as a Spanish instructor.[52] Shortly after arriving there he already foresaw the focus of the narrative he now begins to write:

> . . . me di cuenta de que mi estancia en la ciudad de Oxford sería seguramente, cuando terminara, la historia de una perturbación; y de que cuanto allí se iniciara o aconteciera estaría tocado o teñido por esa perturbación global y condenado, por tanto, a no ser nada en el conjunto de mi vida, que *no* está perturbada.

> (. . . I realized that my time in the city of Oxford would surely be, when it ended, the story of a perturbation; and that everything that initiated or happened there would be touched or tainted by that global and fateful perturbation, and therefore, there could be nothing in the sum of my life that was *not* perturbed.)[53]

Recognizing that perturbations in a system create information, one of the pieces of information conveyed by *Todas las almas* concerns the disquietingly contradictory spatial and temporal essence of human existence.

As the anecdote begins, the emphasis seems to be more on space than on time as the protagonist learns what it is like to cross borders and live in a foreign country. His colleagues and mentors, Cromer-Blake and Toby Rylands, offer him companionship and intellectual stimulus. Yet their friendship cannot prevent him from feeling marginalized, until a love affair with Clare Bayes, the wife of another university colleague, alleviates his anguish. As his tenure draws to a close, she ends their affair. Now as he writes of his Oxford experiences, two and one-half years have passed; he is a successful Madrid businessman, he is married and the father of an infant son, and his two closest British friends are dead. The contrasting spatial separation and temporal contiguity of his friends' deaths and his son's birth

---

52. To date the author has published the following works of fiction: *Los dominios del lobo*, 1971; *Travesía del horizonte*, 1972; *El monarca del tiempo*, 1978; *El siglo*, 1983; *El hombre sentimental*, 1986; *Mientras ellas duermen*, 1990; *Corazón tan blanco*, 1992; and *Mañana en la batalla piensa en mí*, 1994, in addition to *Todas las almas*, 1989. Other than reviews, I am unaware of any critical essay published on *Todas las almas*.

53. Javier Marías, *Todas las almas*, 69. Subsequent citations will indicate the page number in parentheses.

seem to have inspired his writing project. He apparently hopes that the act of narrating will help him reconcile the incongruity between the mortal essence of the individual and the immortal perseverance of the species— the contradiction experienced by all humans between their ego and their communal instinct, between their need to feel unique from and yet identical to all souls—past, present, and future.

Having uprooted himself for the opportunity to work at Oxford, he quickly discovers that his career move has more serious consequences than he had anticipated: "me veía de pronto *fuera del mundo*" (I found myself suddenly *outside the world*). He goes on to explain that "there is no one here who has known me when I was a young man or a child. That is what perturbs me, to no longer to be in the world and to have not existed before in *this* world. That there is no witness to my continuity" (70). By immigrating and crossing national borders he constitutes a perturbation in the system for himself and for his British acquaintances. A stranger in a strange land, he feels he has been detached from the chain linking him to the other members of the community called Spain. Even for those who live in Oxford, he is something of an oddity, or "a decorative character" (15), who disrupts ever so slightly their routine existence.

Finding himself isolated and with no human witness to his daily activities, he becomes convinced that he can only measure his being in terms of waste, of what he discards; without companionship, only what ends up at the end of each day in the wastebasket bears testimony to his quotidian existence: "La bolsa y el cubo son la prueba de que ese día ha existido y se ha acumulado y ha sido levemente distinto del anterior y del que seguirá, aunque es asimismo uniforme y el nexo visible con ambos" (The garbage sack and the wastebasket are proof that a certain day has existed and accumulated and has been slightly distinct from the day before and from the one that will follow, although by the same token it is uniform and the visible link between one and the other, 88). Thus the wastebasket serves as a negative sign that paradoxically affirms his existence.[54] But the affirmation is in another sense a negation, for it affirms only mental decisions and physical acts of what *not* to keep, use, and produce. In rhetorical terms,

54. The classic example of a negative that affirms is the command: "Do not think about elephants." Bertice Bartlett, "Negatives and the Reader," offers an insightful discussion of the affirming function of negatives.

the wastebasket can be interpreted as a trope signifying what happens when an ego is divorced from its link to community, perhaps a metaphor for the triviality of an individual's existence viewed within the spectrum of humanity as a whole.

Although Clare plays a key role in rescuing him from his despair and sense of insignificance, initially he views her as merely another object to be used and discarded. In a comical parody of the male gaze, the protagonist first lays eyes on her during a High Table of his Oxford college. She is seated across from him and from her husband, a seating arrangement that allows the speaker to look at her surreptitiously during the course of the meal. But his gaze, "filled with sexual admiration," is challenged by that of the High Table warden, Lord Rymer, who stares at Clare with a look "of fierce and undisguised lasciviousness" (54). The protagonist wins this ogling contest when Lord Rymer, having drunk himself into a stupor, so overplays his hand that he becomes the center of everyone else's gaze. The protagonist, ever alert, takes advantage of this general focus on the head of the table: "Then I looked openly at Clare Bayes's face and, without knowing her, I saw her as someone who already belonged to my past" (62). Freed from subterfuge and male competition, his ogle becomes a contemplation.

Clare reciprocates by gazing at him: "It was that she was looking also, and she looked at me as if she knew me as a little boy in Madrid . . . my nocturnal fears . . . And that act of seeing myself as she saw me made me see her in a similar manner" (63–64). Clare has managed to maneuver herself from the position of object into that of subject and him from subject to object, and vice versa. Rather than serving exclusively as a mirror for his adult virility, she acts as a speculum that refracts his gaze back to his childhood vulnerability. Apparently because she forces him to look at the boy hiding behind a man's disguise, her ricocheting gaze creates for him a feeling of community:

> Así me miraba Clare Bayes y yo la miraba a ella, como si fuéramos los ojos vigilantes y compasivos el uno del otro, los ojos que vienen desde el pasado y que ya no importan porque ya saben cómo están obligados a vernos, desde hace mucho: tal vez nos mirábamos como si fuéramos hermanos ambos.
>
> (Clare Bayes looked at me like that and I at her, as if we were the vigilant and compassionate eyes of each other, eyes that come from the past and to whom it no longer matters because they have known for

some time now how they are obligated to look at us: perhaps we looked at one another as if we were brother and sister.)[55] (66)

The physical body that initially attracted him now serves also as a sign pointing at that ethereal body labeled *humankind*. By virtue of Clare's gaze, he regains for the first time since arriving at Oxford his sense of continuity and community with the rest of his species.

But if initially Clare seems to represent a resolution of the contradiction between the demands of his ego and of his generic instinct, in retrospect the resolution dissolves and ideality gives way to reality. According to both classical and popular culture, glorified love is essentially egocentric. Discursive tradition would have both participants in an idealized reciprocal love relationship believe themselves and each other to be unique. Yet as he contemplates his relationship with Clare from the present, the speaker subverts this particular love myth:

> Siempre me ha parecido un exceso de ingenuidad pensar que nadie— porque nos ama, esto es, porque *a solas* ha *determinado* amarnos transitoriamente y *luego* nos lo ha *anunciado*—va a comportarse con nosotros de manera distinta de como lo vemos comportarse con los demás, como si nosotros no estuviéramos destinados a ser los demás inmediatamente después de la determinación solitaria y la anunciación del otro, como si de hecho no fuéramos siempre también los demás además de nosotros.

> (It has always struck me as excessively ingenuous to think that anybody —because he or she loves us, that is to say, because *in private* he or she has *determined* to love us temporarily and *then* has *informed* us of it—is going to behave differently with us than how we have seen him or her behave with others, as if we were not destined to be the others immediately after the solitary determination and the revelation of the existence of the other, as if indeed we were not always also the others in addition to ourselves.) (32–33)

Although this declaration can be read as an expression of his resentment of Clare taking the initiative in ending their relationship (in which case it would echo another long-standing discursive practice, misogyny), the context indicates that the speaker intends it as a concession of his own

---

55. In yet another expression of iteration, this passage is repeated verbatim as the two lovers say good-bye for the final time (231).

insignificance. By identifying himself as a mere representative of a universal category, he subverts the egocentrism that discursive tradition has posited as the very cornerstone of a romanticized love relationship. In spite of what the arts through the ages would have him believe about this type of perfect love, now he can only mock the notion of his or anyone else's uniqueness. This is but the first in a list of discoveries in the novel serving to demythologize the cult of the individual.

The problematic issue of individual identity takes on a more bizarre aspect, as his foreignness in Oxford inspires him to occupy himself with a solitary research pursuit. During a period when Clare's son is ill and the protagonist cannot see her, he visits bookstores in search of works written by Arthur Machen. In his searches he encounters a fellow Machen collector, Alan Marriott, who in a conversation explains that for their Gaelic author, certain associations and pairings create horror. As explained by Marriott, Machen argues that whereas a person may strike us as perfectly normal and sympathetic, when that same person is associated or paired with something or someone else, the pairing constitutes a perturbation, and the result can be horrific. Marriott goes on to explain his research on a contemporary of Machen, John Gawsworth, who used a series of aliases. By virtue of his name changes, Gawsworth's true identity had become fused with that of several people. The text then offers a photo of the "real" Gawsworth (a mimetic representation) followed on the next page by another photo of his mortuary mask (a mimetic representation of a nonmimetic representation) (129, 131). This story of fused identities serves to underscore how essentially identical each of us is to an infinite number of other people. In addition, the juxtaposition or pairing of the photos suggests how an individual acts as a palimpsest on which an observer can detect in the current image the traces of that individual's past life and future death as well as the traces of the lives and deaths of previous and future generations. The total annihilation of the ego inherent in these examples helps explain the horror for Machen and now the protagonist of such associations.

Initially dismissed by the speaker, this concept comes back to haunt him when one day he happens to find Clare in the company of a young boy and an old man. In the case of the man, "I knew immediately that he was her father because of the astonishing resemblance. (Because of the perhaps frightening resemblance.)" (185). When he manages to get a clear view of the boy, Eric, "what I saw was the same face for the third time, identical,

Clare Bayes's face that I knew perfectly and that I had kissed and that had kissed me so many times" (186). As he observes this repetition in three generations, he comes to a disturbing realization: "I have kissed and I have been kissed also by the boy and the old man . . . for the face is the same although the ages and sex vary, incarnations or representations or simulacra or manifestations" (196). The comfort of community has now become the horror of anonymity. Although the realization of interconnectedness earlier soothed his sensation of being marginalized and perturbed, now it creates the opposite effect. The connecting lines do not merely lead from one point to another, but they backtrack, forming a vertiginous communal web. Identities, even genders, are erased; Clare is not merely Clare, she is simultaneously her father and her son, the three fused into simulacra of each other. What is more, since he now realizes that Clare alone was not the object of the sexual passion he felt and expressed, that passion seems not merely ridiculous but also somehow horribly perverse.[56] In effect, the fusion of Clare with her son and father represents another disturbance in the system; it serves to subvert another pillar of our Western discursive tradition: the feminine object of desire.

The horror experienced in the face of Clare's metamorphosis becomes even more personal for the speaker with the birth of his own son, only months old as he writes this story. The speaker now contemplates the mystery of this progeny who cannot yet walk or talk and who has no memory: "Hace poco *no era.* Ahora es un niño eterno . . . me pregunto qué precisará este niño para causar horror, me preocupa la fantasía de poder ser yo mismo—su padre—la idea precisa, la idea justa para que infundamos horror" (A little while ago he *did not exist.* Now he is an eternal child . . . I wonder what will be necessary for this child to create horror, the fantasy worries me that I—his father—could constitute the precise idea, the very idea for us to implant horror, 108). Again, the pairing of himself with his son creates horror. The infant alone, in his completely dependent state, could never elicit such a negative reaction. But when he is paired with his father, the association or fusion can become horrific, if not for others then at least for the father himself. As a result, the speaker confesses to wishing

56. This episode echoes the movie *The Crying Game.* In the movie, the protagonist vomits in horror when he discovers that the person with whom he has been intimate and fallen in love is really a man, a transvestite.

at times that he could return to a state of childlessness—he cannot allow himself to wish for the disappearance of his son, only to find himself again as he was before his son was born: "de *ser sin hijos,* de ser un hombre sin prolongación, de poder encarnar siempre y sin mezcla la figura filial o fraterna, las verdaderas, las únicas a las que estamos acostumbrados, las únicas en las que estamos o podemos estar instalados naturalmente desde el principio" (of being *childless,* of being a man without an heir, of being able to incarnate purely the filial or fraternal symbol, the truths, the only ones of which we are or can be naturally placed in possession from the beginning, 108). Once again he is torn by a contradiction: He would like to return to a state of preparenthood uniqueness but without renouncing the existence of his son and the continuity implicit in that existence.

The Alan Marriott character in the novel demonstrates how a force that perturbs a system creates information. By virtue of his presence, readers experience the conflict of the uniqueness of the individual and the universality of the species. The protagonist experienced anguish when he arrived at Oxford and found himself severed from the continuity of his Spanish roots. Clare provided him with a sense of interconnectedness. But thanks to Marriott, he also discovered, when he saw her in the company of her son and father, that continuity can also be grotesque. The perturbation created by this encounter points to the conflict between the needs of the ego (needs reinforced, if not created, by discourse) and the inclination to form part of a larger community (an inclination also reinforced, if not created, by discourse). It is a conflict between the time-bound individual and the essentially timeless species. The protagonist wants to be unique and temporal as well as universal and eternal.

There is one character above all who incarnates the conflict I have just defined: Will, the doorman for the Oxford building where the protagonist has his office and holds his classes. "Will literally did not know what day he was living, and thus, without anyone being able to predict the date of his choice let alone knowing what determined it, he spent every morning in a different year, traveling through time backward and forward at his own free will, or, more accurately, probably unwillingly" (11). As a result of his flexible time frame, Will confuses the identity of the current staff with previous generations. Depending on the time zone in which he finds himself, he refers to the protagonist as Mr. Trevor, Dr. Nott, Mr. Renner, Dr. Ashmore-Jones, Mr. Brome, Dr. Myer, and Dr. Magill, all former faculty members, and occasionally as Mr. Branshaw, a name unknown to anyone else and that "made me wonder if Will's capacity to project himself in time might also include the future" (14). The speaker even admits to admiring the doorman at times because Will is constantly "repeating what he has known. It is a way of not discarding anything, although he is not aware of it and although from my point of view his life in a booth has been anything but fulfilling" (163). Although technically sane, the speaker admits to being *perturbado* (one of whose synonyms in Spanish, nevertheless, is *loco* or crazy). Will, on the other hand, quite obviously is technically deranged yet he does not feel *perturbado*. In fact, thanks to his insanity, what are perturbations for others are natural phenomena for him. Since for Will specific moments and individuals repeat themselves and he does not have to file anything in the archives of the past, he is free from the conflict between the temporality of the individual and the atemporality of the universe. He does not suffer, therefore, from the anxieties created when systems inevitably deviate from predictable patterns into strange loops. Yet he pays a price for his freedom, for he cannot process the information such deviations in the system provide concerning the contradictory essence of human existence.

Since he has no built-in mechanism, such as Will's mental disorder, for ignoring the realities of life and death, the speaker's response is to write about his experiences. He begins his narration by announcing that two of his three close friends from Oxford have died since he left, and only in the final pages does he identify the deceased: Cromer-Blake and Toby Rylands. Yet for Will, who still lives, there can be no death: "he will continue saying good day and raising his hand and confusing time and my time and perhaps calling someone by my name (because for him I have not left, and for him all souls are alive)" (242). By means of his narrative the speaker, like Will, can resurrect those who have died and ensure that all his Oxford acquaintances will take their place among all souls. But of course there still remains a basic difference between the abstraction of a soul and the reality of a person and between a linguistic representation and a living being.

Indeed, the novel leads readers to the conclusion that the issue of representation lies at the core of the protagonist's writing project. On the very first page he draws a distinction between his past and present self: "Although the one who speaks is not the same one who was there" (9). Even his use of first-person narration responds merely to convenience and convention: "it is only because I prefer to speak in the first person, not because I believe that memory suffices for someone to continue being the same person in different times and spaces" (9–10). Crossing borders, both temporal and spatial, changes being. When he goes on to emphasize, therefore, that he is not an extension, or a shadow, or an heir, or even the appropriator of his past being, it is clear that he wants to make his readers aware of the existence of two distinct people. As his project unfolds, the reason for that distinction becomes clearer: "It is possible that I have lied about everything, I don't know, but it doesn't matter, my life now runs along a different course, I am no longer the person who spent two years in the city of Oxford, at least I don't think I am. I am no longer perturbed . . ." (238–39). Notwithstanding a hesitant note in this statement, the speaker claims to have found the solution to his anguish in the act of narrating. Unlike Will, he cannot deceive himself into believing that Cromer-Blake and Rylands are still alive, even though the characters he has created for them are now timeless. Their egos have perished, but the linguistic representations of their human essence persevere. So also the representations of Clare, Will, and the others are now fixed in an eternal present, while back in Oxford he knows very well that they are undergoing the inevitable aging process just as he is in Madrid. In his dual role as narrator and protagonist, the speaker incarnates the temporal/atemporal polarity. The speaking subject can never become the object about which he or she speaks, nor can the individual solve the problem of the ego by joining a community of souls. Yet while the act of narrating has not eliminated the contradiction between the time-bound individual and the timeless natural order, at least it has provided the speaker with a means of reconciling himself to it by allowing him aesthetically to participate in this contradiction.

The type of accommodation implicit in the narrating act in *Todas las almas* can be associated with something Cromer-Blake wrote in his diary, which the narrator quoted near the beginning of the novel: "death not only takes from us our own life, but also the lives of others" (44). In the throes of what turned out to be a fatal illness, Cromer-Blake's statement invites both an egotistic and an altruistic reading. While the object pronoun and verb "takes from us" places the focus on the ego, the second object, "the lives of others," expresses a concern for fellow human beings. Rather than resolving the contradiction, Cromer-Blake found a means of accommodating it. That acceptance seems to be what the narrator-protagonist has discovered in the process of writing his story. And of course in doing so, he has provided his readers with the aesthetic experience of unresolved contradiction, an experience as frustrating and enriching as existence itself.

Javier Marías's project, similar to that of his contemporaries, clearly is to demonstrate the extent to which discourse has contributed to, if not created, such institutions as love, desire, beauty, and even parenthood. Yet perhaps more than the works of the other authors examined in this study, with the possible exception of that of Luis Goytisolo, *Todas las almas* tries to point us beyond the level of discourse to its underlying human values and instincts. The title itself points at spiritual as opposed to social values. But of course, he cannot address spirituality without contributing further to its textualization, and he cannot represent instinct without becoming a slave of language. For example, one night the protagonist meets a young woman in a discotheque, and they end up in his bed: " 'I have my dick in her mouth,' I thought as I had it there, and I thought it with these words, for only those words come to mind when thoughts about what one is doing are put into words . . ." (145–46). This example of textualizing, of what Foucault describes as the "putting into discourse of sex,"[57] underscores how language tends to obliterate instinct and feeling. In this case, an instinctive act is transformed by discourse into a vulgar and trivial text. Language has displaced experience. His partner then intensifies that effect when she asks him to repeat the words she says for him: " 'I desire you,' I said. 'I desire you,' I thought, and I stopped thinking after this thought" (149). His only escape from the vulgarity and nonreality of a text is to stop textualizing, which can only occur if he stops the thinking process itself. This is, perhaps, the ultimate contradiction presented in the novel. The power of discourse allows us to define ourselves as humans, yet discourse also threatens to deprive us of what it is to be human.

The process of narrating the perturbation the speaker both represents and experienced during his two years at Oxford serves as the informational essence of the novel. But of course now he is back in Madrid and a wealthy businessman with wife and child. Therefore when he declares almost at the end of the novel that "I am no longer perturbed" (239), he announces that he has nothing more of interest or surprise to tell his readers. Naturally the novel then ends.

---

57. Michel Foucault, *The History of Sexuality I: An Introduction,* 12.

Todas las almas is an appropriate work with which to conclude this study of discursive fields in post-totalitarian Spanish fiction. The other works published between the years 1985 and 1989 that we have examined here emphasize the relationship between discourse and popular culture or canonized texts. In his novel Javier Marías shifts the emphasis from the fashionable to the aberrant; he focuses on the inevitable but unpredictable disturbances in seemingly unperturbable discursive systems. But by virtue of such perturbations, we are provided the occasional opportunity to apprehend surprising new, or more accurately, merely forgotten or ignored information concerning human existence.

Todas las almas appeared the same year as the breakup of the Soviet bloc. Many believe that those political events ensure that history will record the year 1989 as the victory of capitalism and democracy over socialism and totalitarianism. But as Jacques Latour notes that same year conferences were held in Amsterdam, London, and Paris to protest the environmental destruction of the planet. Latour suggests that some day history may also point to 1989 as the year when the world recognized the failure of capitalism.[58] Whatever the judgment will be, and it is all but ensured that the initial consensus eventually will be followed by disagreement, historians nevertheless will find in the monumental political perturbations of that year significant sources of information.

But as this century ends and the next millennium approaches, the world may well witness a new means of defining information itself. In a thought-provoking article, N. Katherine Hayles argues that we are now experiencing an epistemic shift in our sources of information. In the computer age, the dialectic presence/absence has been replaced by pattern/randomness. Rather than possession, the key word today is *access*. Perturbations now and in the immediate future may send a system into turmoil (or what happens when you strike the wrong function key on a computer), but they may also rescue it from sterility. As Hayles states it: "Information is produced by a complex dance between predictability and unpredictability, repetition and variation."[59] Without minimizing the epistemic shift Hayles defines, it is highly significant that the informational potential of perturbations is essentially the same in the emerging episteme as defined by Hayles as it has

58. Bruno Latour, *We Have Never Been Modern.*
59. Hayles, "Virtual Bodies and Flickering Signifiers," 78.

been in the one just ending. Since literature itself constitutes a disturbance in a cultural system, I now would like to draw this study to a close by shifting the emphasis to this function of literature as a unique source of knowledge in the emerging cybernetic age.

Epilogue

In current literary studies, as in most other areas of scholarship, it is no longer fashionable to draw sweeping or definitive conclusions. This is a fashion change I applaud, and consequently I have opted for the word *epilogue* (from the Greek *epilogos*, "to say in addition") as a label for this final section. The emphasis here falls much more on contextualization and speculation than on summation and totalization.

As the reader who has followed me to this point very well knows, textual analyses constitute the core of this study. Although I have attempted to relate each close reading to its epistemic context, no doubt some will find this book much too tied to what is now pejoratively labeled *conventional literary studies*. As one means for mounting a defense against the attack on the study of literature, I now propose to contextualize the method of analysis I have applied here vis-à-vis two of the more prominent new theoretical approaches. Then I will use that comparison as a point of departure for speculating on the role literary studies may be able to play in the next millennium.

For some critics literary studies has a pejorative connotation because they believe that, as now defined and practiced, the field cannot survive in the twenty-first century. As I say this I am fully aware that the present embattled status of literary studies is not unique even in my time. After Sputnik the emphasis in the 1950s shifted dramatically to space technology and science, and with the exception of foreign-language study the humanities in general were relegated to a marginal status. The next attack came on the heels of the social upheavals of the late 1960s and early 1970s when literary studies were only one of a number of disciplines labeled *irrelevant*. Although the present attacks, therefore, are not really new, there is as much need now as there was in the 1950s and early 1970s to make sure we have an answer to the charges leveled against us. I feel we cannot afford merely to remain silent or to repeat the cultural continuity arguments from the past. It seems clear to me that if we hope to be effective, our defense must correspond to the present context.

A few of the more committed cultural-studies advocates qualify as the more vociferous adversaries today of literary studies. Yet in fairness, their programs for reform respond to what seem to be their sincere fears and forecasts of doom for literature as an academic discipline. For example, John Mowitt resurrects the concept of text posited by Derrida, Barthes, Kristeva, and others, in part perhaps to divorce himself from his more marxist-oriented colleagues, and above all to discredit the divisions formed by academic disciplines.[1] Since a text is all-encompassing and we must textualize all our knowledge and experience, Mowitt argues that divisions into academic disciplines contradict the very concept of a text. He proselytizes for the need to create an antidisciplinary academic community where the pursuit of knowledge transcends current institutional structures. In this utopian world where anti- will replace inter-, intra-, and all other forms of disciplinary demarcations, literature will be integrated into the study of law, economics, politics, philosophy, history, music, art, film, and whatever else comes to define a text for a particular individual or group. Although there is much to be said for any proposal to broaden what in some cases clearly have become excessively narrow academic pursuits, some cultural-studies advocates run the danger of making those pursuits so all encompassing that rather than a cadre of specialists we will have an army of dilettantes. If cultural studies is carried to the extreme some—but by all means not all—advocate, one can easily imagine literary studies becoming absorbed by rather than integrated into more utilitarian or purely conceptual cultural registers.[2]

Related to cultural studies is the new historicism as defined and practiced by historians such as Hayden White and Dominick LaCapra, and literary scholars such as Stephen Greenblatt and Brook Thomas, among a host of others. In the final analysis, the new literary historicism movement is, to a large degree, a reaction against marxism and its totalizing worldview. More precisely, in the words of Thomas, "The question of how to put versions of the past to present uses is a central one for any movement calling itself a

---

1. John Mowitt, *Text: The Genealogy of an Antidisciplinary Object.*
2. For an example of a felicitous blending of literary and cultural studies, see Mark I. Millington and Paul Julian Smith, eds., *New Hispanisms: Literature, Culture, Theory.*

new historicism."[3] Similar to my approach here, the new historicists, as well as many cultural study advocates, concern themselves with demonstrating how certain discursive practices fit into a common episteme. Greenblatt, for example, argues that what Bakhtin labels authoritative discourse in fiction is an expression of an increased need by the modern state to control society, the individual, and art. To one degree or another every one of my analyses attempts to demonstrate that thesis. In addition, when Greenblatt and his disciples claim that it is impossible to find a position from which to represent a context that is not a part of that context, they are echoing words voiced by Hayles and repeated earlier in these pages. For them also, then, literature serves as a register and not a reflection of the "social energy" of a given society.[4] Insofar as this new approach manages to broaden the scope of the literary text without sacrificing it in the process, I think that new historicism along with cultural studies has a great deal of potential in reference to how we might better practice our chosen field in the future. In their extremes, however, both approaches threaten to reduce that same text to a documentary function.

Whether the answer for the future of our craft is cultural studies, or new historicism, or the kind of literary *épistémocritique* I have attempted here, or some kind of amalgamation of these and other approaches, remains very much an open question. But most of what I have read and observed has convinced me that the relationship of literary studies to knowledge is more crucial at this moment than the debate on critical methodologies. No doubt my concern with this relationship helps account for the importance I place in this study on works such as *Tiempo de silencio,* by Martín-Santos; *Teoría del conocimiento,* by Luis Goytisolo; and *El año de Gracia,* by Fernández Cubas. Rather than allowing the study of literature to become fused with other types of inquiries, or the literary text to be reduced to a document of past discursive practices, I would like to join those few who advocate that we should direct our primary efforts to exploring how and what the literary text helps us learn.

As noted, some twenty-five years ago certain scholars and students were suggesting that literature was an "irrelevant" academic subject and that perhaps sociohistorical studies should replace it on the curriculum. John S.

---

3. Brook Thomas, *The New Historicism: And Other Old-Fashioned Topics,* 24.
4. See H. Aram Veeser, ed., *The New Historicism,* for essays by Greenblatt, Thomas, Vesser, and a host of others on various definitions and explanations of this "new" approach.

Brushwood answered that argument by pointing out how we learn different things from different disciplines. He convincingly reasoned that "the nature of a piece of knowledge acquired through one discipline is not the same as the nature of a piece of knowledge acquired through another discipline. In other words, different ways of learning produce different ways of knowing."[5]

William Paulson essentially echoes Brushwood's argument when recently he proposes that as teachers and critics we need to concern ourselves with "what literary texts *know,* or can contribute to the domain of knowledge, that other cultural forms and practices cannot—what in the domain of knowledge is favored or inhibited, made possible or excluded, by the literary text."[6]

Following a line of thinking similar to Paulson's, Gerald Graff advocates juxtaposing one way of knowing with another in his program for an integrated curriculum.[7] I suspect that all three scholars would concede that many aspects of cultural studies and new historicism are now and will continue to be integrated effectively into literary studies, yet clearly Brushwood and Paulson are especially concerned first and foremost with defining what is unique to literature, for that uniqueness may prove to be the only thing preventing the literary text from being absorbed by textuality itself.[8]

The new labels themselves, which foreground culture and history with no mention at all of literature, underscore what I see as the danger of our craft becoming obliterated. As many of us have witnessed, when academic lines are crossed or erased under the rubric of inter- or antidisciplinary approaches, all too often the literary text is reduced to the role of sociopolitical document. The work of literature is then used to isolate and document sociological, anthropological, psychological, philosophical, ideological, and

---

5. John S. Brushwood, "Latin-American Literature and History: Experience and Interpretation," 98.

6. William Paulson, "Literature, Knowledge, and Cultural Ecology," 31.

7. See the chapter "Turning Conflict into Community" in *Beyond the Culture Wars: How Teaching the Conflicts Can Revitalize American Education,* by Gerald Graff.

8. Deleuze and Guattari in *What Is Philosophy?* (though without stating the problem precisely in these terms) also address the issue of how and what one learns in different disciplines—in their case in philosophy, science, and literature. For them the key to philosophy is the creation of concepts, to science the creation of functions that are presented as propositions (117)—"science is paradigmatic, whereas philosophy is syntagmatic" (124)—and to literature the creation of a bloc of sensations. Of particular relevance to my thesis here is their chapter "Percept, Affect, and Concept" (163–99).

so on, currents. With this type of documentary approach, little or no effort goes into analyzing how these currents are woven into the work's textual fabric. At least as I understand the term and have tried to employ it in this study, the literary work serves as a *register* only to the extent that it lends aesthetic expression to a given referent. Deleuze and Guattari explain in the following way how a literary aesthetic experience is created: "The writer uses words, but by creating a syntax that makes them pass into sensation that makes the standard language stammer, tremble, cry, or even sing: this is the style, the 'tone,' the language of sensations, or the foreign language within language that summons forth a people to come" (176). The words and syntax of *El cuarto de atrás* enmesh the reader in the recent gender-coded history of postwar Spain, while the language of *La verdad sobre el caso Savolta* transports its reader to the revolutionary, corrupt, and contradictory turn-of-the-century Barcelona; the style of *Para no volver* allows its reader to confront the male-defined world of psychoanalysis, while the "foreign language within language" of *El invierno en Lisboa* enables the reader to experience how the make-believe world of film and jazz constitutes the only viable reality for the characters. Of course these as well as all the other works analyzed in this study could be used as sociocultural-political histories. As she writes her personal chronicle, the fictitious Queen Urraca challenges the way Spain (and other countries) wrote and continue to write their national chronicles. But most would agree that the novel *Urraca* is not the best source for studying medieval Spanish history. If the goal is a purely contextual or conceptual understanding of some historical, philosophical, or scientific principle, people will almost certainly gain more information by consulting works on the topic in the fields of history, philosophy, or science. A literary work on the same subject certainly can enrich that information, but not effectively replace it.

As I have just indicated, the efficacy of doing research in specialized areas to gain specialized knowledge does not negate the argument, made by Brushwood among many others, that historians, philosophers, scientists, and literary critics can better understand their own fields if they also explore others. Along with discovering the various ways one learns in different academic subjects, cross-disciplinary inquiries are essential for enriching one's awareness of the temporal or epistemic relationships among these modes of learning. But I remain convinced that better understanding and enrichment should not serve as a substitute for the kind of expertise to be gained by an in-depth study of a phenomenon or concept within its specialized field.

The degree of specialization I have just advocated is not essential, however, if the goal is to gain epistemic awareness rather than conceptual mastery. For example, I think literary critics should be encouraged to talk about a specific aspect of a philosopher's ideas expressed in a literary work without feeling obliged at the same time to define and historicize that idea within the spectrum of philosophy in general. We may even find a case, such as in *Tiempo de silencio,* where there are expressions of power hierarchies and panoptic systems, two primary concerns of Foucault, that predate the philosopher's published theses on the same subjects. When we come to a work published after *Discipline and Punish,* such as *Visión del ahogado* in which the panopticon plays a fundamental structural and thematic role, the need to provide an entire philosophical contextualization of Foucault still would strike me as highly questionable. Indeed, one could argue that Millás's source for the panoptic concept may well have been Martín-Santos (or someone else) rather than Foucault. Yet, perhaps it goes without saying, if any author expresses the concept of the panopticon in his or her literary text, it is appropriate if not mandatory for the critic to include documented reference to Foucault's ideas, for he is the person who has developed most fully the historical roots and the philosophical implications of that phenomenon. But above all I want to argue for maintaining the focus of literary studies on the literary text itself. Instead of attempting to discover and contextualize sources—something that scholars who consider the literary work a document may feel obliged to do—I have tried to practice in the preceding pages a juxtaposition of literary expressions with theories from other disciplines. By means of such a juxtaposition, I believe we can best gain insight into how people in different fields but within a common time frame approach reality.

But juxtaposition can sometimes lead to another problem, which is a formulaic application of a psychoanalytic, philosophic, or scientific theory to a work of literature. When that happens, there is a tendency to make the work appear to be a reflection rather than a register of the theory being applied. In some cases the work may indeed be a self-conscious attempt to reflect a particular theoretical concept, but generally that is not so, and when it is, the results tend to be infelicitous. As I see it, the danger of formulaic applications of theories to works of literature is to denigrate literature itself, to deprive it implicitly of any uniqueness it has as a source, and not just a mirror, of knowledge.[9]

Up to recent times, literary critics argued that literature is unique because it provides a vital link to our cultural past (the great-books defense). In the final chapter of *The Noise of Culture*, Paulson makes the heretical suggestion that rather than trying to argue that the study of literature continues to form a central role in our cultural system, we may be better off conceding its marginality and concentrating on the importance of that alienated position vis-à-vis current discursive practices. He reasons that because it is marginal, literature constitutes a perturbation in our cultural system, and as such it has tremendous potential to create and convey information.[10]

The whole thesis of literature as an expression of marginality could even have a pragmatic function, for political, military, and corporate leaders can ill afford to be unaware of the feelings of the have-nots if they hope to protect their leadership positions. But Paulson's project is not concerned in any obvious way with pragmatic applications. In his more recent essay "Cultural Ecology," he makes it clear that he wishes to address the issue of alterity as an ontological dilemma: "if one tries to distance oneself radically from the dominant episteme one becomes marginalized, and if one does not try to do so, one reduces the Other to the Same and opposition to recuperation" (35). Art in general and literature in particular allow us to experience marginality without having to surrender our central position—and with it our power base, however fragile it may be—within the institution and state. The social sciences facilitate our efforts to conceptualize the economic, social, political, and psychological implications of marginalization, but I continue to believe that only art has the unique capacity to transform those implications into personal experience.

Recently some have begun to discredit the very concept of aesthetic experience. Yet teaching has convinced me that literature involves *experiencing*

9. For example, Luis Goytisolo stated to me on February 24, 1993, that he did not even know about fractal theory when he wrote *Teoría del conocimiento*. Yet some of his verbal images and conceits are strikingly similar to the fractal patterns and geometrical concepts that Mandelbrot presents in the edition of his book published just after Goytisolo's novel. I cite this as an example of a similar view of reality appearing in two apparently unrelated subject areas, but within a common temporal frame.

10. I think it is epistemically significant that perturbation is the central theme of Marías's novel *Todas las almas*, which appeared just one year after Paulson's study.

what cognitive processes have allowed us to learn (experience precedes cognition in this equation), while the other disciplines mentioned generally aspire to achieve cognition—I am using the term in the sense of conceptualizing information.[11] That division changed somewhat when Hayden White began to demonstrate how some of the tools of literary analysis have encouraged and facilitated the shift from the study of history to that of historiography. Yet when historiographers such as White, LaCapra, and others incorporate into historical studies the strategies we employ to analyze fiction, they mean to imply that only the representation of history is a fiction, not history itself; although the written version cannot recreate the historical reality, the referent itself is real. As far as I am aware, even the most blatantly self-conscious historiography strives to respect referential truth. Dominick LaCapra, for example, never questions the reality of the holocaust, but he does argue that there are as many versions of the event as there are subject positions reporting it.[12] Fiction, on the other hand, either invents its referent or fictionalizes the one history has to offer. In the words of Deleuze and Guattari, "The work of art is a being of sensation and nothing else: it exists in itself" (164). Fiction revels in its own fictionality.

In addition to the experiential essence literature shares with other art forms, as Jonathan Culler noted almost twenty years ago, it has a unique quality in reference to language itself: "Insofar as literature turns back on itself and examines, parodies, or treats ironically its own signifying procedures, it becomes the most complex account of signification we possess."[13] As if in anticipation of Culler's thesis, Juan Goytisolo offers us *Juan sin Tierra* and its ingenious sign system. Indeed, since the majority of the readers of this study almost certainly belong to the general field known as foreign-language study, we can lay claim to working with yet another level of linguistic complexity. The majority of our students must decode a language foreign to them before they can even begin to unravel what Deleuze

---

11. A practical demonstration of this thesis is to read aloud a humorous passage from a poem, story, or play to a class, and if some members smile or laugh, ask them to explain why it is funny. Generally it requires an effort from students to analyze or subject to a cognitive process what they initially experience in reading. Those who do not laugh or smile most certainly have missed out on the experiential dimension and consequently have even more difficulty moving to the cognitive level.

12. Dominick LaCapra, "Representing the Holocaust: Reflections on the Historian's Debate."

13. Culler, "In Pursuit of Signs," 106.

and Guattari explain as "the foreign language within language" (176) that we call literature.

Against the threat posed by an increasingly nonreading culture, the teaching of literature and language may be the last bastion we have for safeguarding what we know as literacy. Increasingly I hear people concerned with the possibility that we may be facing an end to criticism as a discipline grounded in language and writing. By subjecting students to language in its most sophisticated expression, during the next millennium we may be able to help stem the tide flowing against criticism and the written word; we may be able to play a vital role for our colleagues in other disciplines who, in spite of technological advances, may not be able to operate effectively, if at all, unless their students achieve a reasonable level of literacy. As reading itself becomes as marginalized in our cultural system as foreign languages by definition already are, the teaching of literature and language as a marginalized discipline may, paradoxically, ensure our central position in institutions of learning at all levels.

Although literature is merely one among a plethora of registers of a given episteme, I think it is important that we not ignore the unique manner in which *each* register projects the temporal relationship it has with the others. In the case of art in general and literature in particular, that uniqueness lies, at the risk of repeating myself, in its capacity to create from language an experience that is both imaginary and real. Deleuze and Guattari express that experience as follows: "We are not in the world, we become with the world; we become by contemplating it. Everything is vision, becoming" (169). But I doubt that aesthetic experience itself is enough. We also need literary studies to analyze how language operates at its most sophisticated and satisfying level, thereby ensuring that the reality of imagination does not become lost as we enter into the always uncertain future. I have dedicated this book from the moment of its conception to a celebration of the uniquely creative force of fiction. Literary criticism, I believe, provides us with the essential means to celebrate that vital force.

Bibliography

Ahrari, Mohammed E. "OPEC and the Hyperpluralism of the Oil Market in the 1980s." *International Affairs* 61 (1985): 263–77.

Alborg, Concha. "Metaficción y feminismo en Rosa Montero." *Revista de Estudios Hispánicos* 22 (1988): 67–76.

Alonso, Santos. "Desperdiciada fabulación." *Insula* 516 (December 1989): 21.

———. *Guías de lectura: "La verdad sobre el caso Savolta."* Madrid: Alhambra, 1988.

Alsina, Jean. "Une couverture: *Ya* (17–2-70)." In *Le discours de la presse,* ed. Arnaud Corvaisier, 15–20. Rennes: Presses Universitaires de Rennes, 1989.

———. "Valeurs matrimoniales et roles feminins dans trois publicités espagnoles entre 1973 et 1986." *Hispanistica 20* 5 (1987): 323–31.

Althusser, Louis. *Lenin and Philosophy and Other Essays.* Trans. Ben Brewster. New York: Monthly Review Press, 1971.

Altisent, Marta E. "El erotismo en la actual narrativa española." *Cuadernos Hispanoamericanos* 468 (June 1989): 128–44.

Amell, Alma. "Una crónica de la marginación: La narrativa de Rosa Montero." *Letras Femeninas* 18 (1992): 74–82.

———. *Rosa Montero's Odyssey.* Columbus: University Press of America, 1994.

Amell, Samuel. "Literatura e ideología: El caso de la novela negra en la España actual." *Monographic Review/Revista Monográfica* 3 (1987): 192–201.

———. "El motivo del viaje en tres novelas del posfranquismo." In *Estudios en homenaje a Enrique Ruiz Fornells,* ed. Juan Fernández Jiménez, José Labrador Herraiz, and Teresa L. Valdivieso, 12–17. Erie: Asociación de Licenciados y Doctores Españoles en Estados Unidos, 1990.

Bakhtin, M. M. *The Dialogic Imagination: Four Essays.* Trans. Caryl Emerson and Michael Holquist. Austin: University of Texas Press, 1981.

Barrero Pérez, Oscar, ed. *Historia de la literatura española contemporánea.* Madrid: Istmo, 1992.

Barthes, Roland. "From Work to Text." In *Textual Strategies: Perspectives in Post-Structuralist Criticism,* ed. Josué V. Harari, 73–81. Ithaca: Cornell University Press, 1979.

Bartlett, Bertice. "Negatives and the Reader." Paper presented at Mellon Faculty Development Seminar, Lawrence, Kans., February 1984.

Bellver, Catherine G. "*El año de Gracia* and the Displacement of the Word." *Studies in Twentieth-Century Literature* 16 (1992): 221–32.

———. "Assimilation and Confrontation in Esther Tusquets' *Para no volver.*" *Romanic Review* 8 (1990): 368–76.

———. "Intertextuality in *Para no volver.*" In *The Sea of Becoming: Approaches to the Fiction of Esther Tusquets,* ed. Mary S. Vásquez, 103–22. New York: Greenwood, 1991.

Beloff, Max. "1989, A Farewell to Arms?: A Rejoinder." *International Affairs* 65 (1989): 415–17.

Benn, David Wedgwood. "Glasnost, Dialogue and East-West Relations." *International Affairs* 65 (1989): 273–303.

Benveniste, Emil. *Problems in General Linguistics.* Trans. Mary Elizabeth Meek. Coral Gables: University of Miami Press, 1971.

Bergmann, Emilie L. "Letters and Diaries as Narrative Strategies in Contemporary Catalan Women's Writing." In *Critical Essays on the Literature of Spain and Spanish America,* ed. Luis González-del-Valle and Julio Baena, 19–28. Boulder: Society of Spanish and Spanish-American Studies, 1991.

Bersani, Leo. "The Subject of Power." *Diacritics* 7 (1977): 2–21.

Booth, Wayne C. *The Rhetoric of Fiction.* Chicago: University of Chicago Press, 1961.

Bové, Paul A. *Mastering Discourse: The Politics of Intellectual Culture.* Durham: Duke University Press, 1992.

Bravo, María-Elena. "Literatura de la distensión: El elemento policíaco." *Insula* 472 (March 1986): 1, 12–13.

Bretz, Mary Lee. "Cristina Fernández Cubas and the Recuperation of the Semiotic in *Los altillos de Brumal.*" *Anales de la Literatura Española Contemporánea* 13 (1988): 177–88.

Brooks, Cleanth, and Robert Penn Warren. *Understanding Fiction.* New York: Crofts, 1943.

Brooks, Peter. *Body Work: Objects of Desire in Modern Narrative.* Cambridge: Harvard University Press, 1993.

——. *Reading for the Plot: Design and Intention in Narrative.* New York: Vintage, 1985.

Brown, Joan Lipman. "The Challenge of Martín Gaite's Woman Hero." In *Feminine Concerns in Contemporary Spanish Fiction by Women,* ed. Roberto Manteiga, Carolyn Galerstein, and Kathleen McNerney, 86–98. Potomac: Scripta Humanistica, 1988.

——. "Rosa Montero: From Journalist to Novelist." In her *Women Writers of Contemporary Spain,* 240–57. Newark, N.J.: University of Delaware Press, 1991.

——. *Secrets from the Back Room: The Fiction of Carmen Martín Gaite.* Jackson: University of Mississippi Press, Romance Monographs, 1987.

——, ed. *Women Writers of Contemporary Spain.* Newark, N.J.: University of Delaware Press, 1991.

Brownlow, Jeanne P. "Epochal Allegory in Galdós's *Torquemada:* The Ur-Text and the Episteme." *PMLA* 108 (1993): 294–307.

Brushwood, John S. "Latin-American Literature and History: Experience and Interpretation." *Hispania* 54 (1971): 98–99.

Buck, Carla Olson. "Speaker/Reader: Dialogic Relationships in the Novels of Carmen Martín Gaite." Ph.D. diss., University of Kansas, 1986.

——. "The World Turned Upside Down: The Carnivalesque in Carmen Martín Gaite's *Retahílas* and *El cuarto de atrás.*" In *Romance Languages Annual.* Forthcoming.

Campbell, Jeremy. *Grammatical Man: Information, Entropy, Language, and Life.* New York: Simon and Schuster, 1982.

Cano Ballesta, Juan. *Literatura y tecnología (Las letras españolas ante la revolución industrial 1900–1933).* Madrid: Orígines, 1981.

Carracedo, Argelia F. "Síntesis del tiempo en *Urraca* de Lourdes Ortiz." *Journal of Interdisciplinary Literary Studies/Cuadernos Interdisciplinarios de Estudios Literarios* 2 (1990): 97–108.

Castillo, Debra. "Never-Ending Story: Carmen Martín Gaite's *The Back Room.*" *PMLA* 102 (1984): 814–28.

Cate-Arries, Francie. "Lost in the Language of Culture: Manuel Vázquez

Montalbán's Novel Detection." *Revista de Estudios Hispánicos* 22 (1988): 47–56.

Cela, Camilo José. *La familia de Pascual Duarte.* Barcelona: Destino, 1976.

Chambers, Ross. *Room for Maneuver: Reading Oppositional Narrative.* Chicago: University of Chicago Press, 1991.

Cillán Apalategui, Antonio, ed. *Discursos y mensajes del jefe del estado (1968–1970).* Madrid: Publicaciones Españolas, 1971.

———. *El léxico político de Franco en las cortes españolas.* Zaragoza: Tipo-Línea, 1970.

Ciplijauskaité, Biruté. "Historical Novel from a Feminine Perspective: *Urraca.*" In *Feminine Concerns in Contemporary Spanish Fiction by Women,* ed. Roberto Manteiga, Carolyn Galerstein, and Kathleen McNerney, 29–42. Potomac: Scripta Humanistica, 1988.

———. "Lyric Memory, Oral History and the Shaping of the Self in Spanish Narrative." *Forum for Modern Language Studies* 28 (1992): 390–400.

———. *La novela femenina contemporánea (1970–1985): Hacia una tipología de la narración en primera persona.* Barcelona: Anthropos, 1988.

Clark, John W. "Views from the Ivory Tower's Basement. A Commentary on 'The Clock and the Cloud: Chaos and Order in *El diablo mundo.*'" *Revista de Estudios Hispánicos* 26 (1992): 227–50.

Cohan, Steven, and Linda M. Shires. *Telling Stories: A Theoretical Analysis of Narrative Fiction.* New York: Routledge, 1988.

Colmeiro, José F. "E. Mendoza y los laberintos de la realidad." *Romance Languages Annual* 1 (1989): 409–12.

———. "La narrativa policíaca posmodernista de Manuel Vázquez Montalbán." *Anales de la Literatura Española Contemporánea* 14 (1989): 11–32.

———. *La novela policíaca española.* Barcelona: Anthropos, 1994.

Compitello, Malcolm A. "Luis Martín-Santos: A Bibliography." *Letras Peninsulares* 2 (1989): 249–69.

———. "Spain's 'nueva novela negra' and the Question of Form." *Monographic Review/Revista Monográfica* 3 (1987): 182–91.

Constitución Española. Madrid: Boletín Oficial del Estado, 1985.

Conte, Rafael. "Antonio Muñoz Molina o la conquista del estilo." *Insula* 490 (September 1987): 15.

———. "El precursor." *Quimera* 75 (March 1988): 45–48.

Costa, Luis F. "*Para no volver:* Women in Franco's Spain." In *The Sea of*

Becoming: Approaches to the Fiction of Esther Tusquets, ed. Mary S. Vásquez, 11–28. New York: Greenwood, 1991.

Craig, Betty Jean. "*Tiempo de silencio:* Le grand bouc, and the maestro." *Revista de Estudios Hispánicos* 13 (1979): 99–113.

Culler, Jonathan. "In Pursuit of Signs." *Daedalus* 106 (1977): 95–111.

Davidson, Sara. *Rock Hudson, His Story.* New York: William Morrow, 1986.

Deleuze, Gilles. "Rhizome versus Trees." In *The Deleuze Reader,* ed. Constantin V. Boundas, 27–36. New York: Columbia University Press, 1993.

Deleuze, Gilles, and Félix Guattari. *What Is Philosophy?* Trans. Hugh Tomlinson and Graham Burchell. New York: Columbia University Press, 1994.

Derrida, Jacques. *The Postcard: From Socrates to Freud and Beyond.* Trans. Alan Bass. Chicago: University of Chicago Press, 1987.

Dolgin, Stacey L. *La novela desmitificadora española (1961–1982).* Barcelona: Anthropos, 1991.

Encinar, Angela. "*Urraca:* Una recreación actual de la historia." *Letras Femeninas* 20 (1994): 87–99.

Epps, Brad. "The Space of Sexual History: Reading Positions in *El cuarto de atrás* and *Reivindicación del Conde don Julián.*" In *Critical Essays on the Literature of Spain and Spanish America,* ed. Luis González-del-Valle and Julio Baena, 75–87. Boulder: Society of Spanish and Spanish-American Studies, 1991.

Espadas, Elizabeth. "An Annotated Bibliography of Works by and about Esther Tusquets." In *The Sea of Becoming: Approaches to the Fiction of Esther Tusquets,* ed. Mary S. Vásquez, 189–226. New York: Greenwood, 1991.

Falange Publications. *Franco y España: 25 años de Caudillaje.* Jaén: Falange Publications, 1961.

———. *El Movimiento Nacional: Textos de Franco.* Madrid: Falange Publications, 1966.

———. *Palabras del Caudillo.* Barcelona: Falange Publications, 1939.

Fernández Cubas, Cristina. *El año de Gracia.* Barcelona: Tusquets, 1985.

———. Interview by Julie Gleue. Barcelona, Spain. March 24, 1994.

Foucault, Michel. *The Archaeology of Knowledge and the Discourse on Language.* Trans. A. M. Sheridan Smith. New York: Pantheon, 1972.

————. *Discipline and Punish: The Birth of the Prison.* Trans. Alan Sheridan. New York: Vintage, 1979.

————. *The Foucault Effect: Studies in Governmentality,* ed. Graham Burchell, Colin Gordon, and Peter Miller. Chicago: University of Chicago Press, 1991.

————. *The History of Sexuality I: An Introduction.* Trans. Robert Hurley. New York: Vintage, 1980.

————. *Power/Knowledge: Selected Interviews and Other Writings 1972–1977.* Trans. Colin Gordon, Leo Marshall, John Mepham, and Kate Soper. New York: Pantheon, 1980.

Fraser, Nancy. *Unruly Practices: Power, Discourse and Gender in Contemporary Social Theory.* Minneapolis: University of Minnesota Press, 1989.

Gallagher, Charles F. "Culture and Education in Spain Part 6: Franco Spain (1936–1975)." *American Universities Field Staff Reports* 24 (1979): 1–17.

————. "Paradoxes and Problems in the Spanish Economy." *American Universities Field Staff Reports* 33 (1978): 1–12.

García, José. "*Juegos de la edad tardía,* apoteosis del discurso literario." *Anales de la Literatura Española Contemporánea* 20 (1995): 101–25.

Gardiner de Arias, Beckie. "Cosmogonic Myth in *Antagonía* by Luis Goytisolo: A Creation of Creations." Ph.D. diss., University of Kansas, 1989.

Gardner, Anthony. "The Media under Gorbachev (Interview with Vitalii Alekseevich Korotich, Editor of *Ogonek).*" *Journal of International Affairs* 42 (1989): 357–62.

Gascón Vera, Elena. "Rosa Montero ante la escritura femenina." *Anales de la Literatura Española Contemporánea* 12 (1987): 59–78.

Gautier Gazarián, Marie-Lise, ed. *Interviews with Spanish Writers.* Elmwood Park, Ill.: Dalkey Archive, 1991.

Genette, Gérard. *Narrative Discourse: An Essay in Method.* Trans. Jane E. Lewin. Ithaca: Cornell University Press, 1980.

Giménez, Viviana Claudia. "Subversión en *Te trataré como a una reina* de Rosa Montero." *Romance Languages Annual* 3 (1991): 454–59.

Girling, J. L. S. "'Kissingerism': The Enduring Problems." *International Affairs* 51 (1975): 323–43.

Glenn, Kathleen M. "'Alusión al tiempo' and Hitchcock's *Rear Window:* Voyeurism and Self-Reflexivity." *Monographic Review/Revista Monográfica* 4 (1988): 16–24.

———. "Authority and Marginality in Three Contemporary Spanish Narratives." *Romance Languages Annual* 2 (1990): 426–30.

———. "Gothic Indecipherability and Doubling in the Fiction of Fernández Cubas." *Monographic Review/Revista Monográfica* 8 (1992): 125–41.

———. "Victimized by Misreading: Rosa Montero's *Te trataré como a una reina.*" *Anales de la Literatura Española Contemporánea* 12 (1987): 191–202.

Gleue, Julie. "The Epistemological and Ontological Implications in Cristina Fernández Cubas' *El año de Gracia.*" *Monographic Review/Revista Monográfica* 8 (1992): 142–56.

Goñi, Javier. "Entrevista con Ignacio Martínez de Pisón." *Insula* 479 (September 1986): 15–16.

González-del-Valle, Luis, and Julio Baena, eds. *Critical Essays on the Literatures of Spain and Spanish America.* Boulder: Society of Spanish and Spanish-American Studies, 1991.

González Echevarría, Roberto. *Myth and Archive: A Theory of Latin American Narrative.* New York: Cambridge University Press, 1990.

Gorrochategui Gorrochategui, Pedro. "Una bibliografía global de Luis Martín-Santos." *Cuadernos Universitarios* 8 (1990): 195–234.

Goytisolo, Juan. *Juan sin Tierra.* Barcelona: Seix Barral, 1975.

———. "Reading and Rereading." Paper presented at Novel of the Americas Symposium, Boulder, Colo., September 24, 1992.

———. "Texto literario y producto editorial." Paper presented at Círculo de Lectores, Madrid, March 12, 1993.

Goytisolo, Luis. *La cólera de Aquiles.* Barcelona: Seix Barral, 1979.

———. *Teoría del conocimiento.* Barcelona: Seix Barral, 1981.

Graff, Gerald. *Beyond the Culture Wars: How Teaching the Conflicts Can Revitalize American Education.* New York: Norton, 1992.

Greenblatt, Stephen. "Towards a Poetics of Culture." In *The New Historicism,* ed. H. Aram Veeser, 1–14. New York: Routledge, 1989.

Grugel, Jean. "Spain's Socialist Government and Central American Dilemmas." *International Affairs* 63 (1987): 603–15.

Guelbenzu, José María. *El río de la luna.* Madrid: Alianza, 1981.

Gullón, Germán. "El novelista como fabulador de la realidad: Mayoral, Merino, Guelbenzu." In *Nuevos y novísimos: Algunas perspectivas críticas sobre la narrativa española desde la década de los 60,* ed.

Ricardo Landeira and Luis González-del-Valle, 71–81. Boulder: Society of Spanish and Spanish-American Studies, 1987.

Gutiérrez, Fabián. *Cómo leer a Juan José Millás*. Madrid: Júcar, 1992.

Handelman, Susan A. *The Slayers of Moses: The Emergence of Rabbinic Interpretation in Modern Literary Theory*. Albany: State University of New York Press, 1982.

Hart, Patricia. *Spanish Sleuth: The Detective in Spanish Fiction*. Rutherford, N.J.: Fairleigh Dickinson University Press, 1987.

Hart, Stephen M. *The Other Scene: Psychoanalytic Readings in Modern Spanish and Latin-American Literature*. Boulder: Society of Spanish and Spanish-American Studies, 1992.

Hayles, N. Katherine. *Chaos Bound: Orderly Disorder in Contemporary Literature and Science*. Ithaca: Cornell University Press, 1990.

———. *The Cosmic Web: Scientific Field Models and Literary Strategies in the Twentieth Century*. Ithaca: Cornell University Press, 1984.

———. "Virtual Bodies and Flickering Signifiers." *October* 66 (1993): 69–91.

Herpoel, Sonja. "El Vosk de Goytisolo, ¿Prisionero de su presunción?" *Letras Peninsulares* 4 (1991): 423–34.

Herzberger, David K. *Narrating the Past: Fiction and Historiography in Postwar Spain*. Durham: Duke University Press, 1995.

———. "Narrating the Past: History and the Novel of Memory in Postwar Spain." *PMLA* 106 (1991): 34–45.

———. "The 'New' Characterization in José María Guelbenzu's *El río de la luna*." In *Nuevos y novísimos: Algunas perspectivas críticas sobre la narrativa española desde la década de los 60*, ed. Ricardo Landeira and Luis González-del-Valle, 83–95. Boulder: Society of Spanish and Spanish-American Studies, 1987.

Howard, Michael. "1989: A Farewell to Arms?" *International Affairs* 65 (1989): 407–13.

Hutcheon, Linda. *A Poetics of Postmodernism: History, Theory, Fiction*. New York: Routledge, 1988.

Ichiishi, Barbara F. *The Apple of Earthly Love: Female Development in Esther Tusquets' Fiction*. New York: Peter Lang, 1994.

Iser, Wolfgang. *The Implied Reader: Patterns of Communication in Prose Fiction from Bunyan to Beckett*. Baltimore: Johns Hopkins University Press, 1974.

Jameson, Fredric. *Postmodernism, or, the Cultural Logic of Late Capitalism.* Durham: Duke University Press, 1991.

Jerez-Farrán, Carlos. "'Ansiedad de influencia' versus intertextualidad autoconsciente en *Tiempo de silencio* de Martín-Santos." *Symposium* 42 (1988): 119–32.

Johnson, Roberta L. "Voice and Intersubjectivity in Carmé Riera's Narratives." In *Critical Essays on the Literature of Spain and Spanish America,* ed. Luis González-del-Valle and Julio Baena, 153–59. Boulder: Society of Spanish and Spanish-American Studies, 1991.

Joll, James. "The Ideal and the Real: Changing Concepts of the International System, 1815–1982." *International Affairs* 58 (1982): 210–24.

Jones, Margaret E. W. *The Contemporary Spanish Novel, 1939–1975.* Boston: Twayne, 1985.

Jordan, Barry. *Writing and Politics in Franco's Spain.* New York: Routledge, 1990.

Kielinger, Thomas. "Waking Up in the New Europe—with a Headache." *International Affairs* 66 (1990): 249–63.

Knickerbocker, Dale F. "*Tiempo de silencio* and the Narration of the Abject." *Anales de la Literatura Española Contemporánea* 19 (1994): 11–31.

Kundera, Milan. *The Book of Laughter and Forgetting.* Trans. Michael Henry Heim. New York: Penguin, 1981.

Labanyi, Jo. *Myth and History in the Contemporary Spanish Novel.* Cambridge: Cambridge University Press, 1989.

Lacan, Jacques. *Ecrits: A Selection.* Trans. Alan Sheridan. New York: Norton, 1977.

LaCapra, Dominick. "Representing the Holocaust: Reflections on the Historian's Debate." In *Probing the Limits of Representation: Nazism and the "Final Solution,"* ed. Saul Friedlander, 108–27. Cambridge: Harvard University Press, 1992.

Landeira, Ricardo, and Luis González-del-Valle, eds. *Nuevos y novísimos: Algunas perspectivas críticas sobre la narrativa española desde la década de los 60.* Boulder: Society of Spanish and Spanish-American Studies, 1987.

Landero, Luis. *Juegos de la edad tardía.* Barcelona: Tusquets, 1989.

Latour, Bruno. *We Have Never Been Modern.* Trans. Catherine Porter. Cambridge: Harvard University Press, 1993.

López, Ignacio Javier. "Novela y realidad: En torno a la estructura de *Visión del ahogado* de Juan José Millás." *Anales de la Literatura Española Contemporánea* 13 (1988): 37–54.

Lubbock, Percy. *The Craft of Fiction.* New York: Viking, 1957.

Luciani, Frederick. Review of *The Truth about the Savolta Case,* by Eduardo Mendoza. *New York Times Book Review* (November 29, 1992): 10.

Lyotard, Jean-François. *The Postmodern Condition: A Report on Knowledge.* Trans. Geoff Bennington and Brian Massumi. Minneapolis: University of Minnesota Press, 1989.

Mandelbrot, Benoit B. *The Fractal Geometry of Nature.* New York: W. H. Freeman, 1982.

Mandrell, James. "Peninsular Literary Studies: Business as Usual." *Revista de Estudios Hispánicos* 27 (1993): 291–307.

Manteiga, Roberto C. "The Dilemma of the Modern Woman: A Study of the Female Characters in Rosa Montero's Novels." In *Feminine Concerns in Contemporary Spanish Fiction by Women,* ed. Roberto Manteiga, Carolyn Galerstein, and Kathleen McNerney, 113–23. Potomac: Scripta Humanistica, 1988.

Manteiga, Roberto C., Carolyn Galerstein, and Kathleen McNerney, eds. *Feminine Concerns in Contemporary Spanish Fiction by Women.* Potomac: Scripta Humanistica, 1988.

Marco, José María. "El espacio de la libertad." *Quimera* 66–67 (March 1986): 48–52.

———. "El espacio del deseo: La grieta y el mercado." *Quimera* 75 (1988): 53–57.

———. "La verdad sobre el caso Mendoza." In *Historia de la literatura española contemporánea,* ed. Oscar Barrero Pérez, 305–8. Madrid: Istmo, 1992.

Margenot, John B., III. "Parody and Self-Consciousness in Cristina Fernández Cubas' *El año de Gracia.*" *Siglo XX/Twentieth Century* 11 (1993): 71–87.

Marías, Javier. *Todas las almas.* Barcelona: Anagrama, 1989.

Martín, Sabas. "*El río de la luna,* de J. M. Guelbenzu, o la doble pasión." *Cuadernos Hispanoamericanos* 383 (1982): 414–19.

Martínez Bonati, Félix. *La estructura de la obra literaria: Una investigación de filosofía del lenguaje y estética.* Barcelona: Seix Barral, 1972.

Martínez de Pisón, Ignacio. *Alguien te observa en secreto.* Barcelona: Anagrama, 1985.

Martín Gaite, Carmen. *El cuarto de atrás.* Barcelona: Destino, 1982.

———. *Usos amorosos de la posguerra española.* Barcelona: Anagrama, 1987.

Martín-Santos, Luis. *Tiempo de silencio.* Barcelona: Seix Barral, 1987.

Masoliver Ródenas, Juan Antonio. "Antonio Muñoz Molina: Un paisaje del tiempo." *Las Nuevas Letras* 8 (1988): 96–97.

McGovern, Lynn. "A 'Private I': The Birth of a Female Sleuth and the Role of Parody in Lourdes Ortiz's *Picadura mortal.*" *Journal of Interdisciplinary Literary Studies* 5 (1993): 251–79.

McHale, Brian. *Constructing Postmodernism.* New York: Routledge, 1992.

———. *Postmodernist Fiction.* New York: Methuen, 1987.

Mendoza, Eduardo. Presentation at homage to Juan Benet, Círculo de Bellas Artes, Madrid, February 23, 1993.

———. *La verdad sobre el caso Savolta.* Barcelona: Seix Barral, 1986.

Miguel, Amando de. *Sociología del franquismo: Análisis ideológico de los ministros del régimen.* Barcelona: Euros, 1975.

Miguel Martínez, Emilio de. *La primera narrativa de Rosa Montero.* Salamanca: Universidad de Salamanca, 1983.

Millás, Juan José. *Visión del ahogado.* Madrid: Alfaguara, 1977.

Millington, Mark I., and Paul Julian Smith, eds. *New Hispanisms: Literature, Culture, Theory.* Ottawa: Dovehouse Editions, 1994.

Milner Garlitz, Virginia. "Teosofismo en *Tirano Banderas.*" *Journal of Spanish Studies Twentieth Century* 2 (1974): 21–29.

Miranda, Marta Isabel. "Modos de comunicación en *Visión del ahogado,* de Juan José Millás." *España Contemporánea* 7 (1994): 49–60.

Moi, Toril. *Sexual/Textual Politics: Feminist Literary Theory.* New York: Routledge, 1985.

Molinaro, Nina. *Foucault, Feminism, and Power: Reading Esther Tusquets.* Lewisburg, Penn.: Bucknell University Press, 1991.

———. "Resistance, Gender, and Mediation of History in Pizarnik's *La condesa sangrienta* and Ortiz's *Urraca.*" *Letras Femeninas* 19 (1993): 45–54.

Montero, Rosa. *Te trataré como a una reina.* Barcelona: Seix Barral, 1988.

Morán, Fernando. *Explicación de una limitación: La novela realista de los años cincuenta en España.* Madrid: Taurus, 1971.

Mowitt, John. *Text: The Genealogy of an Antidisciplinary Object.* Durham: Duke University Press, 1992.

Muñoz Molina, Antonio. *El invierno en Lisboa.* Barcelona: Seix Barral, 1987.

———. "El jazz y la ficción." *Revista de Occidente* 93 (February 1989): 21–27.

Navajas, Gonzalo. "Civilization and Fictions of Love in *Para no volver.*" In *The Sea of Becoming: Approaches to the Fiction of Esther Tusquets,* ed. Mary S. Vásquez, 123–36. New York: Greenwood, 1991.

———. "El *Ubermensch* caído en Antonio Muñoz Molina: La paradoja de la verdad reconstituida." *Revista de Estudios Hispánicos* 28 (1994): 213–33.

Navarro, José María. "El lenguaje coloquial en *Te trataré como a una reina,* de Rosa Montero." In *Actas de las Jornadas Hispánicas de la Asociación Alemana de Profesores/as de Español,* ed. Karl Heinz Joppich, 13–24. Bonn: Romanisfischer, 1986.

Nichols, Geraldine C. *Escribir, espacio propio: Laforet, Matute, Moix, Tusquets, Riera y Roig por sí mismas.* Minneapolis: Institute for the Studies of Ideologies and Literature, 1989.

———. "Minding Her Ps and Qs: The Fiction of Esther Tusquets." *Indiana Journal of Hispanic Literature* 2 (1993): 159–79.

Ordóñez, Elizabeth J. "*Para no volver:* Through the Mirror and over the Threshold of Desire." In *The Sea of Becoming: Approaches to the Fiction of Esther Tusquets,* ed. Mary S. Vásquez, 137–56. New York: Greenwood, 1991.

———. "Rewriting Myth and History: Three Recent Novels by Women." In *Feminine Concerns in Contemporary Spanish Fiction by Women,* ed. Roberto Manteiga, Carolyn Galerstein, and Kathleen McNerney, 6–28. Potomac: Scripta Humanistica, 1988.

———. *Voices of Their Own: Contemporary Spanish Narrative by Women.* Lewisburg, Penn.: Bucknell University Press, 1991.

Ortega, José. "La dimensión fantástica en los cuentos de Fernández Cubas." *Monographic Review/Revista Monográfica* 8 (1992): 157–63.

———. "La dimensión temporal en dos novelas de Antonio Muñoz Molina." *Letras Peninsulares* 4 (1991): 381–99.

Ortiz, Lourdes. *Urraca.* Barcelona: Puntual, 1982.

Otero, Carlos P. "The Cognitive Revolution and the Study of Language: Looking Back to See Ahead." In *Current Studies in Spanish Linguistics,* ed. Héctor Campos and Fernando Martínez-Gil, 3–69. Washington, D.C.: Georgetown University Press, 1992.

Paulson, William R. "Literature, Knowledge, and Cultural Ecology." *Substance* 71–72 (1993): 27–37.

———. *The Noise of Culture: Literary Texts in a World of Information.* Ithaca: Cornell University Press, 1988.

Pedraza, Pilar. *La bella, enigma y pesadilla (Esfinge, Medusa, Pantera).* Barcelona: Tusquets, 1991.

Pérez Firmat, Gustavo. "Repetition and Excess in *Tiempo de silencio.*" *PMLA* 96 (1981): 194–209.

Pope, Randolph D. "Una brecha sobrenatural en *Teoría del conocimiento* de Luis Goytisolo." *Monographic Review/Revista Monográfica* 3 (1987): 129–36.

———. "Postmodernismo en España: El caso de Antonio Muñoz Molina." *España Contemporánea* 5 (1992): 111–19.

Prince, Gerald. "Introduction á l'étude du narrataire." *Poétique* 14 (1973): 178–96.

Ragland-Sullivan, Ellie. *Jacques Lacan and the Philosophy of Psychoanalysis.* Urbana and Chicago: University of Illinois Press, 1987.

Riera, Carmen. *Cuestión de amor propio.* Barcelona: Tusquets, 1988.

Roberts, Gemma. "Amor sexual y frustración existencial en dos novelas de Guelbenzu." In *Nuevos y novísimos: Algunas perspectivas críticas sobre la narrativa española desde la década de los 60,* ed. Ricardo Landeira and Luis González-del-Valle, 151–68. Boulder: Society of Spanish and Spanish-American Studies, 1987.

Rodríguez, Mercedes M. "Narrative Strategies in the Novels of Esther Tusquets." *Monographic Review/Revista Monográfica* 7 (1991): 124–34.

———. "*Para no volver:* Humor vs. Phallocentrism." *Letras Femeninas* 16 (1990): 29–35.

Rodríguez-García, José María. "Gatsby Goes to Barcelona: On the Configuration of the Post-Modern Spanish Novel." *Letras Peninsulares* 5 (1992–1993): 407–24.

Rodríguez Padrón, Jorge. "La narrativa de José María Guelbenzu." *Cuadernos Hispanoamericanos* 428 (1986): 71–90.

Rodríguez Puértolas, Julio. *Literatura fascista española: I/Historia.* Madrid: Akal, 1986.

Roman, Isabel. "La coherencia de *El río de la luna,* de José María Guelbenzu." *Anales de la Literatura Española Contemporánea* 10 (1985): 111–22.

Rosenberg, John R. "The Clock and the Cloud: Chaos and Order in *El diablo mundo.*" *Revista de Estudios Hispánicos* 26 (1992): 203–25.

Rueda, Ana. "Cristina Fernández Cubas: Una narrativa de voces extinguidas." *Monographic Review/Revista Monográfica* 4 (1988): 257–67.

———. "El cuento español: Balance crítico de una década (1980–1990)." *Ojáncano* 5 (1991): 3–12.

Rutledge Southworth, Herbert. "The Falange: An Analysis of Spain's Fascist Heritage." In *Spain in Crisis: The Evolution and Decline of the Franco Régime,* ed. Paul Preston, 1–22. Sussex: Harvester, 1976.

Saladrigas, Robert. "Bajo el signo de la búsqueda." *Quimera* 75 (March 1988): 48–52.

Sánchez, Elizabeth. "*La Regenta* as Fractal." *Revista de Estudios Hispánicos* 26 (1992): 251–76.

———. "Spatial Forms and Fractals: A Reconsideration of Azorín's *Doña Inés.*" *Journal of Interdisciplinary Literary Studies* 5 (1993): 197–220.

Sanz Villanueva, Santos. "Prólogo." In *Ultimos narradores: Antología de la reciente narrativa breve española,* ed. Joseluís González and Pedro de Miguel, 7–23. Pamplona: Hierbaola, 1993.

Schaefer-Rodríguez, Claudia. "Realism Meets the Postmodern in Post-Franco Spain's 'novela negra.'" *Hispanic Journal* 2 (1990): 133–46.

Schumm, Sandra J. "'Borrowed' Language in Carmen Riera's *Cuestión de amor propio.*" *Anales de la Literatura Española Contemporánea* 20 (1995): 199–214.

———. "Metaphor, Metonymy, and Mirrors: Female Self-Reflection in Contemporary Spanish Novels by Women." Ph.D. diss., University of Kansas, 1993.

Servodidio, Mirella, and Marcia L. Welles, eds. *From Fiction to Metafiction: Essays in Honor of Carmen Martín Gaite.* Lincoln: Society of Spanish and Spanish-American Studies, 1983.

Sherzer, William. "An Appraisal of Recent Criticism of *Tiempo de silencio.*" *Letras Peninsulares* 2 (1989): 233–48.

———. "Tiempo e historia en la narrativa de Antonio Muñoz Molina." *España Contemporánea* 4 (1991): 51–57.

Sieburth, Stephanie. "Memory, Metafiction and Mass Culture in *El cuarto de atrás.*" *Revista Hispánica Moderna* 43 (1990): 78–92.

Silverman, Kaja. *The Subject of Semiotics.* New York: Oxford University Press, 1983.

Six, Abigail Lee. *Juan Goytisolo: The Case for Chaos.* New Haven: Yale University Press, 1990.

Smith, Paul. *Discerning the Subject.* Minneapolis: University of Minnesota Press, 1988.

Sobejano, Gonzalo. "Juan José Millás, fabulador de la extrañeza." In *Nuevos y novísimos: Algunas perspectivas críticas sobre la narrativa española desde la década de los 60,* ed. Ricardo Landeira and Luis González-del-Valle, 195–216. Boulder: Society of Spanish and Spanish-American Studies, 1987.

———. *Novela española de nuestro tiempo (En busca del pueblo perdido).* Madrid: Prensa Española, 1970.

———. "La novela poemática y sus alrededores." *Insula* 464–65 (July–August 1985): 1 and 26.

Soldevila Durante, Ignacio. *La novela desde 1936.* Madrid: Alhambra, 1980.

Soria Olmedo, Andrés. "Fervor y sabiduría: La obra narrativa de Antonio Muñoz Molina." *Cuadernos Hispanoamericanos* 458 (August 1988): 107–11.

Spanos, William V. "The Detective and the Boundary: Some Notes on the Postmodern Literary Imagination." *Boundary 2* 1 (1972): 147–68.

Spires, Robert C. *Beyond the Metafictional Mode: Directions in the Modern Spanish Novel.* Lexington: University Press of Kentucky, 1984.

———. "El concepto del antisilogismo en la novelística del posfranquismo." *España Contemporánea* 5 (1992): 9–16.

———. "The Dialogic Structure of *Para no volver*." In *The Sea of Becoming: Approaches to the Fiction of Esther Tusquets,* ed. Mary S. Vásquez, 93–102. New York: Greenwood, 1991.

———. "Lourdes Ortiz: Mapping the Course of Postfrancoist Fiction." In *Women Writers of Contemporary Spain,* ed. Joan Lipman Brown, 198–216. Newark, N.J.: University of Delaware Press, 1991.

———. *La novela española de posguerra: Creación artística y experiencia personal.* Madrid: Planeta, 1978.

———. "A Play of Difference: Fiction after Franco." *Letras Peninsulares* 1 (1988): 285–98.

Stanzel, Franz. *Narrative Situations in the Novel: "Tom Jones," "Moby-Dick,"*

"The Ambassadors," "Ulysses." Trans. James P. Pusack. Bloomington: Indiana University Press, 1971.

Steemeijer, Maarten. "El relevo del mito: Sobre *Para no volver* de Esther Tusquets." In *España, teatro y mujeres,* ed. Martín Gosman and Hub Hermans, 155–61. Amsterdam: Rodopi, 1989.

Suñén, Luis. "José María Guelbenzu y su camino de perfección." *Insula* 464–65 (July–August 1985): 21.

———. "La realidad y sus sombras: Rosa Montero y Cristina Fernández Cubas." *Insula* 446 (June 1984): 5.

Talbot, Lynne K. "Journey into the Fantastic: Cristina Fernández Cubas's *Los altillos de Brumal.*" *Letras Femeninas* 1–2 (1989): 37–47.

———. "Lourdes Ortiz's *Urraca:* A Re-Vision/Revision of History." *Romance Quarterly* 38 (1991): 437–48.

Tébar, Juan. "Novela criminal española de la transición." *Insula* 464–65 (July–August 1985): 4.

Thomas, Brook. *The New Historicism and Other Old-Fashioned Topics.* Princeton: Princeton University Press, 1991.

Trevelyan, Humphrey. "Reflection on Soviet and Western Policy." *International Affairs* 52 (1976): 527–34.

Tsuchiya, Akiko. "The Paradox of Narrative Seduction in Carmen Riera's *Cuestión de amor propio.*" *Hispania* 75 (1992): 281–86.

Tusell, Javier. *La dictadura de Franco.* Madrid: Alianza, 1988.

Tusquets, Esther. *Para no volver.* Barcelona: Lumen, 1985.

Valls, Fernando. "Para una bibliografía completa de Luis Goytisolo." *La Página* 11–12 (1993): i–xvi.

———. "El renacimiento del cuento en España (1975–1993)." In his *Son cuentos: Antología del relato breve español, 1975–1993,* 9–78. Madrid: Espasa Calpe, 1993.

van Alphen, Ernst. "The Heterotopian Space of the Discussions on Postmodernism." *Poetics Today* 10 (winter 1989): 819–39.

Vásquez, Mary S., ed. *The Sea of Becoming: Approaches to the Fiction of Esther Tusquets.* New York: Greenwood, 1991.

Vázquez de Parga, Salvador. *La novela policíaca en España.* Barcelona: Ronsel, 1993.

———. "Viaje por la novela policíaca actual." *El Urogallo* 9–10 (January–February 1987): 20–25.

Vázquez Rial, Horacio. "El tormento de los años mozos." *Quimera* 75 (March 1988): 46–49.

Veeser, H. Aram, ed. *The New Historicism.* New York: Routledge, 1989.

Verdín Díaz, Guillermo. *Introducción al estilo indirecto libre en español.* Madrid: Consejo Superior de Investigaciones Científicas, 1970.

Villanueva, Darío. "Como juego y revelación." *Nueva Estafeta* 48–49 (November–December 1982): 118.

———. "La novela." In *Letras Españolas 1976–1986,* ed. Andrés Amorós, 19–64. Madrid: Castalia, 1987.

———. "La novela española en 1978." *Anales de la Narrativa Española Contemporánea* 4 (1979): 91–115.

Zatlin, Phyllis. "The Novels of Rosa Montero as Experimental Fiction." *Monographic Review/Revista Monográfica* 8 (1992): 114–24.

———. "Tales from Fernández Cubas: Adventure in the Fantastic." *Monographic Review/Revista Monográfica* 3 (1987): 107–18.

Index

Agency, 64, 74–75, 78, 83–87, 88, 97, 200, 209; as contrasted with subject, 60*n13*, 121. *See also* Subject; Althusser, Louis
Alborg, Concha, 143*n39*
Alsina, Jean, 22*n18*, 71*n26*
Althusser, Louis, 57*n11*, 188*n30*; on agency, 74; and *El cuarto de atrás,* 63–76; and *El invierno en Lisboa,* 214
Apparatuses, 57*n11*; as employed by Francoist government, 156; as expressed in post-Francoist Spain, 188; in *Tiempo de silencio,* 40; in *El cuarto de atrás,* 50, 63–76, 78; in *El río de la luna,* 131
Archive, 23*n21*. *See also* Foucault, Michel
Atomic bomb: as referent in *Tiempo de silencio,* 35, 36*n9*
Authoritative discourse: as defined by Bakhtin, 55–56; as relates to New historicism, 237; as expressed in novels analyzed, 63, 72, 73, 100. *See also* Bakhtin, M. M.

Bakhtin, M. M.: theory of heteroglossia as expressed in *Juan sin Tierra,* 55–63; in *El cuarto de atrás,* 70, 73; as concerns authoritative discourse, 237; as concerns posited reader/author, 139*n34*. *See also* Authoritative discourse; Chronotope; Double voicing
Barthes, Roland, 139*n35*
Bartlett, Bertice, 224*n54*
Benet, Juan, 54, 173*n18*; as concerns *novela negra,* 105; as concerns neorealism, 31
Benveniste, Emil, 67. *See also* Historical narrative

Bersani, Leo, 111*n12*, 189
Bible, 59, 167, 170, 171
Biblical discourse: and novels analyzed, 45–46, 48, 58–63, 140, 159, 167, 171. *See also* Discursive practices
Bolero: in *El cuarto de atrás,* 72; in *Te trataré como a una reina,* 141, 142, 143*n39*, 144, 145
Book of Daniel, 165*n13*
Boom, 4–5, 32
Booth, Wayne C., 31
Border crossing, 224, 231
Bové, Paul A., 5
Brooks, Peter, 99, 163*n11*. *See also* Object of beauty
Brushwood, John S., 237–38, 239
Buchanan, Pat, 19
Bush, George, 19, 154

Campbell, Jeremy, 26, 112*n13*; as refers to second law of thermodynamics, 25; as ideas relate to *El río de la luna,* 130. *See also* Entropy; Information theory
Cano Ballesta, Juan, 36*n9*
Canon, literary, 7
Carrero Blanco, Luis, 12, 22
Carter, Jimmy, 52, 104
Caudillo, 19*n11*
Cebrián, Juan Luis, 17*n7*
Cela, Camilo José, 54, 105
Cervantes, Miguel de, 41–42, 48
Chambers, Ross, 75; ideas as expressed in *Cuestión de amor propio,* 199–209. *See also* Oppositional reading; Object of desire; Seduction
Chaos theory: and international politics, 23–25, 29; and Spain in 1970s, 53;

Novela negra, 77*n34,* 100, 105. *See also* Detective genre
Novela rosa, 72, 204, 206

Object of beauty, 97, 183. *See also* Brooks, Peter; Lacan, Jacques
Object of desire, 43, 123, 209, 228. *See also* Chambers, Ross; Lacan, Jacques
Oppositional reading: as expressed in *Cuestión de amor propio,* 198–209. *See also* Chambers, Ross
Opus Dei, 12, 21, 33, 34, 36, 43
Orderly disorder, as expressed in *El río de la luna,* 120–31. *See also* Chaos theory; Hayles, N. Katherine
Organic Law of the State, 21
Ortega, David, 154
Ortiz, Lourdes, 131–41; related to other novelists of study, 151, 186, 173
Otero, Carlos, 23*n20*
Other, 27, 43. *See also* Lacan, Jacques; Ragland-Sullivan, Ellie

Panopticon, 15–23, 156; and *Tiempo de silencio,* 40–49, 240; and *Visión del ahogado,* 50, 87–102; and *Alguien te observa en secreto,* 173–85; and *El año de Gracia,* 165. *See also* Disciplining society; Foucault, Michel
Parataxis, 37, 43
Pastiche, 28, 213
Paternalistic hierarchies: and *Tiempo de silencio,* 35–36, 38–39, 41–42, 49
Paulson, William R., 6–7, 26, 61–62*n14,* 112*n13,* 222, 238, 241. *See also* Information theory; Noise; Perturbation
Perestroika. *See* Gorbachev, Mikhail
Pérez Firmat, Gustavo, 109*n10*
Persian Gulf War, 154
Perturbation, 26, 241; as expressed in *Todas las almas,* 222–34. *See also* Entropy; Information theory; Noise
Piquer, Conchita, 72
Posited reader, 8, 139*n34,* 209
Postmodernism, 1, 23, 28, 29, 213*n46;* related to detective genre, 77, 176*n22;* related to novels analyzed, 62–63, 87*n42,* 100, 171, 210*n42*
Poststructuralism, 26, 27*n28. See also* Syllogistic logic

Post-totalitarian society (Spain), 1, 11, 64, 155
Power hierarchies, 7, 15–16, 18, 21, 25, 42; as expressed in novels analyzed, 36, 38–39, 49, 56–57. *See also* Foucault, Michel
Primo de Rivera, José Antonio, 19*n11. See also* Falange
Primo de Rivera, Pilar, 70. *See also* Falange; Feminine Section; Social Service
Prince, Gerald, 139*n34*
Psychoanalytic discourse: and *Para no volver,* 185–98. *See also* Discursive practices

Quantum mechanics, 23–24
Quixote, Don (Cervantes), 41, 48

Racevskis, Karlis, 2
Ragland-Sullivan, Ellie, 27. *See also* Lacan, Jacques
Randomness, 23
Reagan, Ronald, 104, 153, 154
Récit/histoire, as expressed in novels analyzed, 54–55, 78–79, 85, 101, 122, 125, 126, 130, 157
Regenta, La (Clarín), 114*n14*
Register, 1, 5, 6, 8–9, 16, 25, 35, 62, 78, 80, 89, 91, 100, 101, 237, 239, 240, 243. *See also* Episteme
Republican Party (U.S.), 15, 19, 154
Republicans (Spain), 18, 19, 20
Revista Española, 31. *See also* Neorealism
Rhetoric of fiction, 31
Rhizome, 131
Riera, Carmen, 198–209
Roberts, Gemma, 121*n17,* 128*n23*
Rodríguez-García, José, 76–77*n33,* 87*n42*
Roman à clef, 200
Rosenberg, John, 28*n32*
Rueda, Ana, 172*n17*

SALT, 52
Sánchez, Elizabeth, 114*n14*
Sánchez Ferlosio, Rafael, 124
Sanz Villanueva, Santos, 172*n17*
Saussure, Ferdinand de, 49
Schumm, Sandra J., 65*n19,* 207*n39*
Sebeok, Thomas A., 130*n27*